Beating the Sicilian II

A Complete New Repertoire for White

JOHN NUNN

B.T.Batsford Ltd/Trafalgar Square

First published 1990
© John Nunn 1990

ISBN 0 7134 6445 3
A CIP catalogue record for this book is available from the British Library

Typeset by Latimer Trend Co Ltd, Plymouth, Devon
and printed in Great Britain by Dotesios (Printers) Ltd, Trowbridge, Wilts
for the publishers,
B. T. Batsford Ltd,
4 Fitzhardinge Street,
London W1H 0AH

Published in the USA by
Trafalgar Square Publishing
North Pomfret, VT 05053

Contents

Preface

This second edition of *Beating the Sicilian* does not need such a lengthy introduction, as the concept of a 'repertoire' book has become a familiar one. However I will take time to detail some changes which have been made to the original *Beating the Sicilian*. The earlier work was based on the premise that a book like *The Najdorf for the Tournament Player* provides a surfeit of information for the average White player, who only wants to know one good line to play against the Najdorf. It therefore developed a complete repertoire for White against the Sicilian, covered in sufficient detail for most players to meet any line of the Sicilian with confidence. To my surprise I found that the book became popular not only amongst the intended audience of club players, but also at the Grandmaster level.

There were faults in *Beating the Sicilian*. I recommended some unusual sidelines, but this recommendation was self-defeating, because many of these lines were suddenly played in Grandmaster games. At this level the reasons why the lines were in fact sidelines became abundantly clear. Thus the book contributed to its own

rapid dating. This time I have adopted a different policy. In every variation I have recommended one of the current main lines against that variation. Such main lines cannot be refuted, although the whims of fashion may lead to them becoming more or less popular as the years go by. In this way the lines recommended in the book should remain valid for years to come (until the third edition?) and readers may be confident that the effort put into studying them will earn a long-term reward. One side-effect of this policy is that the analysis has become considerably more detailed. You cannot learn the main line of the Yugoslav Attack without studying a fair number of variations, but as we only need to examine Black alternatives the work required is not too onerous. In any case the growth of opening theory at all levels of chess has forced players to devote more effort to the study of opening theory in order to maintain (or increase) their level of success. Unfortunately this has led to scrapping the policy of offering alternative White choices such as 6 a4 against the Najdorf. The book would have grown too big (and expensive) if these had been left in. In any case, these lines have not changed greatly since the first book, so much of the old material is still valid.

I have maintained the arrangement of material from the earlier book. The biggest changes in the repertoire are the abandonment of the Classical Scheveningen (now only the Keres attack is recommended), the switch to 9 ♗xf6 in the Pelikan, adopting the main line of the Yugoslav Attack against the Dragon, and moving to 5 ♘b5 against the Taimanov. Needless to say, all chapters have been thoroughly updated, even if the chosen variation is unchanged. All material up to October 1989 has been consulted, including *Informator* 47, *New in Chess* yearbook 12 and *ChessBase* magazine 13.

In some cases, usually at a fairly late stage of the analysis, I have given more than one move for White where there is genuine doubt as to which is the best alternative. I have devoted special attention to a few relatively unusual lines which in some cases have a 'cult' following. Examples of this are the Pin Variation (Chapter 11) and 2 ... ♘f6 (Chapter 12). These lines are probably not very good for Black, but they are tricky and

are sometimes used as a surprise weapon. All too often a White player, when confronted by one of these unusual lines, will decide to play safe and not enter the main theoretical paths. In doing this he often throws away any chance to gain the advantage. A short survey of the critical lines is enough to enable one to counter such unusual lines, but I have given a fairly detailed coverage for the sake of completeness.

One problem with the division of material into games is that while it is convenient for the reader who starts at page 1 it is not so suitable if the book is to be used as a reference work. Finding which game contains a particular line is not so easy, but an unusually detailed index should help with this problem. I have again included plenty of diagrams at critical moments to provide further assistance.

Finally I would like to thank all those readers of *Beating the Sicilian* who wrote with comments, suggestions and games. Grandmasters are usually only too willing to offer their opinions, and it is useful to get balancing feedback from the club players who provide the main readership of a book such as this.

1 Najdorf Variation

Of all the lines in the Sicilian which Black can adopt, the Najdorf has developed the largest body of theory. Whole books have been written on mere sub-variations of the Najdorf, for example the Polugayevsky variation and the infamous Poisoned Pawn. Devising a counter which is viable in tournament play, while at the same time necessitating relatively slight book knowledge, has proved especially hard. The Najdorf starts with the moves 1 e4 c5 2 ♘f3 d6 3 d4 cxd4 4 ♘xd4 ♘f6 5 ♘c3 a6. Black's first aim is to play ... e5 without allowing the reply ♗b5+, while the secondary point is to prepare queenside expansion by ... b5. Some of White's systems against the Najdorf are specifically aimed at preventing ... e5, while others allow Black to play this move in the hope of exploiting the backward d-pawn later. 6 ♗g5 and 6 ♗e2 are the most common replies, but as both lead to reams of analysis I have settled on a less familiar system which offers good attacking chances while retaining an element of solidity. This system, based on 6 f4, has become more popular since the first edition of this book was published and

games by players such as Belyavsky, Dolmatov and A. Sokolov have shed new light on several lines. In games 1–4 we investigate the replies most commonly encountered in practice. The main division is between those lines involving an early ... e5 and those in which Black delays this move or omits it entirely. We will postpone consideration of the former lines until games 3 and 4, and concentrate first on the alternatives to ... e5.

Game 1
F. Olafsson–Sax
Novi Sad 1976

1	e4	c5
2	♘f3	d6
3	d4	cxd4
4	♘xd4	♘f6
5	♘c3	a6
6	f4 *(1)*	

6 f4 is a flexible move; White gives little away regarding his piece deployment, and waits for Black's reply before deciding where to put his bishops.

6 ...   ♘bd7

This move is designed to reserve the option of playing ... e5 under more favourable circumstances if White should develop his pieces to unsuitable squares. 6 ... ♕c7 is game 2, but there are other playable moves:

(1) **6 ... ♘c6** 7 ♘xc6 bxc6 8 e5 ♘d7 (8 ... dxe5 9 ♕xd8+ ♔xd8 10 fxe5 ♘d5 11 ♗d2 is good for White) 9 ♗c4!? dxe5 10 0-0 e6 11 f5 ♗c5+ 12 ♔h1 with good attacking chances.

(2) **6 ... g6** 7 ♗d3 and after a subsequent ... ♕c7 or ... ♘bd7 there will probably be a transposition into lines considered in game 2.

(3) **6 ... e6** (after this White may transpose into various lines of the Scheveningen, but since these lines do not form part of the repertoire recommended in this book, we suggest an independent alternative which promises good chances for White) 7 ♕f3 (White's advantage over similar lines is that his bishops are not committed, so he can force through g4–g5 very quickly) and now:

(3a) **7 ... ♘bd7** 8 g4 e5 9 ♘f5 is dangerous for Black, for example 9 ... g6 (9 ... exf4?! 10 ♗xf4 ♘e5 11 ♗xe5 dxe5 12 g5 ♘d7 13 ♗c4 gives White a tremendous attack)

10 g5 gxf5 11 exf5 and Black is under heavy pressure.

(3b) **7 ... ♕c7** 8 g4 b5 9 g5 ♘fd7 (9 ... b4 10 ♘cb5 axb5 11 gxf6 gxf6 12 ♗xb5+ ♗d7 13 ♗d3 gave White a good game in Lau–Schuh, West German Ch. 1987) 10 a3 ♗b7 11 ♗e3 (11 ♗g2 g6 12 ♕f2 ♘c6 13 ♘de2 h6 14 f5 was also promising in Smyslov–Kamsky, New York Open 1989) ♘c6 12 ♗h3 b4 13 axb4 ♘xb4 14 0-0 ♘c5 15 ♖ad1 g6 16 ♖d2 ♗e7 17 ♖df2 with advantage to White, Timman–Hjartarson, Belfort World Cup 1988.

(3c) **7 ... ♕b6** 8 ♘b3 ♕c7 9 g4 b5 10 ♗d3 ♗b7 11 g5 ♘fd7 12 ♗e3 ♘c6 13 ♕h3 b4 (13 ... ♘c5 14 0-0 ♘b4 15 ♖ad1 ♘bxd3 16 cxd3 ♘xb3 17 axb3 ♕d7 18 f5 exf5 19 ♗d4! was good for White in Ulybin–Labunsky, USSR 1987) 14 ♘e2 g6 15 0-0-0 ♗g7 16 ♖hf1 0-0-0 17 f5 ♘ce5 18 ♔b1 with a slight plus for White, Ulybin–Magerramov, Uzgorod 1988.

7 ♗e2 *(2)*

This position frequently arises via the move order 6 ♗e2 ♘bd7

(instead of the more common 6 ... e5) 7 f4.

7 ... e5

This move is most common, the following lines being somewhat unpleasant for Black:

(1) **7 ... g6** (an attempt to reach positions akin to the Dragon, but here White can exploit an interesting tactical resource) 8 g4 ♘c5 (8 ... h6 9 f5 ♘c5 10 ♗f3 e5 11 ♘b3 gxf5 12 exf5 e4 13 ♗g2 ♘xb3 14 axb3 ♖g8 15 h3 ♗xf5 16 ♕d4 ♗e6 was unclear in Belyavsky–Ljubojevic, Bugojno 1984, but this line is certainly risky for Black) 9 ♘b3! b6 (not **9 ... ♘fxe4?** 10 ♘xe4 ♘xe4 11 ♕d4 ♘f6 12 g5 winning, nor **9 ... ♘xb3** 10 axb3 ♗g7 11 g5 ♘d7 12 ♗e3 with a clear plus for White, Liberzon–Savon, Sukhumi 1972) 10 g5 ♘fd7, Arnason–Tringov, Plovdiv 1986, and now 11 ♗f3 ♗b7 12 ♕e2 supporting e4 and preparing ♗d2 and 0-0-0 gives White a promising position.

(2) **7 ... ♘c5** 8 ♗f3 ♕b6 9 ♘b3 (once again this move, putting the question to the c5 knight, gives White the advantage) ♘xb3 10 axb3 g6 11 e5 dxe5 12 fxe5 ♘d7 13 ♘d5 ♕d8 14 ♗g5, Gipslis–Quinteros, Olot 1973 and White stands very well since 14 ... ♘xe5? loses to 15 ♘f6+ exf6 16 ♕xd8+ ♔xd8 17 ♗xf6+.

(3) **7 ... ♕b6** 8 ♘b3 g6 9 ♕d3 (preparing ♗e3, when Black is driven back in confusion) ♕c7 10 g4 ♘c5 11 ♘xc5 ♕xc5 12 ♗e3 ♕a5 13 b4! with advantage, Torre–Quinteros, Leningrad IZ 1973.

(4) **7 ... b5** (I suggested this move in 1982 but a few months later found a good reply; 8 ♘d5! ♗b7 (9 ♘c6 was the threat and 8 ... ♘xd5 9 exd5 gives White a superb outpost at c6) 9 ♘xf6+ ♘xf6 (or else White has a positional advantage) 10 e5 dxe5 11 fxe5 followed by e6, when Black has problems developing his kingside pieces.

8 ♘f5

Inexperienced White players sometimes try 8 ♘b3 but after the reply 8 ... b5 White should be thinking about equalizing! Natural moves like 8 ♘b3 quite often turn out badly in the Najdorf, which is one reason why it is so popular with Black players.

8 ... ♘c5
9 ♘g3

White's knight manoeuvre solidly defends the sensitive e4 square and he is now ready to complete his development by 0-0 and ♗e3. If Black does nothing to stop this then White's position will be very promising, so his next move is directed against both the developing moves mentioned above.

9 ... ♕b6

Or 9 ... ♗d7 10 0-0 ♗e7 11 ♗e3 (11 a4 is also possible, when 11 ... g6? 12 ♗e3 ♘c6 13 fxe5! ♘fxe4 14 ♘cxe4 ♘xe4 15 e6! was very good for White in Kiprichnikov–Petkevich, USSR 1975) ♖c8 12 fxe5 dxe5 13 ♘d5 ♗e6!

14 ♘xf6+ (or 14 ♘xe7 ♛xe7 15 ♗g5 ♘cd7 16 c3 with an edge for White) ♗xf6 15 ♛c1 ♗e7 with a small plus for White, Tsesh-kovsky–Tarjan, Riga 1979.

10 ♖b1! *(3)*

It may seem to be a major concession to play such a move merely in order to achieve ♗e3, and for a long time 10 f5 was played in order to delay the painful decision to waste time with ♖b1. However, it is now recognized that White should retain the option of opening up the position by fxe5 and so the immediate ♖b1 is thought best today. The situation in this line is typical of opening variations in which Black plays very actively. If he can keep his initiative going then everything turns out well for him, but if he falters and has to start moving backwards the result is usually disastrous. Which of these alternatives actually occurs frequently depends on obscure tactical points, as happens here.

10 ...   ♗d7

10 ... ♗e7 sets a neat trap

which Karpov once fell into—11 ♗e3?! exf4 12 ♗xf4 ♘cxe4 13 ♘gxe4 ♘xe4 14 ♘xe4 ♛b4+ and Black wins a pawn, although White probably has sufficient compensation to draw. The best line against 10 ... ♗e7 is 11 fxe5 dxe5 12 ♗e3 ♛c6 (12 ... ♛c7 13 0-0 0-0 14 ♔h1 b5 15 ♖xf6! ♗xf6 16 ♘d5 ♛c6 17 ♘xf6+ gxf6 18 ♛e1 is also dangerous for Black) 13 0-0 0-0 14 ♘d5 ♘xd5 15 exd5 ♛c7 16 b4 ♘a4 17 ♘e4 and White's powerful queenside majority gives him a substantial advantage,   Vogt–Fernandez, Halle 1978.

10 ... exf4 11 ♗xf4 ♘e6 is a recent idea for Black, which has had success in two games. After 12 ♗d2 ♘d4 **13 ♗d3** (or 13 ♘d5 ♘xd5 14 exd5 ♗e7 15 ♗c3 ♘f5 with rough equality), Kinder-mann–King, Dortmund 1988, continued 13 ... ♗e7 14 ♘h5 0-0 15 ♘xf6+ ♗xf6 16 ♘d5 ♛d8 17 0-0 ♗e5 18 ♔h5 ♗e6 19 ♗g5 f6 20 ♗e3 b5 with equality, while Vogt–H. Olafsson, Thessaloniki Ol. 1988 went 13 ... ♛c5 14 ♘d5 ♘xd5 15 exd5 ♛xd5 16 0-0 ♘c6 17 ♗e4 ♛c5+ 18 ♔h1 ♘e5 19 ♘f5 ♗xf5 20 ♖xf5 ♛c7 and this too ended in a draw. The second line looks risky for Black, but King's handling of the position affords White few chances for an advantage. However White has an interesting option on move 13, namely **13 ♘h5!?** ♖xh5 14 ♗xh5 ♗e6 (or else ♘d5) 15 0-0!? To castle into a double check appears suicidal, yet this is the only way to make ♗e3 into a threat! After **15 ... g6** 16 ♗e3 ♗g7 17 ♘a4 ♛a7 18 c3 or **15 ... ♘xc2+** 16 ♚h1 ♘e3 17 ♛a4+ White is clearly better, so Black should probably play the safe **15 ... ♘c6+** 16 ♚h1 g6, although even here 17 ♗g4! looks at least slightly better for White.

11	**fxe5**	**dxe5**
12	**♗e3**	

Here, too, this is White's best. The threat of b4 forces Black to move his queen, and since he must try to keep up the momentum it is natural to attack the e4 pawn. Everything then hinges on whether White can successfully gambit this pawn.

12	**...**	**♛c6**
13	**0-0**	**0-0-0**

Black would like to play 13 ... ♘cxe4 14 ♘cxe4 ♘xe4 15 ♗f3 ♗c5 but White wins material by 16 ♘xe4 ♗xe3+ 17 ♚h1 0-0 18 ♘c3 ♛c8 19 ♘d5 ♗c5 20 b4 ♗d6 21 ♘b6. If Black can't take the e-pawn then his whole plan looks suspicious, but he could have minimized his disadvantage by 13 ... ♖d8! As played his king is subjected to a devastating attack.

14 b4!

White forces Black to take the poisoned pawn. This would also have been the reply to 13 ... ♗e7.

14	**...**	**♘cxe4**

14 ... ♘e6 15 ♘d5 threatening c4 and b5 is also horrible.

15	**♘cxe4**	**♘xe4**
16	**♘xe4**	**♛xe4** *(4)*

17	**♗b6**	**♖e8?**

Now Black gets mated. The best practical chance was to jettison the exchange by 17 ... ♗e7, although 18 ♗f3 ♛g6 19 ♗xd8 ♖xd8 20 ♛d5 ♛b6+ 21 ♚h1 f6 22 ♛f7 attacking the vulnerable kingside pawns should win for White in the long run.

18	**♗f3**	**♛g6**
19	**♗xb7+**	**♚b8**

19 ... ♚xb7 20 ♛xd7+ ♚xb6 21 ♛xe8 ♗c5+ is impossible because White takes the bishop with check.

20 ♗e3

The simplest. Material is level and White's attack against the naked Black king must be decisive.

20	**...**	**♗b5**
21	**♗f3**	**♛d6**

21 ... ♗xf1 loses to 22 ♛d7.

22	**♛e1**	**f5**

22 ... ♗xf1 23 ♛xf1 followed by b5 or ♖d1 wins.

23	**c4**	**♗xc4**
24	**b5**	**axb5**
25	**♛a5**	**e4**
26	**♖xb5+**	**Resigns**

26 ... ♗xb5 27 ♕xb5+ ♚c7
28 ♖c1+ ♚d8 29 ♗b6+ ♚e7 30
♗c5 wins.

Game 2
Nunn–Grünfeld
England–Israel Telex Match 1981

1	e4	c5
2	♘f3	d6
3	d4	cxd4
4	♘xd4	♘f6
5	♘c3	a6
6	f4	♕c7

If Black wishes to delay ... e5
(or even dispense with it alto-
gether) then this is probably the
most reliable way to go about it.
Black avoids the tactical problems
resulting from a quick e5 by
White and can continue his development by ... g6, ... ♗g7, ...
♘bd7 and maybe ... b5 and ...
0-0 as well.

7 ♘f3 *(5)*

This is more accurate than 7
♗d3, when 7 ... e5 8 ♘f3 b5
transposes into a relatively comfortable line for Black.

7 ... ♘bd7

After this we reach a standard
position which can arise by a wide

range of move orders. The main
question is whether Black can
exploit White's early ♘f3 by playing **7 ... e6**. The analysis runs 7
... e6 8 ♗d3 and now:

(1) **8 ... b5** 9 e5! dxe5 (**9 ... b4**
10 ♘e4 ♘xe4 11 ♗xe4 d5 12 ♗d3
is slightly better for White, while
Sax–Guerra, Dubai Ol. 1986 continued **9 ... ♘fd7** 10 0-0 ♘c6 11
♚h1 ♗e7 12 ♕e1 0-0 13 ♕g3 f5
14 exf6 ♘xf6 15 ♗d2 with advantage to White) 10 fxe5 ♘fd7 (10
... ♘g4 11 ♕e2 ♗b7 12 ♗e4 also
gives White an edge) 11 0-0 ♘c6
12 ♗f4 ♗b7 13 ♚h1 ♘c5 14 ♘e4
♘xe4 15 ♗xe4 ♘b4, Reeh–
Schulz, West German Ch. 1987,
and now 16 ♘g5!? gives White
dangerous attacking chances.

(2) **8 ... ♘c6** 9 0-0 and now:

(2a) **9 ... ♗e7** 10 ♕e1 and
Black has a range of possibilities.
The passive **10 ... ♘d7** 11 ♕g3
0-0 12 ♚h1 ♖e8?! 13 e5! ♘b4 14
f5! gave White a strong attack in
Hazai–Karolyi, Hungary Ch.
1986, while **10 ... 0-0** is met by 11
e5 dxe5 12 fxe5 ♘d7 13 ♗f4 ♘c5
14 ♕g3 ♘xd3 15 cxd3 ♚h8 16
♘e4 and White is better according to Sax and Hazai. Perhaps the
best line is **10 ... ♘b4** 11 e5 ♘xd3
12 cxd3 ♘d5 13 ♘xd5 exd5 14
♕g3 0-0 15 ♚h1 dxe5 16 fxe5
♗f5 17 ♘d4 ♗g6 18 ♗d2 with a
level position, Sax–de Firmian,
New York Open 1987.

(2b) **9 ... b5** 10 ♕e1 ♗b7 11
♚h1 ♗e7 12 e5! dxe5 13 fxe5
♘d7 14 ♗f4 ♘c5 15 ♘e4! (as in
line 1 above, except that the

moves ♕e1 and ... ♗e7 have been added) ♘xe4 (15 ... ♘xd3 16 cxd3 0-0 17 ♕g3 ♔h8 18 ♘f6! ♕d8 19 ♘g5 is very good for White) 16 ♗xe4 h6?! (16 ... ♘b4 17 ♗xb7 ♕xb7 18 ♕g3 g6 may be better, although 19 ♗h6 cuts Black off from the kingside), Sax–A. Sokolov, Reykjavik 1988, and now 17 a4 b4 18 ♕f2 gives White good attacking prospects.

(3) **8 ... ♘bd7** 9 0-0 ♗e7 (9 ... b5 may be met by the simple 10 ♕e1, or even by 10 e5!? dxe5 11 fxe5 ♘xe5 12 ♘xe5 ♕xe5 13 ♕f3 and now **13 ... ♖b8?!** 14 ♗f4 ♕c5+ 15 ♔h1 ♗b7 16 ♗e4! ♘xe4 17 ♗xb8 f5 18 ♖ae1 was good for White in Nicevski–Markiewicz, Dembica 1987, so Black should have played **13 ... ♖a7** 14 ♗f4 ♕h5 15 ♕g3 with an unclear position) 10 ♕e1 0-0 11 e5! ♘e8 12 ♕g3 ♘c5 13 ♗e3 ♗d7?! 14 ♗xh7+! ♔xh7 15 ♘g5+ ♔g8 (15 ... ♗xg5 16 fxg5 ♖h8 17 ♖xf7 is unpleasant) 16 ♕h4 ♗xg5 17 fxg5 ♗c6, Wedberg–Ionescu, Berlin 1988, and after 18 exd6 ♘xd6 (not 18 ... ♕xd6 19 ♖ad1 ♕e7 20 ♕b4) 19 ♗xc5 ♘f5 Black does not have enough for the pawn.

8	**♗d3**	**g6**

8 ... e5 9 a4 transposes to game 3, while 8 ... e6 is line 3 in the above analysis.

9	**0-0**

White's strategy in this line is rather crude. He intends a straightforward attacking build-up on the kingside by ♕e1–h4, f5, ♗h6, and ♘g5. Of course Black is also playing moves while all this is going on but if he continues naively with his development without taking specific counter-measures he can easily fall victim to White's attack.

9	**...**	**♗g7**
10	**♕e1** *(6)*	

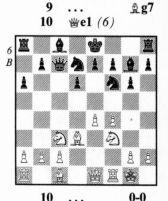

10	**...**	**0-0**

This move is probably already an inaccuracy. The alternatives are:

(1) **10 ... ♘c5** 11 e5 dxe5 12 fxe5 ♘fd7 13 ♗f4 ♘e6 14 ♗g3 ♘b6 (after 14 ... 0-0 15 ♔h1 Black has to find an answer to ♘d5) 15 a4 ♗d7 16 a5 ♘c8 17 ♘e4 and White's initiative proved decisive in Sax–Minic, Rovinj–Zagreb 1975.

(2) **10 ... b5** (probably the best move, aiming to complete Black's development before he gives White a target to attack by castling) 11 e5 (attacking moves like ♕h4 serve no function while Black's king is still in the centre) dxe5 12 fxe5 ♘g4 13 e6 fxe6 14 ♕h4 with an unclear position. For the pawn White has some

initiative and Black has problems finding a refuge for his king. White also has the option of opening lines on the queenside by a timely a4, and in practice Black will not have an easy defensive task ahead of him.

11   ♕h4   b5
12   f5

At one time White invariably played ♔h1 before proceeding with his attack. This type of consolidating move is often a symptom of chess laziness, in that White does not want to be bothered with calculating the consequences of Black's queen check in every variation and so simply rules it out, even though it may cost him a vital tempo.

12   ...   ♗b7?

Black continues to play normal Sicilian moves without realizing how critical his position has become. The point is that after White's fxg6 Black does not want to play ... hxg6 when ♘g5 gives White a permanent mating threat on h7. However, the recapture ... fxg6 invites White's knight to come in at e6 and Black's ... ♗b7 removes a vital defence from this square. 12 ... ♘c5 was essential, when 13 ♗h6 b4 may enable Black to defend.

13   fxg6

In a game Velikov–Valenti, Pernik 1979, White played 13 ♗e3 (laziness again) when Black missed his second chance to play ... ♘c5 and lost after 13 ... b4? 14 ♘d5! ♗xd5 15 exd5 ♘xd5 16

fxg6 hxg6 17 ♘g5 ♘5f6 18 ♖f3 with a crushing attack.

13   ...   fxg6

After 13 ... hxg6 14 ♘g5 Black cannot move either knight since ... ♘h5 is met by g4. White can just build up by ♖f3 and ♖af1 to eliminate the defensive knights at f6.

14   ♘g5   ♘c5 (7)

Too late! 14 ... ♕b6+ (14 ... ♘h5 15 ♗e3 is good for White) 15 ♔h1 ♘h5 was best, but even then 16 ♗d2 threatening both ♘e6 and ♘d5 gives White a promising attack.

15   ♖xf6!   ♖xf6
16   ♕xh7+   ♔f8
17   ♗e3

White's material investment is very slight for such a strong attack. The main threat is 18 ♘d5 ♗xd5 19 exd5 attacking g6 and preparing b4 followed by the occupation of e6 by White's knight.

17   ...   ♘xd3

17 ... e5 18 ♘d5 ♗xd5 19 exd5 e4 20 ♗e2 ♖e8 21 b4 followed by ♘e6+ is also winning.

| 18 | cxd3 | ♛d7 |

Black cannot meet the threat of ♘d5 by 18 ... e6 since 19 ♘xe6+! ♖xe6 20 ♖f1+ ♚e8 (20 ... ♖f6 21 ♖xf6+ wins the queen) 21 ♛g8+ is decisive.

19	♘d5	♗xd5
20	exd5	♛f5
21	♘e6+	♖xe6
22	dxe6	♛xe6
23	♗h6	Resigns

23 ... ♗xh6 24 ♛h8+ ♚f7 25 ♖f1+ wins everything.

Game 3
Nunn–Cserna
Lugano 1984

1	e4	c5
2	♘f3	d6
3	d4	cxd4
4	♘xd4	♘f6
5	♘c3	a6
6	f4	e5

Black's most popular move. After all, ... a6 was designed to prepare ... e5 and the determined Najdorf player will generally play ... e5 unless it is absolutely impossible.

| 7 | ♘f3 | ♛c7 |

At one time it was held that Black should prevent the active development of White's bishop at c4 and so this move was almost universal. But more recently 7 ... ♘bd7 has become the most popular move. We consider this in game 4.

8 a4

The alternative is 8 ♗d3. The continuations after 8 a4 and 8 ♗d3 are rather similar, but there are some important differences. Firstly 8 a4 expends a tempo, but this is not especially serious since White can often omit ♚h1 (after 8 ♗d3 b5 White usually has to play ♚h1 since Black's check on b6 gives him extra defensive possibilities). More significantly, a4 reserves the c4 square for White's use (by ♛e2 and ♗c4 or ♘d2 and ♗c4) and in some lines the added pressure White can exert on f7 by these manoeuvres improves his chances considerably.

| 8 | ... | ♘bd7 |
| 9 | ♗d3 | (8) |

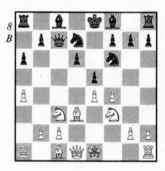

9 ... g6

Black's main decision is whether the f8 bishop should go to e7 or g7. There are two other lines, one in which Black commits himself to ... ♗e7 at once and one in which he postpones the decision:

(1) **9 ... ♗e7** 10 0-0 0-0 11 ♘h4 g6 (this is usually unavoidable in lines where Black plays ... ♗e7, for example 11 ... ♗d8?! 12 ♘f5 g6 13 ♘h6+ ♚g7 14 f5 b6 15 g4 with a dangerous attack, Sax–

Bukic, Vrbas 1980) 12 f5 d5!? 13 exd5 e4 (13 ... ♘xd5? 14 ♘xd5 ♛c5+ 15 ♗e3 ♛xd5 16 fxg6 hxg6, Cramling–Gallagher, Oakham 1984, and now White could have won by 17 ♛g4!, e.g. **17 ... ♘f6** 18 ♘xg6 ♗xg4 19 ♘xe7+ ♚h8 20 ♘xd5 ♘xd5 21 ♗h6, **17 ... ♗c5** 18 ♘xg6 ♗xe3+ 19 ♚h1 ♛e6 20 ♗f5, **17 ... ♘b6** 18 ♛g3 and White has threats at b6 and g6, or finally **17 ... ♗xh4** 18 ♛xh4 followed by ♗c4 and ♗h6, and in every case White has a winning position) 14 ♗e2 ♗d6 15 g3 b6, Sax–Andersson, London 1980, and now 16 ♘g2 is best, followed by ♗h6 and ♘e3 supporting the pawns at d5 and f5, when White should have the advantage.

(2) **9 ... b6** (the problem with this delaying move is that Black may have trouble getting castled) 10 0-0 ♗b7 11 ♛e1 g6 (11 ... ♗e7 12 ♚h1 0-0 13 ♘h4 g6 14 fxe5 dxe5 15 ♗h6 ♖e8 16 ♘f5! ♗f8 17 ♗xf8 ♖xf8 18 ♘e3 is slightly better for White, Sznapik–Ostermeyer, Oslo 1983) 12 fxe5 dxe5 13 ♛h4 ♗e7 (13 ... ♗g7 14 ♗h6 0-0 transposes to the main line) 14 ♗g5 h6 15 ♚h1 (15 ♘d2? ♗c5+ and 16 ... ♘h5) ♚f8 (or 15 ... 0-0-0 16 ♗e3 with an automatic attack against Black's weakened queenside) 16 ♘d2! ♚g7 17 ♗e3 ♘c5 18 ♗c4 ♖af8 19 ♛f2 ♗d8 20 ♗xc5 ♛xc5 21 ♛xc5 bxc5 22 a5 ½-½, Rantanen–Nunn, Helsinki 1981, although White is distinctly

better. This is an example of the advantage of having c4 available for the bishop.

10	0-0	♗g7
11	♛e1	0-0
12	fxe5	dxe5
13	♛h4	b6
14	♗h6	♗b7
15	♘g5 (9)	

This position is the natural result of White's blunt play. Although its evaluation has fluctuated over the years, the scales have recently tipped in White's favour. It is very rarely seen today because Black players steer well clear of it.

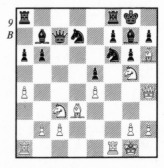

15 ... ♖fc8

The only other reasonable move is 15 ... ♛d6 (**15 ... ♘h5?** 16 ♗xg7 ♚xg7 17 ♖xf7+ and **15 ... ♖ae8** 16 g4! are to be avoided, while **15 ... ♖fe8** 16 ♗xg7 ♚xg7 17 ♘xf7! ♚xf7 18 ♛xh7+ ♚e6 19 ♖xf6+! ♚xf6 20 ♖f1+ ♚e6 21 ♗c4+ ♚d6 22 ♖d1+ ♚c6 ♗d5+ ♚c5 24 ♗xb7 Resigns was Rantanen–Morris, Gausdal 1978), but 16 ♖ad1 causes serious problems. After 16 ... ♘h5 White plays 18 ♗xg7 ♚xg7 19 ♗e2 ♕c5+ 20 ♚h1, when **20 ... ♘hf6** loses to 21 ♖xd7 and **20 ... ♘df6** loses to 21 ♗xh5 ♘xh5 22 ♖xf7+. Other 16th moves are almost as bad.

16   ♚h1

Black intends to meet moves such as 16 g4 and 16 ♖ad1 by ... ♕c5+ and ... ♕f8, when the rook on c8 prevents ♗c4 and Black successfully defends. Unfortunately White has a tactical idea which cuts across Black's plan to bring his queen to f8.

16	**...**	**♕d6**
17	**♗xg7**	**♚xg7**
18	**♘xf7!**	

This hardly counts as a sacrifice, since White immediately gains three pawns for the piece, while Black's king is left floating around in the middle of the board.

18	**...**	**♚xf7**
19	**♕xh7+**	**♚e6**
20	**♕xg6** *(10)*	

There was even a second good line in 20 ♖xf6+ ♘xf6 21 ♕xb7 since the attempt to liquidate by 21 ... ♕c7 allows 22 ♗xa6.

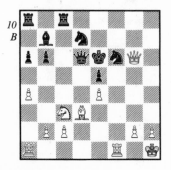

20	**...**	**♕e7**
21	**♖ad1**	

As is so often the case, it is better to spend time cutting off the king's escape route than to give pointless checks which only serve to drive the king into safety.

21	**...**	**♕h7**
22	**♕g3**	**♚e7**

Black cannot play 22 ... ♖g8 because of the check at c4.

23	**♘d5+**	**♗xd5**
24	**exd5**	**♕h6?**

This error allows White to force the king onto the back rank, cutting off both Black rooks from the kingside. However, even the best line 24 ... e4 is good for White after 25 ♖de1 ♖g8 26 ♕c7! ♕g6 27 g3 ♖ac8 28 d6+ ♚e6 29 ♕b7, and with the fall of the e4 pawn White's rooks can get to grips with the Black king.

25	**d6+**	**♚d8**
26	**♗f5!**	**♖a7**

It is hardly surprising that Black has no reasonable move. The immediate threat is 27 ♗xd7 ♚xd7 28 ♕xe5.

27	**♗xd7**	**♖xd7**
28	**♖xf6**	**Resigns**

Game 4
Nunn–King
Bundesliga 1986/7

1	**e4**	**c5**
2	**♘f3**	**d6**
3	**d4**	**cxd4**
4	**♘xd4**	**♘f6**
5	**♘c3**	**a6**
6	**f4**	**e5**
7	**♘f3**	**♘bd7**

In my view this is Black's best response to 6 f4. Although White's bishop can now be developed more actively at c4, Black saves a vital tempo by missing out ... ♕c7 and this gives him good chances to equalize. In fact current theory suggests that White's best plan is to ignore the option to play ♗c4, and to proceed with his normal development by ♗d3. Admittedly Black benefits from missing out ... ♕c7, but it is not clear that the alternatives to ... ♕c7 fully equalize.

8   a4

White cannot do without this as 8 ♗c4 allows 8 ... b5 9 ♗d5 ♖b8 10 ♘g5 (after 10 fxe5 dxe5 11 ♗g5 ♗b4 Black was slightly better in Hort–Andersson, Wijk aan Zee 1979) ♘xd5 11 ♕xd5 ♕e7 12 0-0 h6 with equality, Korchnoi–Hort, Zurich 1984, while 8 ♗d3 allows 8 ... b5, just the line White is trying to avoid.

8   ...   ♗e7

If Black relents by 8 ... ♕c7, we reach game 3. 8 ... d5 is a speculative recent idea, but if White replies 9 exd5 (better than 9 fxe5, as played in Ulybin–Odeev, USSR 1989) e4 10 ♘e5! ♗b4 11 ♗c4 ♘b6 12 ♗b3, he gains the advantage after **12 ... ♘fxd5** 13 a5 ♘xc3 14 ♕xd8+ ♔xd8 15 ♘xf7+ ♔e7 18 bxc3 ♗xc3+ 17 ♔f2 or **12 ... ♘bxd5** 13 0-0 ♗xc3 14 bxc3 0-0 15 ♕d4. This analysis has not been tested in practice, but it looks good.

9   ♗d3   0-0
10   0-0 *(11)*

10   ...   ♘c5

It is risky to take the pawn by 10 ... exf4 11 ♗xf4 ♕b6+ 12 ♔h1 ♕xb2 13 ♕e1, for example 13 ... ♕b4 (13 ... ♘c5 14 ♖b1 ♘xd3 15 cxd3 ♕c2 16 d4 ♖e8 17 ♖f2! ♕d3 18 ♖c1 ♗f8 19 ♖e2 with advantage to White, Ciocaltea–Danner, Timisoara 1982) 14 ♖b1 ♕c5 15 ♘d5 ♘xd5 16 exd5 ♗f6 (16 ... ♗d8 17 c4 ♘f6 18 ♗e3 ♕c7 19 ♗d4 gave White a dangerous attack in Ledermann–Lau, Ramat–Hasharon 1982) 17 c4 (or 17 ♕e4 g6 18 ♗h6 ♗g7 19 ♗xg7 ♔xg7 20 ♘g5 ♘e5 21 ♕h4 h6 22 ♘e4 ♕xd5 with a double-edged position, Korolev–Lipiridi, corr. 1984) ♕c7 (a draw was agreed here in Hazai–Marin, Warsaw 1987) 18 ♕g3! ♘e5 19 ♗g5 ♗xg5 20 ♗xh7+! ♔xh7 21 ♘xg5+ ♔h6 (21 ... ♔g8 22 ♕h4 ♖e8 23 ♖be1 also gives White a winning attack) 22 ♕h4+ ♔g6 23 ♖b3 f5 24 ♖g3 ♘g4 25 ♖xg4 fxg4 26 ♖xf8 ♕e7 27 ♖f7 ♕e8 28 ♕h7+ ♔xg5 29

♜xg7+ ♚f6 30 ♕h6+ ♚f5 31 ♕g5+ ♚e4 32 ♜e7+ 1–0, Vogt–Womacka, E. Germany 1989.

11 ♚h1

This is not the only reasonable move, but judging by recent results it is the most dangerous for Black.

11 ... d5

This is the tactical justification of Black's play, but there are quieter alternatives:

(1) **11 ... ♘xd3** 12 cxd3 ♕a5 13 ♕e1 exf4 14 ♘d5 ♕d8 15 ♘xf4 ♝d7 16 ♝d2 was good for White, Mateo–Byrne, New York 1986.

(2) **11 ... ♕c7** 12 ♕e1 *(12)* (threatening 13 fxe5 dxe5 14 ♕g3, when Black has no natural way to defend the e5 pawn) and now:

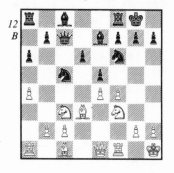

(2a) **12 ... ♝d7** 13 fxe5 dxe5 14 ♕g3 ♜ae8 15 ♕xe5 ♝d6 16 ♕d4, but Black's compensation looks inadequate in view of White's control of d5.

(2b) **12 ... ♝e6** 13 f5 ♝d7 14 g4!? (14 ♝g5 ♝c6 15 ♝xf6 ♝xf6 16 g4 is also slightly better for White) ♝c6 (14 ... ♘xg4 loses to 15 ♘d5 ♕d8 16 ♜g1 ♘f6 17

♝h6 ♘e8 18 ♜xg7+ ♘xg7 19 ♕g3 ♝f6 20 ♜g1 with a winning attack) 15 g5 ♘h5 (retreating to d7 gives White a completely free hand on the kingside, e.g. 15 ... ♘fd7 16 f6 ♝d8 17 ♕h4 ♘e6 18 ♘d5 and wins) 16 f6 ♝d8 (not 16 ... gxf6? 17 ♕h4 winning) 17 ♕h4 g6 18 ♝e3 (White's kingside attack has come to a temporary halt, so the time has come to bring the remaining pieces into play. There is a positional threat of 19 ♝xc5 dxc5 20 ♝c4, followed by the occupation of d5. Thus the c5 knight must move, but 18 ... ♘e6 19 ♘d5 ♝xd5 20 exd5 ♘ef4 21 ♝xf4 exf4 22 ♝f5! followed by ♝g4 is good for White, hence Black's next move) ♘xd3 19 cxd3 ♚h8 20 ♘e2 d5? (a very natural move aiming to weaken e4 and activate the c6 bishop against the White king. However, it also weakens the important e5 pawn and this turns out to balance White's weak spot at e4. 20 ... ♝d7, intending ... ♕c2, is refuted by 21 ♜fc1 when 21 ... ♕a5 surprisingly loses to 22 ♜c4! and Black has no defence to 23 b4; the best defence is **20 ... ♕d7!** aiming for counterplay by attacking a4, when White should continue 21 ♘g3 ♝xa4 22 ♘xh5 gxh5 23 ♕xh5 ♝b5 24 ♜a3 and Black still has to find a defence to the threat of ♜g1–g4–h4) 21 ♘g3 dxe4 (Black cannot play 21 ... ♕d6 because of 22 d4!, when both **22 ... dxe4** 23 ♘xe5 and **22 ... exd4** 23 e5 followed by ♝xd4 leave the c6–h1 diagonal blocked by a Black pawn) 22 dxe4 ♕d6 23 ♖ad1! ♕b4 (23 ... ♕e6 24 ♗c5 ♖g8 25 ♗d6 leads to the loss of e5) 24 ♘xe5 ♘xg3+ 25 hxg3 ♕xe4+ (after 25 ... ♗xe4+ 26 ♔g1 ♗b6 27 ♗xb6 ♕xb6+ 28 ♖f2 Black cannot meet the threats of ♕xe4 and ♕h6) 26 ♕xe4 ♗xe4+ 27 ♔h2 (surprisingly the exchange of queens does not stop the attack. White's immediate threat is 28 ♗c5 and the lines **27 ... ♖c8** 28 ♖d7 ♔g8 29 ♘g4! heading for h6 and **27 ... ♔g8** 28 ♗c5 ♖e8 29 ♘xf7! ♕xf7 30 ♖d7+ ♕e6 31 f7 ♖f8 32 ♖d4 ♖xf7 33 ♖d6+ both win for White) ♗c7 28 ♗c5 ♗xe5 29 ♗xf8 ♖xf8 30 ♖fe1 ♗c2 31 ♖d2 ♗xa4 (Black cannot get two pawns for the exchange since 31 ... ♗xg3+ 32 ♔xg3 ♗xa4 33 ♖e7 threatens both ♖xb7 and ♖xf7) 32 ♖xe5 h6 33 gxh6 ♔h7 34 g4 ♗xh6 35 g5+ ♔h7 36 ♖e4 ♗c6 37 ♖h4+ ♔g8 38 ♔g3 Resigns, Nunn–Portisch, Brussels 1986.

(2c) **12 ... exf4** 13 ♗xf4 ♖e8 (after 13 ... ♗e6 14 ♘d4 ♕b6 15 ♗e3 ♘g4 16 ♗g1 ♘e5 17 ♘f5 ♗xf5 18 ♘d5 ♕d8 19 exf5 ♗f6 20 ♗e2 ♘ed7 21 ♘xf6+ ♘xf6 22 ♗f3 White's two bishops gave him the advantage in Short–Gallagher, British Ch. 1987) 14 ♘d4 ♗d7 15 ♗g5 ♕d8, Hazai–Novikov, Camaguey 1987, and now White should have taken the chance to activate his bishop by 16 ♗c4!, pointing it at the sensi-

tive square f7. The key tactical line 16 ... ♘xa4 17 ♖xa4 ♗xa4 (17 ... b5 18 ♘cxb5 axb5 19 ♖xa8 ♕xa8 20 ♗xb5 is good for White) 18 ♘xa4 b5 19 ♘c6 ♕c7 20 ♘xe7+ ♕xe7 21 ♗xf6 gxf6 22 ♘b6 bxc4 23 ♘d5 ♕e5 24 ♘xf6+ ♔g7 25 ♕h4 h6 (25 ... ♖h8 26 ♕g4+) 26 ♖f5! turns out well for White since 26 ... ♕xb2 loses to 27 ♖g5+!

(3) **11 ... exf4** 12 ♗xf4 ♗d7!? 13 ♕e2 ♖c8 14 a5 ♖e8 15 ♗e3 ♗f8 16 ♗d4! (intending ♘g5) and now:

(3a) **16 ... ♗e7** 17 b4 ♘e6 18 ♗b6, **16 ... h6** 17 ♘d2 ♘g4 18 ♗c4 and **16 ... ♘e6** 17 ♗b6 ♕e7 18 ♘h4 g6 19 ♖ae1 are clearly good for White.

(3b) **16 ... ♗g4** 17 ♕e3 ♗h5 18 ♗xf6 ♕xf6 19 ♘d5 ♕d8 20 ♘d4 ♗g6 21 ♘f5 ♕e5 22 b4! ♘xe4 23 ♗xe4 ♖c4 24 ♖ae1 ♖cxe4 25 ♕xe4 ♖xe4 26 ♖xe4 was very promising for White in Ulybin–Pigusov, Pavlodar 1987.

(3c) **16 ... ♘fxe4** (Ulybin's recommendation in *Informator*, but it appears to have a tactical flaw) 17 ♘xe4 ♘xe4 18 ♗xe4 ♗b5 19 c4! (Ulybin only considered 19 ♕e3, which leads to a draw) ♖xc4 (or 19 ... ♗xc4 20 ♕c2 ♗xf1 21 ♗xh7+ ♔h8 22 ♕f5 with a winning attack) 20 ♕d3 ♖c5 21 ♗xh7+ ♔h8 22 ♕b3 ♗xf1 23 ♗xc5 dxc5 24 ♖xf1 ♔xh7 25 ♕xf7 with a large advantage for White.

12 ♘xe5 *(13)*

12   ...   ♘fxe4

Black has two important alternatives:

(1) **12 ... ♘cxe4** 13 ♗xe4 dxe4 14 ♕e2 and now:

(1a) **14 ... ♗f5** 15 g4 ♗c8 16 ♖d1 ♕e8 17 g5 ♘d7 18 ♘c4 e3 (**18 ... ♘c5** 19 b4 ♘e6 20 ♘d5 and **18 ... b6** 19 ♗e3 ♗b7 20 ♘d5 are also good for White) and now there are two favourable lines for White, either **19 ♗xe3** b5 20 axb5 ♗b7+ 21 ♔g1 axb5, Kengis–Loginov, Pavlodar 1987, and now 22 ♖xa8 ♗xa8 23 ♘xb5 ♕c8 24 ♘cd6 ♕c6 25 ♔f2 leaves Black with inadequate play for the two pawns, or the simple **19 ♕xe3**.

(1b) **14 ... ♕d4** 15 ♖d1 ♕b4 16 a5 ♗d8 17 ♖a4 ♕e7 is Loginov's suggestion in *Informator*, but now 18 b3! appears good for White.

(2) **12 ... dxe4** 13 ♗e2 (Black gains time, but the pawn on e4 obstructs Black's pieces) ♕c7 (13 ... ♕xd1 14 ♖xd1 ♗e6 15 ♗e3 ♖fd8 16 g4 g6 17 g5 ♘d5 18 ♘xd5 ♗xd5 19 b3 ♘e6 20 ♘c4 ♗xc4 21 ♗xc4 ♗c5 22 ♗xc5 ♘xc5 23 ♔g2 ♖ac8 24 ♔f2 was

marginally better for White in Kindermann–de Firmian, Biel II 1986, but 19 b4 ♘e6 20 c4 ♗c6 21 ♘xc6 bc 22 ♖xd8 ♖xd8 23 c5 looks more dangerous) 14 ♗e3 (White may also play 14 ♕e1 first, so as to meet 13 ... ♘e6 by 14 ♗d1 attacking e4) b6 15 ♕e1 ♗b7 16 ♕g3 and now:

(2a) Belyavsky–Chandler, Vienna 1986 continued **16 ... ♘e6?!** (with the idea of exchanging bishops by ... ♗c5, but this plan fails tactically) 17 ♖ad1 (not 17 f5 ♗d6!, but now f5 is a serious threat) ♗c5? (Black's position was uncomfortable in any case) 18 f5! ♗d6 (the point is that 18 ... ♗xe3 19 fxe6 fxe6 loses to 20 ♖xf6! ♖xf6 21 ♖d7) 19 ♖xd6 ♕xd6 20 fxe6 and White won.

(2b) Black tried **16 ... ♖ad8** in Psakhis–Balashov, Irkutsk 1986, but 17 ♖ad1 ♘cd7 18 ♗d4 ♘xe5 19 fxe5 ♘d7 20 b3! (20 ♗xa6! was even stronger) followed by ♗c4 gave White a decisive attack. Black should have played for exchanges by 17 ... ♖xd1 18 ♖xd1 ♖d8, but White is still slightly better.

13 ♗xe4 dxe4
14 ♘d5 *(14)*

Better than 14 ♗e3, played in Belyavsky–Portisch, Tilburg 1986, when 14 ... f6 15 ♗xc5 ♗xc5 16 ♘xe4 ♕xd1 17 ♖axd1 fxe5 18 ♘xc5 ♗g4 19 ♖de1 exf4 led to equality. The idea of 14 ♘d5 is to eliminate the e7 bishop; Black's remaining bishop will be obstructed by the e4 pawn, while

White's can become active along the b2–g7 diagonal.

14
B

14 ... ♗e6

Or:

(1) **14 ... ♗d6** 15 ♘c4! and Black has immediate difficulties since the only natural developing move 15 ... ♗e6 loses a piece to 16 ♘xd6. Otherwise White can proceed with ♘db6, or b4 followed by ♗b2.

(2) **14 ... f5** 15 b4 ♘d7 16 ♗e3! is good for White, when both 16 ... ♘f6 and 16 ... ♘xe5 17 fxe5 ♗e6 lose material to ♘xe7+ and ♗c5.

(3) **14 ... f6!** 15 ♘xe7+ ♕xe7 16 ♘c4 ♗e6 17 ♘e3 f5 leads to a typical position. White continues with moves such as b3, ♗b2 and ♕e1 when White's bishop is more effective than Black's. However the opposite coloured bishops will exert a drawish tendency, particularly if Black can exchange knights by ... ♘d7–f6–d5.

15 ♘xe7+ ♕xe7
16 f5 f6

16 ... ♖ad8 17 ♕g4 ♗c8 (17 ... f6 18 fxe6 fxe5 19 ♗g5 ♖xf1+

20 ♖xf1 ♖f8 21 ♖xf8+ ♕xf8 22 h3 is very good for White) 18 ♕g3 (not 18 f6 ♕xf6!) f6 19 ♘g4 leads to a position much like the game, except that Black's bishop is on c8 instead of f7. Although Black is exerting pressure on f5 from c8, in my view the bishop will be needed for defending the kingside and therefore the game continuation is better.

17 ♘g4

17 fxe6 fxe5 18 ♗e3 ♘xe6 19 ♕d5 may give White a minute advantage, but the move played is much more interesting. The reply 17 ... ♗c4 is ineffective after 18 ♖f4 and the bishop will soon be driven away by b3 in any case.

17 ... ♗f7
18 ♕e1?!

I decided that it was time to start developing my queenside pieces, but I should have spent just one more tempo improving my position by 18 a5! It looks strange to put a pawn on a black square when White's plan is to imprison Black's bishop using the pawns on c2, b3, a4, e4 and f5, but it is very useful to have the option of attacking the knight on c5. Not only may White push it away by b4 at a later stage, but by preventing ... b6 White can also attack it by ♗a3. The extra possibility of winning the e-pawn by getting rid of this knight (e.g. after a5, b3, ♗b2, ♕h4 and ♖ae1) would have made Black's position even more uncomfortable.

18 ... a5!

Black seizes on the mistake and secures the c5 square.

19 b3   ♖fd8

This is not very logical, since in a few moves Black decides that he needs a rook on f8 to support f6, so he could have saved time by 19 ... b6 followed by ... ♖ad8–d6.

20 ♗b2   ♖d6
21 ♕g3   ♚h8
22 ♖ae1   b6
23 ♕h4   ♖f8
24 ♖e3 *(15)*

White tries a little trick; perhaps Black won't notice the threat of 25 ♖h3 ♗g8 26 ♘e5.

24 ...   ♕d8

Unfortunately he does! Now White has to decide on a plan. At first sight his position looks very promising: since both f6 and h7 are weak, the knight on c5 cannot move without losing the e-pawn and Black has no real counterplay. However it is hard to find a concrete way White can improve his position, since almost all his pieces are already on their best possible squares. Black's potential counterplay down the d-file limits

the action of White's rooks and although White can hope to win the e-pawn by a timely ♘f2xe4, this would not be enough to win the game. I could only conceive of two possible ideas, namely ♘f2–h3–f4 coupled with ♖h3 to aim at the weak g6 square, or g4–g5 to open up the long diagonal. If White wants to play g4 the knight must move, so it seems natural to play ♘f2, which keeps both plans open. White therefore aims for the optimum arrangement of rook on e3 and knight on f2, with the bishop on c3 to prevent counterplay by ... ♖d2. Black tries to prevent White arriving at this setup.

25 ♚g1

Avoiding immediate back rank problems and future long diagonal troubles after g4. White does not need to play ♗c3 straight away because 25 ... ♖d2 loses to 26 ♘xf6 ♗g8 27 ♘h5!

25 ...   ♗g8

Now, however, 26 ... ♖d2 is a threat.

26 ♗c3

If Black does nothing White will be able to play 27 ♘f2, so he deflects the rook away from e3.

26 ...   ♖d1
27 ♖ee1   ♖d6

If correctly followed up this is a perfectly good defence. 27 ... ♖xe1 28 ♖xe1 ♕d6 29 ♘e3 ♖d8 30 ♖d1 ♕e7 31 ♖d4! ♖xd4 32 ♗xd4 is still not completely equal, since if the Black queen leaves the defence of the e-pawn,

♗xc5 and ♕xe4 wins it, while otherwise White intends ♕f4–b8. Thus Black's choice was probably correct.

28   ♘f2

Sometimes an oversight is the best chance to win! It seemed to me that this was the moment to set up the position with ♘f2 and ♖e3, but it fails for tactical reasons. However, there seems to be no other winning attempt.

28   ...   ♕c8!

Since Black obviously cannot play ... ♕xf5 because of ♘xe4, I decided to continue with my plan. There was nothing better in any case.

29   ♖e3

After having made this move I suddenly noticed that Black could play 29 ... ♕xf5 30 ♘xe4 ♕e6! with an immediate draw, but the confident way I had made the move evidently led my opponent to accept that the pawn was invulnerable.

29   ...   ♖d5?
30   g4!

White not only achieves the position he has been aiming for, but does so in a very favourable form since the rooks on d5 and f8 are both vulnerable to the manoeuvre ♘h3–f4–g6.

30   ...   ♕c7

Black could perhaps have offered more resistance, but the twin possibilities of ♘h3–f4 and g5 make this position very unpleasant.

31   ♘h3   ♘d3

After 31 ... ♗f7 32 ♘f4 ♖d6, the continuation 33 ♘g6+ ♗xg6 34 fxg6 h6 35 g5 blows up Black's position.

32   cxd3   ♕xc3
33   ♘f4   g5
34   ♘xd5   ♗xd5
35   ♕e1

Thanks to the earlier ♔g1 Black has no real counterplay and he is soon forced to give up.

35   ...   ♕d4
36   dxe4   ♗xe4
37   ♕c3   ♕d5
38   ♕c4   Resigns

2 Scheveningen Variation

This line is popular with many of the world's leading players, including Kasparov, and so one would hardly expect there to be a clear way for White to obtain an advantage. The characteristic feature of the Scheveningen is Black's pawn centre at d6 and e6 covering all the central squares on Black's 4th rank. Thus Black avoids the slight weakness at d5 inherent in the Najdorf and Dragon systems. Behind the cover of his modest but solid pawn centre Black intends to complete his development in peace. The most common move order for Black to adopt if he is aiming for a Scheveningen is 1 e4 c5 2 ♘f3 e6 3 d4 cxd4 4 ♘xd4 ♘f6 5 ♘c3 d6, but Black can invert his second and fifth moves in this line.

The amount of theory in the Scheveningen has increased dramatically since the first edition of the book, so it is no longer feasible to cover two major systems within the confines of a relatively short book. Therefore I have decided to concentrate on the Keres Attack, which is currently considered a more critical test of the Scheveningen than the Classical System. The Keres Attack starts 1 e4 c5 2 ♘f3 e6 3 d4 cxd4 4 ♘xd4 ♘f6 5 ♘c3 d6 6 g4. This kingside pawn push aims firstly to drive the knight from f6, thereby making it harder for Black to break open the centre by ... d5, and secondly to gain space on the kingside and dissuade Black from castling there. Although White often obtains good attacking chances with this system he must not neglect his development since Black can often break the position open by ... d5 and even if this loses a pawn White can find his own king stuck in the centre. In other words, a balance must be struck between furthering White's own kingside ambitions and restraining Black in other sectors of the board.

There are two major options for Black after 6 g4. He may either prevent the further advance of the pawn by 6 ... h6, as covered in games 5, 6, and 7, or he may continue his own plans and allow the knight to be driven back to d7. In this case Black may choose 6 ... a6, 6 ... ♗e7 or 6 ... ♘c6. The specific choice of sixth move may not be very important because there are many transpositions. In game 8 we deal with lines specific to 6 ... ♘c6 (i.e. those involving an early ... ♛c7), and the other lines may be found in game 9. Apart from these two major options, there is a third possibility for Black, namely to counterattack by 6 ... e5. With this move Black loses a tempo, but he hopes to prove that White's g4 has only served to weaken his kingside. This move is a lot better than its reputation, and it has recently seen a surge of popularity; it is covered in game 8.

Game 5
Nunn–Bischoff
Lugano 1986

1	e4	c5
2	♘f3	e6
3	d4	cxd4
4	♘xd4	♘f6
5	♘c3	d6
6	g4	h6 *(16)*

Black avoids having his knight driven away from f6. For a long time White almost played 7 g5 hxg5 8 ♗xg5, Anatoly Karpov being one supporter of White's point of view. Although this continuation gives White a lead in development it has defects, not the least being that Black's rook on h8 is activated and presses down on White's weak h-pawn. Now 7 h4 is considered to give White better chances than 7 g5 and is currently the most popular line. White wants to continue with ♖g1 and g5, driving away the knight after all. Black can either aim for counterplay by preparing ... d5 (game 6), or he can aim to nip White's kingside play in the bud with a timely ... h5 (game 7).

7	h4	a6!?

Although this is a natural move, it has only become popular recently. The main variation is 7 ... ♘c6, and this will be examined in games 6 and 7, but there is one other important possibility, namely 7 ... ♗e7 (7 ... e5 8 ♘f5! ♗e6 9 g5 ♘xe4 10 ♘xg7+ ♗xg7 11 ♘xe4 d5 12 gxh6 ♗xh6 13 ♗xh6 ♖xh6 14 ♕d2 ♖xh4 15 ♗b5+ ♘c6 16 0-0-0 was very good for White in Stanciu–Vegh, Ulan Bator 1986) 8 ♕f3 *(17)* and now:

(1) 8 ... ♘fd7 9 ♕g3 ♘c6 10 ♗e3 a6 11 0-0-0 ♕c7, Ljubojevic–

Timman, Brussels SWIFT 1986, and now Ljubojevic recommends 12 Be2 as slightly better for White.

(2) **8 ... g6!?** 9 g5 hxg5 10 Bxg5 a6 11 0-0-0 e5 12 Nde2 Bg4 13 Qg3 Nbd7 14 f3 Be6 15 Bh3 Bxh3 16 Rxh3 Rc8 17 f4 was unclear in De Wit–Oll, Groningen 1984/5. This interesting idea does not seem to have been repeated. Perhaps 14 f4 is better, hoping to prove that the exposed position of the g4 bishop is a liability.

(3) **8 ... h5** 9 gxh5 and now:

(3a) **9 ... Nc6** 10 Bb5 (an attempt to exploit Black's move order; 10 Nxc6 bxc6 11 Bg5 may be better, when Black has to prove that he has something better than 11 ... Nxh5 transposing to line 3b) Bd7 11 Bxc6 bxc6 12 e5 Nd5?! (12 ... dxe5 13 Nxc6 Bxc6 14 Qxc6+ Kf8 15 h6 gxh6 16 Bd2 Rb8 17 0-0-0 Qb6 18 Qxb6 Rxb6 is equal according to Ljubojevic) 13 exd6 Bxd6 14 Bg5 Qb6 15 0-0-0 Be5 16 Nxd5 cxd5 17 c3 with an edge for White, Ljubojevic–Timman, Bugojno 1986.

(3b) **9 ... Nxh5** 10 Bg5 (10 Be3!? is an interesting untested idea, offering the h-pawn in return for a quick attack with 0-0-0) Nc6 11 Nxc6!? bxc6 12 0-0-0 Bxg5+?! (accepting the sacrifice turns out to be too risky; Black should develop by 12 ... Rb8) 13 hxg5 Qxg5+ 14 Kb1 Ke7 (not 14 ... d5? 15 exd5 cxd5 16 Nxd5 exd5 17 Rxd5 nor 14 ... Qc5? 15

e5! and White wins in both cases, while 14 ... Qe5 15 Be2 g6 16 Qe3 intending f4 gives White a dangerous initiative) 15 Be2 g6 16 Rxd6! Qxd6 17 Qxf7! (somewhat surprisingly Black has no defence) a5 18 Rd1+ Ke5 19 Bxh5 Rxh5 20 f4+ Qxf4 21 Qg7+ Resigns, Sobura–Pieniazek, Poland 1988.

8   Bg2

White abandons his plan to play Rg1 and g5 because after 8 Rg1 d5 9 exd5 Nxd5 10 Nxd5 Qxd5 11 Bg2 Qc4 12 c3 Be7 13 g5 Nd7 14 Qe2 Qxe2+ 15 Kxe2 Nb6 White had no advantage in Karpov–Kindermann, Vienna 1986.

8 ... Nc6

Or:

(1) **8 ... g6** 9 g5 hxg5 10 Bxg5 Be7 11 Qd2 e5 12 Nde2 Be6 13 0-0-0 Nbd7 14 f4 Qa5 (or 14 ... Qc7?! 15 fxe5! dxe5 16 Nd5 Bxd5 17 exd5 Rc8 18 Rhf1! with advantage for White, Ghinda–Bonsch, Halle 1987) 15 Kb1 Nb6 16 b3 with some advantage for White, Gufeld–Georgadze, USSR 1981.

(2) **8 ... d5** 9 exd5 Nxd5 10 Nxd5 exd5 is given as unclear by *ECO*. However in distinction to 8 Rg1 d5, White's rook is still defending the h-pawn, so White might consider 9 e5 Nfd7 10 f4, when 10 ... Be7 11 h5 and 10 ... h5 11 gxh5 look good for White, so the critical reply is probably 10 ... Qb6. 8 ... d5 9 g5 is also interesting.

9	g5	hxg5
10	hxg5	♖xh1+
11	♗xh1	♘d7 *(18)*

If Black attacks the g5 pawn White continues 11 ... ♘xd4 12 ♕xd4 ♘h7 13 e5! ♘xg5 (13 ... dxe5 14 ♕h4 traps the knight) 14 exd6 ♗xd6 15 ♕xg7 (15 ♗xg5 ♕xg5 16 ♕xd6 ♕g1+ is less clear) with a tremendous attack for no material loss.

18
W

12   ♗g2

This move was the result of lengthy thought, but even so it wasn't the best. White has very few constructive moves apart from g6 and 12 g6 ♘xd4 13 gxf7+ ♔xf7 14 ♕xd4 ♕h4 (this represents the main advantage of 7 ... a6 over 7 ... ♗e7, since in the corresponding position with the bishop on e7, White's g6 is much more effective) 15 ♗g2 ♘e5 is obscure. White might be able to claim a slight plus after 16 ♗e3 ♕g4 17 ♔f1, but both kings are unhappily placed and I wanted to find something clearer. 12 ♗e3 is bad after 12 ... ♘de5 threatening ... ♘c4 (13 ♕e2 ♘xd4 loses a pawn). Thus the only direct alternative to

12 g6 is 12 f4, but I was reluctant to create a huge empty space around my king. However after the next move White finds himself committed to f4 in any case, so it would have been better to play it at once. As a result of Nunn–Bischoff, subsequent White players took my advice and played the more accurate 12 f4!, with the continuation 12 ... ♕b6 (or 12 ... ♘xd4 13 ♕xd4 ♕b6 14 ♕xb6 ♘xb6 15 a4!? ♗d7 16 a5 ♘c8 17 ♗e3 ♗c6 18 0-0-0! ♔d7 19 ♗f3 ♘e7 20 ♗g4 with a clear plus for White, Ghinda–Vogt, Halle 1987) 13 ♘de2 g6 14 b3 ♕c5 (14 ... ♕c7 15 ♗b2 b5 16 ♕d2 ♗b7 17 ♘d1 0-0-0 18 ♘e3 ♗e7 19 0-0-0 ♘b6 20 ♔b1 ♔b8 21 ♘c1 was also a little better for White in Grünfeld–Bischoff, Munich 1987) 15 ♕d2 b5 16 ♗b2 ♗b7 17 0-0-0 0-0-0 18 ♔b1 ♕f2!? (or 18 ... ♗e7 19 ♘c1! f6 20 gxf6 ♘xf6 21 ♘d3 with an edge) 19 ♖e1! ♗e7 20 ♘d1 ♕c5 21 ♘e3 and White has a small but permanent advantage, Short–Kindermann, Dortmund 1986. 12 ♗g2 and 12 f4 lead to similar positions, so it is well worth studying Nunn–Bischoff even if you intend to play 12 f4.

12   ...   g6!

The point of 12 ♗g2 is that White improves the position of his bishop (particularly in the g6 line given above) while Black lacks useful moves. 12 ... ♘de5 allows 13 f4 with gain of tempo (13 ... ♘c4 14 b3 ♕b6 15 ♘ce2), 12 ... ♕c7 (or ♗e7) allows 13 g6 and 12 ... ♕b6 13 ♘b3 leads to a loss of time after a subsequent ♗e3. Black's move is the best, cutting out g6 by White and again posing the question as to how White can improve his position.

13   f4

Now the defect of 12 ♗g2 is revealed. In the analysis of 12 f4 we saw that Black generally plays ... g6 in any case, while White's ♗g2 is usually not necessary. Therefore Black gains a tempo, although in this type of position an extra move is not especially valuable. Now that e5 is denied to Black's knights, White threatens simply ♗e3 so Black's rely is more or less forced.

13   ...   ♕b6
14   ♘de2

White can only complete his development by ♕d2 (or ♕d3), b3, ♗b2 and 0-0-0, so before playing f4 I had to make sure that Black couldn't use the four free tempi to harass White's central-ized king.

14   ...   ♕c5

Black settles for finishing his own development by ... b5 and ... ♗b7. There wasn't much choice, as if the queen quits the b6–g1 diagonal White can play ♗e3.

15   ♕d3

It would have been slightly better to play ♕d2 as the position of the queen gives Black a tactical opportunity in a few moves.

15   ...   b5
16   b3

16 ♗e3 is countered by 16 ... ♘b4!

16   ...   ♗b7
17   ♗b2   ♖c8

A provocative move. Black de-cides to keep his king in the centre to help c-file counterplay. After 17 ... 0-0-0 18 0-0-0 White has a very slight advantage as in the ex-amples given after 12 f4.

18   0-0-0   ♘b4

Black goes in for tactics and given his choice last move there was no other consistent continua-tion, for otherwise he has no compensation for the long-term handicap of a poor king position.

19   ♕d2   ♘xc2
20   ♔xc2   b4
21   ♔b1   ♕f2!

This is the point of Black's combination. The immediate 21 ... bxc3 22 ♘xc3 leaves Black in a very poor position as the exchanges have not created any weak spots in White's position to provide counterplay.

22   ♗h1   bxc3

At this stage Black offered a draw but although White must adopt the much less satisfactory recapture with the bishop, thus leaving e4 weak, I decided to play on.

23   ♗xc3   ♕a7?

A misjudgement. The main merit of Black's combination is that his queen has become a nui-sance by taking up residence in the heart of White's position, the more so as White cannot contem-plate a queen exchange which would relieve Black of any worries about his king. Bischoff retreats it to the passive square a8 in return for inconvenient but not really serious pressure on e4. He should have played 23 ... ♘c5 24 ♗d4 ♕h2! (24 ... ♘xe4 25 ♕d3! loses a piece while 24 ... ♕h4 25 ♘c3 e5 26 ♗e3 looks good for White) when White has problems with his e4 pawn. 25 ♕e3 e5 26 ♗b2 ♗g7 creates a very awkward threat of ... exf4, so White would prefer 25 ♘c3 ♕xd2 26 ♖xd2 with equality.

24	**♗b2**	**♕a8**
25	**♕e3**	**♘c5**
26	**♘c3**	

26 ♘g3 with the idea of f5 is also promising.

26 ...   ♗g7 *(19)*

After 26 ... a5 the reply 27 ♕d4 ties Black up by preventing ... ♗g7.

27   ♘d5!

Before playing 26 ♘c3 I had to think very carefully about the tactics initiated by this move, since if White had been reduced to the passive 27 ♖e1 (27 ♖xd6 ♗xc3 is

bad since Black wins after 28 ♗xc3 ♗xe4+ 29 ♗xe4 ♕xe4+ 30 ♕xe4 ♘xe4 or 28 ♕xc3 ♗xe4+ 29 ♗xe4 ♕xe4+ 30 ♔a1 ♕h1+ 31 ♗c1 ♘xb3+) he would have no advantage.

27 ...   ♗xb2

The most natural move. 27 ... exd5 (27 ... ♗xd5 28 exd5 ♗xb2 29 dxe6 wins) 28 ♗xg7 ♘xe4 (28 ... dxe4 29 ♖xd6 is worse as the undefended ♘c5 prevents ... ♖d8, while 29 ... ♘d3 allows ♖xd3) 29 ♗xe4 dxe4 gives White a strong attack on the black squares and Black's queen is buried on a8. However it is not easy to find a concrete way to continue. 30 ♖xd6 ♖d8! 31 ♕d4 ♖xd6 32 ♕xd6 ♕d8 (or else ♗f6) 33 ♕f8+ ♔d7 34 ♕xf7+ wins a pawn, but in view of the opposite coloured bishops and Black's passed e-pawn this might not be enough to win. White should therefore prefer the slow build-up by 30 ♗f6, with many defensive problems for Black.

28 ♘b6   ♗xe4+

After 28 ... ♕a7 29 ♘xc8 ♗xc8 White can't take the bishop, but 30 b4 picks up the knight instead, when Black has insufficient compensation for the lost exchange.

29 ♔xb2   ♕a7

The only defence. Now 30 ♘c4 d5 31 ♕d4 (31 ♘d6+ ♔d7 and 31 ♗xe4 dxe4 also seem satisfactory for Black) fails to 31 ... ♘a4+! 32 bxa4 ♖b8+ followed by ... ♕xd4 and ... ♗xh1.

30 ♖xd6 ♘d3+

Black's moves continue to be forced. 30 ... ♗xh1 31 ♕d4! (attacking the ♖c8 and threatening ♕h8+) ♖b8 (31 ... ♖c7 32 ♕h8+ and mate at d8) 32 ♕xc5 (threat ♖d7) ♖d8 (32 ... ♕e7 33 ♘d7 ♖a8 34 ♕e5 wins) 33 ♕e5 gives White a decisive attack, e.g. 33 ... ♖xd6/♕e7/♕b8 34 ♕h8+ or 33 ... ♖b8 34 ♖xe6+ fxe6 35 ♕h8+.

31 ♔a3

31 ♖xd3 is met by 31 ... ♗xd3.

31 ... ♖c6!

I had overlooked this ingenious defence when I played 26 ♘c3. Other moves lose quickly:

(1) **31 ... ♖c5** 32 ♖xd3 ♖a5+ (32 ... ♕xb6 33 ♗xe4) 33 ♔b2 ♗xd3 (33 ... ♗xh1 34 ♕d4) 34 ♗c6+ ♔d8 (or else a knight check wins the queen) 35 ♕d4+ ♔c7 36 ♘a8+ ♔b8 37 ♕d8 mate.

(2) **31 ... ♕c7** 32 ♖xd3 ♗xd3 33 ♘xc8 ♕xc8 34 ♕xd3 ♕c1+ 35 ♔b4 ♕xh1 36 ♕xa6 with a won ending.

(3) **31 ... ♗xh1** 32 ♕h3 ♖b8 33 ♖xe6+ fxe6 34 ♕h8+ winning the queen.

32 ♖xc6

The best, as 32 ♘d5 ♕xe3 33 ♘f6+ is a draw and 32 ♖xd3 (32 ♕xd3 ♗xd3 33 ♗xc6+ ♔f8 is fine for Black) ♗xh1 33 ♘c4 is about equal.

32 ... ♕e7+ *(20)*

33 ♕c5!

This move was a visible shock for my opponent. 33 ♖c5 ♗xh1

34 b4 ♘xc5 35 ♕xc5 is not so good as Black can avoid the exchange of queens by 35 ... ♕d8.

33 ... ♕xc5+

33 ... ♘xc5 34 ♖c8+ ♕d8 35 ♖xd8+ ♔xd8 transposes except for the position of Black's king, which makes no real difference.

34 ♖xc5 ♘xc5

35 b4!

White is aiming for a good knight v bad bishop ending, but he must avoid 35 ♔b4 ♘d3+ 36 ♔c3, which allows 36 ... ♘f2! Knight v knight endings are still slightly better for White, but far less promising than the position arising in the game.

35 ... ♗xh1

36 bxc5 ♗d5?

With very little time left to reach move 40 Black blunders. He should have tried 36 ... ♔e7 (not 36 ... f6 37 gxf6 ♔f7 38 ♘d7 and ... ♗c6 is impossible, while even if Black's king were on d8 as in the note to Black's 33rd, 36 ... ♔c7 37 ♔b4 ♔c6 38 ♔c4 followed by ♔d4 and ♘c4–e5 wins) 37 ♔b4 e5! (37 ... f6 38 ♔a5 ♗b7 39 ♘c4 followed by ♚b6 should win) 38 fxe5 ♚e6, but even here White wins: 39 ♘c4 ♗d5 40 a3! ♗xc4 (there is not much choice as 40 ... ♗ moves allows ♚a5 and 40 ... ♚e7 41 ♘e3 and 42 ♚a5 wins) 41 ♚xc4 ♚xe5 42 ♚b4! (42 a4? f5 43 gxf6 ♚xf6 44 ♚d5 ♚e7! 45 ♚c6 g5 46 ♚b7 g4 47 c6 leads to an ending of ♛+a-♗ v ♛, which should be a draw, but Black must avoid 44 ... g5? in this line, when 45 ♚d6 g4 46 c6 g3 47 c7 g2 48 c8 (Q) g1 (Q) 49 ♛f8+ wins his queen) ♚d5 (42 ... f5 43 gxf6 ♚xf6 44 ♚a5 g5 45 c6 wins) 43 a4 and Black is in zugzwang.

| 37 | ♘xd5 | exd5 |

White wins because Black's a-pawn has moved, while White's can still advance either one or two squares.

| 38 | ♚b4 | ♚d7 |
| 39 | ♚c3 | |

and Black lost on time, but 39 ... ♚c6 40 ♚d4 a5 41 a4 and 39 ... ♚c7 40 ♚d4 ♚c6 41 a3 a5 42 a4 lead to the same fatal zugzwang.

Game 6
Karpov–Spassky
Tilburg 1980

1	e4	c5
2	♘f3	e6
3	d4	cxd4
4	♘xd4	♘f6
5	♘c3	d6
6	g4	h6
7	h4	♘c6 (21)

For 7 ... a6 and 7 ... ♗e7 see game 5.

| 8 | ♖g1 | d5 |

Another idea is 8 ... ♘d7 (for 8 ... h5 see game 7) 9 g5 hxg5 and now White had a good game after both **10 ♗xg5** ♛b6 11 ♘b3 a6 12 h5 ♛c7 13 ♛e2 b5 14 0-0-0, Tseshkovsky–Zarubin, Sochi 1981, and **10 hxg5** ♘de5 11 ♗e3 ♗d7 12 ♗e2 a6 13 f4, Matulovic–Simic, Smederevo 1981—my personal preference is for 10 ♗xg5, since Black's knight is badly placed at d7

9	♗b5	♗d7
10	exd5	♘xd5
11	♘xd5	exd5
12	♗e3!	

Karpov's play in this game forced a reassessment of the whole line. Hitherto White had played 12 ♛e2+, with rather uninspiring results, but Karpov's idea of ♗e3, ♛d2 and 0-0-0 launching a direct attack (even if this means giving up the h4 pawn) strengthens White's play considerably.

| 12 | ... | ♗e7 |

12 ... ♛xh4 13 ♛e2 ♘xd4 14 ♗xd4+ ♛e7 15 ♗xd7+ ♚xd7 16 ♗e5 ♖d8 is not so clear, but 13 ♛d2 ♗e7 14 0-0-0 followed by

♘f5 gives White a strong attack as in the game. It is curious that Kasparov recommends 12 ... ♕xh4 both in *ECO* and in his book with Nikitin on the Scheveningen, but in neither case does he mention 13 ♕d2, even though it was given in *Informator* 30.

13   ♕d2 *(22)*

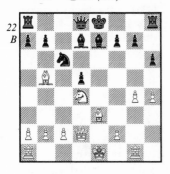

13   ...   ♗xh4?!

13 ... 0-0 14 ♘f5 ♗xf5 15 gxf5 ♔h7 16 0-0-0 is also very good for White, but Black has better survival chances after **13 ... ♘xd4** 14 ♗xd7+ ♕xd7 15 ♕xd4 ♗f6 16 ♕b4 ♗e7, when he went on to draw in Marjanovic–Cebalo, Yugoslav Ch. 1982, although he needed to defend accurately until move 64 to achieve this!

14   0-0-0   ♗f6

14 ... ♘xd4 15 ♗xd7+ ♕xd7 16 ♗xd4 0-0 17 f4! followed by g5 and 14 ... 0-0 15 g5! hxg5 16 ♗xg5 ♗xg5 17 ♖xg5 ♘xd4 18 ♖dg1 g6 19 ♕xd4 both give White a winning attack.

15   ♘f5   ♗xf5
16   gxf5   a6

Black could not castle without losing his vital h6 pawn, but now his king is permanently pinned down in the centre.

17   ♗xc6+   bxc6
18   ♗c5!

Now White only needs to rip open the d-file by c4 to finish Black off. Although Spassky launches an ingenious counterattack his inability to bring the h8 rook into the game enables Karpov to repulse the threats.

18   ...   ♖b8
19   b4   ♖b5

Black's only chance is to eliminate the deadly bishop.

20   ♖ge1+   ♔d7
21   c4   ♖xc5
22   bxc5   ♗g5

After 22 ... ♕b8 23 cxd5 ♗g5 24 ♖e3 ♗xe3 25 fxe3 ♕e5 26 dxc6+ ♔xc6 27 ♕d7+ White should win easily enough.

23   f4   ♕f6 *(23)*

With the point that 24 fxg5 ♕a1+ 25 ♔c2 ♕xa2+ 26 ♔d3 ♕xc4+ 27 ♔e3 hxg5 gives Black four pawns and a tremendous attack for the rook.

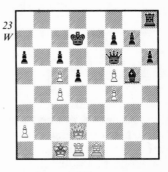

24   cxd5!

Liquidating to a winning ending.

24	...	♛a1+
25	♔c2	♛xa2+
26	♔d3	♛xd2+

26 ... ♛b3+ 27 ♛c3 also forces the queens off.

27	♖xd2	♝xf4

Although Black has two pawns for the exchange all White's pieces are very active and Black is unable to organize himself against the advance of the c-pawn.

28	♖a2	cxd5
29	♖xa6	h5
30	♔d4	h4
31	♔xd5	♖b8
32	f6	gxf6
33	♖xf6	♝g3
34	♖xf7+	♔d8
35	♖f8+	**Resigns**

As 35 ... ♔d7 36 c6+ ♔c7 37 ♖e7+ ♔b6 38 ♖xb8+ ♝xb8 39 ♖b7+ ends the game.

Game 7
Nunn–Sax
Rotterdam 1989

1	e4	c5
2	♘f3	e6
3	d4	cxd4
4	♘xd4	♘f6
5	♘c3	d6
6	g4	h6
7	h4	♘c6
8	♖g1	h5

This is currently the most fashionable move. White's best reply is to take on h5 and since the recapture ... ♘xh5 leaves the knight badly placed, Black normally returns it to f6. The net effect of this is to reach a position similar to that after 6 g4 h6 7 g5 hxg5 8 ♝xg5, but with White having the two extra tempi h4 and ♖g1. This might seem to be a great improvement, but in fact the disadvantages almost balance the advantages. White has two problems: firstly the h-pawn can become weak without the defence of the rook and secondly Black's ... ♛b6 effectively pins the f-pawn against the undefended ♖g1, so it is hard for White to play f4.

9	gxh5	♘xh5

Black players have been known to try 9 ... ♖xh5 10 ♝g5 ♖h8, but this is quite pointless. Black reaches the same position as in the main line, but having forfeited the right to castle kingside.

10	♝g5 *(24)*

24
B

10	...	♘f6

The alternative is the immediate 10 ... ♛b6, which attempts to avoid the loss of time inherent in 10 ... ♘f6. The problem is that the knight is genuinely badly placed at h5, so Black gains nothing by keeping it there. After 10 ... ♛b6 11 ♘b3 a6 12 ♗e2 g6 (12 ... ♘f6 transposes to the analysis of 11 ... ♛b6 in the main line) 13 ♛d2 Black may play:

(1) **13 ... ♗e7** 14 ♖g2! (White need not offer his f-pawn by castling immediately) ♗d7 15 0-0-0 ♖c8 16 ♚b1 ♛c7 17 a3 b5 18 ♗xb5 axb5 19 ♘xb5 ♛b8 20 ♗xe7 ♛xb5 21 ♗xd6 with a clear plus for White, Lobron–Marjanovic, Reggio Emilia 1985/6.

(2) **13 ... ♗d7** 14 ♖g2! ♛c7 15 0-0-0 b5 16 a3 ♘e5 17 ♛d4! ♖h7 18 f4 ♘c4 19 ♗xh5 ♖xh5 20 ♖e1 ♗c6 21 ♘d5 ♗xd5 22 exd5 e5 23 ♛d3 ♗e7 24 ♘d4! and again White stands well, Motwani–Roca, Dubai Ol. 1986.

(3) **13 ... ♛c7** (this is even worse than the lines above because White need not spend time on ♖g2) 14 0-0-0 b5 15 a3 ♗d7 ♗xb5! axb5 17 ♘xb5 ♛b8 18 ♘xd6+ ♖xd6 19 ♛xd6 ♛xd6 20 ♖xd6 with advantage to White, Govedarica–Mokry, Trnava 1987.

11 ♗e2

This flexible move, which prepares a possible h5, has gained in popularity, even though White sometimes has to sacrifice his f2 pawn after ♛d2 and 0-0-0. In reply the immediate ... ♛b6 turns out badly because h5–h6 becomes strong, so Black normally bides his time with ... a6.

11 ... a6

Or:

(1) **11 ... ♗e7** 12 ♛d2 ♘xd4 13 ♛xd4 ♛b6 14 ♗b5+ ♚f8 (14 ... ♗d7 15 ♗xd7+ ♚xd7 16 ♛d2 is good for White) 15 ♛xb6 axb6 16 0-0-0 e5 was unclear in Ljubojevic–Adorjan, Linares 1985, but it is hard to believe that there is no way White can exploit the weak b-pawns. Perhaps 16 ♘a4! is best.

(2) **11 ... ♛b6** 12 ♘b3 a6 13 h5 ♛c7 (or 13 ... ♗d7 14 h6 ♖h7 15 ♛d2 ♘g8 16 ♗e3 ♛c7 17 hxg7 ♖xg7 18 0-0-0 with a plus for White, Alzate–Frias, Dubai Ol 1986) 14 h6 ♘d7 15 hxg7 ♗xg7 16 ♛d2 ♗f8 17 0-0-0 b5 18 a3 ♗b7 19 ♖h1 ♖xh1 20 ♖xh1 ♘ce5, Hellers–Sax, New York Open 1987, and now 21 ♖h8! ♘g6 22 ♖h7 would have given White a very dangerous attack.

12 ♛d2 ♗d7

Playing for ... b5 is a new idea, but the critical continuation is probably he older 12 ... ♛b6 13 ♘b3 *(25)* and now:

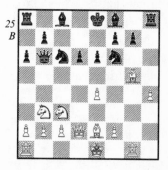

25 B

(1) **13 ... ♛c7** (this doesn't make much sense; Black may as well keep his queen on b6 and dare White to offer his f-pawn) 14 h5 ♘xh5 (14 ... b5 15 a3 ♗b7 16

0-0-0 b4 17 axb4 ♘xb4 18 ♕d4 d5
19 h6! ♖xh6 20 ♗xh6 e5 21 ♗f4!
won for White in Luthar–Bonsch,
East German Ch. 1989) 15 ♖h1
g6 16 ♗xh5 gxh5 17 ♕e2 b5 18
♖xh5 ♖xh5 19 ♕xh5 ♗b7 20
0-0-0 b4 21 ♘e2 ♖c8! 22 ♖d2
♘e5 23 ♘g3! a5 24 f4 with a clear
plus for White, A. Rodriguez–
Douven, Amsterdam 1987.

(2) **13 ... ♗d7** 14 h5 ♘xh5
(Black should take everything on
offer; the passive 14 ... 0-0-0 15
h6 ♖h7 16 0-0-0! ♗e7 17 ♗e3
♕c7 18 ♖xg7 ♖xg7 19 hxg7 ♖g8
20 ♖g1 ♘e5 21 ♗d4 ♘g6 22
♕h6 ♗c6 23 ♗d3 was very good
for White in Korolev–Agzamov,
USSR 1983) 15 ♖h1 g6 16 0-0-0
♕xf2 (once again the crucial
move; 16 ... ♕c7 17 ♗xh5 gxh5
18 ♕e2! ♗e7 19 ♗xe7 ♘xe7 20
♖xh5 ♖xh5 21 ♕xh5 ♘g6 was
played in Tseshkovsky–Mokry,
Trnava 1986, and now 22 ♕h2!
was promising for White) 17 e5!
♕f5! (17 ... ♘xe5 18 ♘e4 ♕f5 19
♕e3! ♗c6 20 ♘bd2! gives White
a crushing attack) and the evaluation of the whole line depends
critically on this position. In A.
Rodriguez–Grooten, Dieren
1987, White played **18 exd6** ♕xg5
19 ♕xg5 ♗h6 20 ♕xh6 ♖xh6 21
♘c5 ♘e5! 22 ♘3e4 0-0-0 23
♘xd7! ♔xd7 24 ♖h3 ♖e8, and
although Rodriguez gives 25 b4!
as unclear, in my opinion this line
is not convincing. Therefore in
Chandler–Hellers, Thessaloniki
Ol. 1988 White tried **18 ♗xh5**, but
after 18 ... ♖xh5 19 ♖xh5 gxh5

20 exd6 ♘e5 21 ♘d4 ♕g4 22 ♗e7
♘c4 23 ♕d3 ♘e5 24 ♕e3 ♘c4 25
♕d3 ♘e5 there was only a draw
by repetition. It seems to me that
White's best chance is to follow
the Rodriguez–Grooten game,
but instead of 21 ♘c5 play 21
♘e4! white intends a combination
of ♘f6 and ♘bc5, while after 21
... 0-0-0 22 ♘f6 ♖dh8 23 ♘xd7
♔xd7 24 ♘c5+ ♔c8 25 ♗f3
White has dangerous threats.

13   0-0-0   b5
14   ♘xc6!

The immediate 14 ♕e3 is met
by 14 ... ♕b6.

14   ...   ♗xc6
15   ♕e3 *(26)*

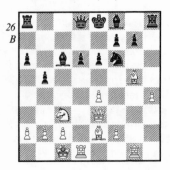

White has the unpleasant
threats of 16 e5 and 16 ♘d5, while
after 15 ... ♕a5 White can afford
to take time out for 16 ♔b1
because 16 ... b4 may be met by
17 ♘d5 ♘xd5 18 exd5 ♗xd5 19
♖xd5 ♕xd5 20 ♗f3. Black is
therefore forced into the unpala-
table 15 ... ♕c7.

15   ...   ♕c7
16   ♘d5   ♗xd5
17   exd5   e5

After 17 ... ♖c8 White replies 18 c3, and Black has achieved nothing positive, while giving away the chance to castle queenside. 17 ... e5 is better, but even so White's lead in development and Black's exposed king give him dangerous attacking chances.

18   ♔b1?!

Chess laziness. Of course ♔b1 is a desirable move, but by giving Black a free tempo White's attack loses much of its momentum. The immediate 18 f4! was correct, when White has a clear advantage. Now by accurate defence Black survives the immediate crisis.

18   ...   ♘h7

Eliminating the g5 bishop makes it easier to flee with the king, should that prove necessary, and ultimately the opposite-coloured bishops might provide a drawing mechanism.

19   f4   ♘xg5

Not 19 ... f6 20 fxe5 dxe5 21 ♗h5+ ♔d8 22 d6 ♗xd6 23 ♖xd6+ ♕xd6 24 ♖d1 ♕xd1+ 25 ♗xd1 fxg5 26 ♕xe5 with an excellent position for White.

20   ♖xg5

A difficult choice, as although White may win a pawn by 20 fxe5 (20 hxg5 g6 21 f5!? is probably also slightly better for White) dxe5 21 ♖xg5 0-0-0! 22 ♖xe5 ♗d6, Black completes his development and the opposite-coloured bishops become an important factor.

20   ...   ♖c8

Now 20 ... 0-0-0 is bad because of 21 a4!, so Black must adopt a different defensive plan.

21   c3   ♕c5

Of course this is only possible when White had not exchanged on e5. Black gains time to reorganize his defences.

22   ♕g3   exf4
23   ♕xf4   ♖c7! *(27)*

An excellent move. Black's rook covers the vulnerable square f7 and when it arrives at e7 the attack on the bishop will gain more time for Black.

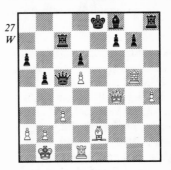

24   a4!

White's only chance to make something of his waning initiative is to create a new target on the queenside.

24   ...   ♖e7
25   ♗d3   g6
26   axb5   axb5

Not 26 ... ♗h6? 27 ♕f6.

27   ♕d4

The ending now represents the best winning chance for White. Although White's gain of a pawn is only temporary, the passed b-pawn combined with an exposed

Black king gives White a nagging advantage.

27	...	♕xd4
28	♗xb5+	♔d8
29	♖xd4	♖e1+
30	♔a2	♗e7
31	♖gg4	♖h1

The h-pawn is doomed, so White switches to harassing Black's king. In this the opposite-coloured bishops prove a big help.

32	♖a4	♖8xh4
33	♖xh4	♖xh4

33 ... ♗xh4 34 ♖a7 is worse, since White threatens the f-pawn directly and the d-pawn indirectly via ♖d7+.

34	♖a8+?

A careless check which drives the Black king to a better square. White should have cut the king off by 34 ♖a7! (threat ♖d7+) ♖e4 (after 34 ... g5 35 ♖d7+ ♔e8 36 ♖xd6+ ♔f8 37 ♖c6 the d-pawn becomes dangerous) 35 ♗c6! with some winning chances because Black cannot challenge White to a pawn race (35 ... g5 36 b4 g4 37 b5 g3 38 b6 wins because the mate threat gains a tempo).

34	...	♔c7
35	♗c6	

35 ♖a7+ ♔b6 36 ♖xe7 ♔xb5 37 ♖xf7 ♔c5 is an easy draw.

35	...	♖e4!

White is effectively a tempo down over the above line since after 36 ♖a7+ ♔b8 White must waste time with his rook. This tempo makes all the difference and Black can now draw comfortably.

36	b4	♗f6
37	♖a7+	♔b8
38	♖xf7	♗xc3
39	b5	♖b4
40	♔a3	♖b1
41	♖b7+	♔c8
42	b6	♗d4
43	♖c7+	♔b8
44	♖b7+	
	Draw	

Game 8
Karpov–Dorfman
USSR Ch. 1976

1	e4	c5
2	♘f3	e6
3	d4	cxd4
4	♘xd4	♘f6
5	♘c3	d6
6	g4	♘c6 *(28)*

I must confess to have taken some liberties with the move order of Karpov–Dorfman, which actually continued 6 ... ♗e7. We transpose back in a few moves, but this move order makes it easier to explain the proposed repertoire. Of the sixth move alternatives, we only consider 6 ... e5 here; the others may be found in game 9. After 6 ... e5 (played by Murei and Suba) 7 ♗b5+ ♗d7 8 ♗xd7+ ♕xd7 (8 ... ♘bxd7 9 ♘f5 is awful for Black) 9 ♘f5 h5 10 f3 hxg4 11 fxg4 ♖h3!? 12 ♕e2 (better than 12 ♘e3 ♕c6 13 ♘ed5 ♘bd7 14 ♕e2, Howell–Suba, London 1988, and now 14 ... ♘xd5 15 ♘xd5 ♘b6 is unclear) ♕c6 (12 ... ♖xc3?! 13 bxc3 ♕c6 14 0-0 ♕xe4 15 ♕xe4 ♘xe4 16 ♖e1

♘c5 17 ♗a3 ♘ba6 18 ♖ad1 ♖d8 19 h4 g6 20 ♘e3 is good for White, Wahls–Mainka, Luxembourg 1989) 13 0-0 ♘bd7 14 g5 ♖xc3, Tisdall–Suba, Preston 1989, and now 15 ♘xg7+ ♗xg7 16 gxf6 ♖xc2 (16 ... ♘xf6 17 bxc3 ♕xe4 18 ♕d3 d5 19 ♕g3 is promising) 17 fxg7 ♔e7 (17 ... 0-0-0 18 ♕g4) 18 ♗g5+! f6 19 ♕f3 is very good for White.

7 g5 ♘d7
8 h4 a6

Or 8 ... ♘xd4 9 ♕xd4 ♘e5 10 ♗e2 ♘c6 11 ♕d3 ♗e7 (or 11 ... a6 12 ♗f4 ♕c7 13 0-0-0 ♘e5 14 ♕d4 ♗d7 15 h5 with strong pressure for White, Lutikov–Malich, Leipzig 1977) 12 ♗f4 (were it not for this move, exposing the weakness of d6, Black's scheme would be viable—this is one of the few situations in the Sicilian where a direct attack on d6 works) 0-0 13 0-0-0 e5 14 ♗e3 ♗e6 15 ♘d5 ♕a5 16 a3 ♗xd5 17 ♕xd5 ♕xd5 18 ♖xd5 with the type of ending Sicilian players have nightmares about, Nunn–Jansa, Dortmund 1979.

9 ♗e3 ♕c7

The repertoire proposed in this book involves meeting lines without ... ♕c7 by the new idea ♗c4 (see next game), while if Black plays ... ♕c7 preventing ♗c4 then White replies with ♕e2 and 0-0-0. Unfortunately White cannot guarantee to play ♗c4 in every line, because if White plays ♗c4 without preparing it by ♗e3 then the reply ... ♘de5 is very awkward.

10 ♕e2

Karpov's move is very logical in that it prepares queenside castling as quickly as possible, while the f1 bishop and h1 rook are left at home since it is not yet clear which square is best for these pieces. At e2 the queen sets up tactical chances down the e-file and avoids attack from a black knight arriving at c4.

10 ... ♗e7

We are now back in Karpov–Dorfman.

11 0-0-0 b5

Tactical ideas for White are already in the air, for example 12 ♘f5 exf5 13 ♘d5 ♕d8 14 exf5, but although this is quite good for White Black can improve by 12 ♘f5 b4!

12 ♘xc6 ♕xc6
13 ♗d4 b4 *(29)*

Black forces White to sacrifice on d5, but this move was itself virtually forced as 13 ... 0-0 14 ♖g1 gives White a crushing attack, e.g. 14 ... b4 15 ♘d5 exd5 16 exd5 ♕xd5 17 ♕xe7 ♕xa2 18 g6 hxg6 19 ♖xg6 and wins.

29
W

14	♘d5	exd5
15	♗xg7	♖g8
16	exd5	♕c7
17	♗f6	

The position of White's bishop at f1 is shown up as a defect since 17 ♖e1 ♘e5 18 ♗xe5 dxe5 19 f4 exf4 achieves nothing when d6 is impossible. If the other rook could come to e1 Black would be finished.

17	...	♘e5
18	♗xe5	dxe5
19	f4	

Now White wins a third pawn for the piece since 19 ... e4 fails to 20 d6 ♗xd6 21 ♕xe4+. Black's king must remain stuck in the centre so one must consider Karpov's sacrifice correct, although in the subsequent play Black's resourceful defence almost saves the game.

19	...	♗f5
20	♗h3	

White takes time out to neutralize Black's counterplay as 20 fxe5 at once allows the unclear 20 ... ♖c8 21 ♖h2 ♕a5.

| 20 | ... | ♗xh3 |

21	♖xh3	♖c8
22	fxe5	

After this Black activates his queen and Karpov is obliged to play with extreme accuracy to maintain his advantage. In his notes Karpov suggested 22 b3 to prevent the following manoeuvre.

22	...	♕c4!
23	♖dd3	♕f4+

23 ... ♕xa2 24 d6 (threat d7+) ♖c4 (24 ... ♖c5 25 ♕f2 and 26 dxe7) 25 dxe7 ♕a1+ 26 ♔d2 ♕xb2 27 ♖d8+ ♔xe7 28 ♖d7+ ♔xd7 29 ♕xc4 and 23 ... ♖xg5 24 hxg5 ♕xa2 25 d6 ♗xg5+ 26 ♖he3 ♖c4 27 ♕g2 are good for White.

| 24 | ♔b1 | ♖c4! |

The rook follows the queen's path with the aim of causing White some problems on the back rank.

25	d6	♖e4
26	♖he3	♖xe3
27	♖xe3	♕xh4 (30)

If Black attempts to save his bishop by 27 ... ♗d8 (27 ... ♗f8 28 ♕xa6 is even worse) he is crushed after 28 ♖f3 ♕g4 29 e6

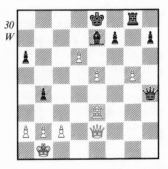

30
W

fxe6 30 d7+ winning the queen, so he quite rightly decides to grab as many pawns as he can while White is taking his bishop.

28   ♕f3!

Naturally not 28 dxe7 at once since Black exchanges queens by 28 ... ♕h1+. White's advantage lies in the insecure black king, which causes trouble even when Black restores material equality.

28   ...   ♕xg5

28 ... ♗xg5 29 e6 fxe6 30 ♖xe6+ ♔d8 (30 ... ♔d7 31 ♕f7+) 31 ♕c6! and 28 ... ♖xg5 29 ♕c6+ ♔f8 30 dxe7+ ♔xe7 31 a3 win for White.

29   ♖e1

29 ♕c6+ ♔f8 30 dxe7+ ♕xe7 31 ♕h6+ ♖g7 is a little better for White and this may in fact be his best line.

29   ...   ♕g2?

29 ... ♕g4 was better, when it is far from clear if White can do more than draw.

30   ♕f5   ♖g6
31   ♖f1   ♕d5
32   dxe7   ♔xe7

Material equality is re-established but Black's king position makes his defensive task difficult. Detailed analysis of this position would take us too far afield, but Black does not seem to have any real improvements hereafter and the task of defending both his king and his pawns soon overstretches his forces.

33   ♕f4   a5
34   ♕h4+   ♔e8
35   ♕xh7   ♕f3

36   ♕h8+   ♔e7
37   ♕h4+   ♔e8
38   ♕c4   ♕b7
39   b3

One of the most impressive features of this game is the way Karpov managed to conduct all the tactical operations with a vulnerable black rank. Many players, through nervousness or laziness, would have wasted a tempo on b3 earlier, and this might well have cost the game (note that although b3 was a good idea at move 22, the point was to prevent the ... ♕c4–f4 manoeuvre rather than to give the king air).

39   ...   ♖e6 *(31)*

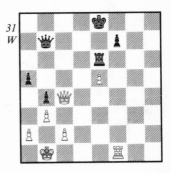

40   ♖g1?!

Perhaps Karpov assumed that the exposed king must succumb quickly to the combined attack of White's queen and rook, but the task is much more difficult than appears at first. I suspect that if Karpov had realized this he would not have been so hasty in giving back the pawn, because he could have waited for a more favourable moment.

40	...	♖xe5
41	♖g8+	♔e7
42	♕h4+	♔d7
43	♕f6!	♖e7
44	♕f5+	♔d6
45	♕xa5	♖e5

45 ... ♕e4 would have lasted longer, but the result is not in doubt.

46	♕d8+	♔e6
47	♔b2!	f6
48	♖f8	♕g7
49	♕c8+	♔d5
50	♕c4+	**Resigns**

Game 9
Nunn–Thorsteins
Lugano 1986

1	e4	c5
2	♘f3	e6
3	d4	cxd4
4	♘xd4	♘f6
5	♘c3	d6
6	g4	*(32)*

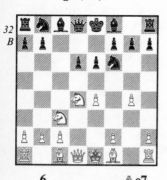

32
B

| 6 | ... | ♗e7 |

We also need to consider those lines which are special to 6 ... a6. After 6 ... a6 7 g5 ♘fd7 8 h4 b5 (8 ... ♘c6 9 ♗e3 will lead to game 8 or to the main line of this game) 9 a3 ♗b7 (9 ... ♘b6 is less accurate since after 10 h5 White may meet 10 ... ♗e7 with the dangerous piece sacrifice 11 ♕g4 e5 12 ♘f5 g6 13 hxg6 fxg6 14 ♗e3! gxf5 15 exf5; in Nunn–Walden, Nottingham 1983, the continuation 10 ... ♘8d7 11 ♖h3 ♘c5 12 g6 f6 13 ♖g3 e5 14 ♘c6 ♕c7 15 ♘b4 was good for White) 10 ♗e3 (10 h5 at once is not so good since 10 ... ♗e7 awkwardly attacks the g5 pawn) ♘b6 (**10 ... ♘c6** 11 ♕e2 ♘de5 12 0-0-0 ♘c4 13 ♘xc6 ♗xc6 14 f4 ♕a5?! 15 ♘d5! gave White a crushing attack in Alexander–Lundholm, corr. 1970–1, while **10 ... ♘c5** 11 ♕g4!? ♘bd7 12 0-0-0 ♘e5 13 ♕g2 ♘c4 14 ♗xc4 bxc4 15 h5 intending g6 is good for White according to Boudy) 11 h5 ♘d7 12 ♖h3! (the discovery of this move led to a reassessment of many lines in the Keres Attack—the point is to defend the rook in preparation for g6) Black may play:

(1) **12 ... ♘e5** 13 g6 hxg6 14 hxg6 ♖xh3 15 gxf7+ ♘xf7 (Black avoids the displacement of his king) 16 ♗xh3 and Black's weak pawn at e6 gives White a good game, Torre–Vogt, Polanica Zdroj 1977.

(2) **12 ... d5** 13 g6 e5 reaches a complex position. In two games White played 14 ♘f5, and after **14 ... hxg6** 15 hxg6 ♖xh3 16 gxf7+ ♔xf7 17 ♗xh3 ♘f6 18 ♗xb6 ♕xb6 19 ♘xd5 ♗xd5 20 exd5 ♖d8 21 ♘e3 ♗c5 22 ♗e6+, Yakovic–Espig, Leipzig 1986 and

14 ... d4 15 h6 hxg6 16 hxg7 ♗xg7 17 ♘xg7+ ♔e7 18 ♗xd4! exd4 19 ♕xd4 ♖xh3 20 0-0-0!, Fogarasi–Espig, Budapest Open 1987, White had a clear advantage. However, as Lukacs and Hazai point out, the improvement **14 ... ♘f6!** leads to a totally unclear position. I therefore suggest **14 exd5!?** exd4 (14 ... ♘xd5 15 ♘xd5 ♗xd5 16 ♘xb5) 15 ♗xd4 with an enormous attack, e.g. 15 ... ♘xd5 16 ♘xd5 ♗xd5 17 ♖e3+ ♗e6 18 ♕f3! winning.

(3) **12 ...** ♗e7 13 g6 ♗f6 14 ♕g4 ♕e7 15 gxf7+ ♔xf7 16 f4 ♖hc8 (16 ... ♖ac8 17 f5 e5 18 ♘e6 ♖hg8 19 h6! g6 20 ♖g3 is also good for White) 17 f5 ♘e5 18 fxe6+ ♔f8 19 ♕g2 ♖xc3! 20 bxc3 ♘a4 21 ♖g3! ♘xc3 22 ♗d3 ♕c7 23 e7+! turned out well for White in Fernandez Garcia–D. Cramling, Barcelona 1986.

(4) **12 ...** ♘c5 3 g6 ♕e7 14 gxf7+ ♕xf7 15 ♕g4 ♗c8 16 e5! dxe5 17 ♖f3 ♕b7 18 ♘de2! ♕c7 19 0-0-0 ♗d7 20 ♗g5 a5? 21 ♘g3! with a massive advantage for White, Idelstein–Barash, Israel 1987.

7	g5	♘fd7
8	h4	♘c6
9	♗e3	0-0

If Black plays 9 ... a6 White may again reply 10 ♗c4, with play similar to that in the main line. Black has one more possibility, namely 9 ... ♘b6 10 f4 and now:

(1) **10 ... 0-0** 11 ♕f3 d5 12 0-0-0 ♗d7?! 13 exd5 exd5 14 ♗d3! ♗c5 15 ♘xc6 ♗xe3+ 16 ♕xe3 bxc6 17 h5 ♖e8 18 ♕d4 ♕e7 19 h6 ♕e3+ 20 ♕xe3 ♖xe3 21 hxg7 with a decisive advantage for White, Lanka–Strautinsh, corr. 1986.

(2) **10 ... d5** 11 ♗b5 (11 e5!? is possible) ♗d7 12 exd5 exd5 13 ♕f3 ♗b4 14 0-0 ♗xc3 15 bxc3 ♘xd4 16 ♗xd7+ ♕xd7 17 ♗xd4 0-0 18 f5 ♘c4, Tseitlin–Lukin, Leningrad 1987, and now 19 ♖f2! intending h5–h6 should be good for White.

10 ♗c4!? *(33)*

An intriguing new idea. White plans a similar strategy to that in the Velimirovic Attack, which arises after 1 e4 c5 2 ♘f3 ♘c6 3 d4 cxd4 4 ♘xd4 ♘f6 5 ♘c3 ♘c6 6 ♗c4 e6 7 ♗e3 ♗e7 8 ♕e2 0-0 9 0-0-0, one typical variation being 9 ... a6 10 ♗b3 ♕c7 11 g4 ♘xd4 12 ♖xd4 b5 13 g5 ♘d7 14 h4, with an obvious similarity to Nunn–Thorsteins. One major difference stands out. In the Velimirovic Attack White cannot play g4 under the most favourable possible circumstances; he must either waste time preparing g4 by 11 ♖hg1, or he must reconcile himself to the relatively unfavourable recapture with the rook on d4 (the reason being that 11 g4 ♘xd4 12 ♗xd4 fails to 12 ... e5). In the Keres Attack position White has already achieved g4–g5 without playing ♖hg1, and there is no reason why he should not take on d4 with his bishop. Therefore if Black plays just as in the Velimirovic Attack, he will end up with an unfavourable version of that system, and White's kingside breakthrough by h5 and g6 will have added force. On the other hand White is two moves away from castling, so the question is whether Black can do something quickly while White's king is still in the centre. It is worth adding that 10 ♕e2 is perfectly playable here, just as in Karpov–Dorfman above, but having played ... 0-0 instead of ... ♕c7 improves Black's prospects.

10 ...   ♘xd4

Perhaps the most natural attempt to exploit White's king position is to open the centre by 10 ... ♘b6 11 ♗b3 d5, but after 12 ♕e2 it is not clear what Black's next move is. **12 ... e5** loses a pawn and **12 ... ♘xd4** 13 ♗xd4 dxe4 14 0-0-0 followed by ♘xe4 prepares a sacrifice on f6. Maybe **12 ... ♗b4!?** is best, with an unclear position.

11   ♕xd4?!

Inconsistent. White should stick to his idea and play 11 ♗xd4. I rejected this because of 11 ... d5 12 exd5 exd5 13 ♘xd5 ♖e8, but a little more thought would have shown that after 14 ♘e3! Black has no real compensation for the pawn. Indeed, after 14 ... ♕c7 (intending ... ♘e5) White can go over to the attack himself by 15 ♗xf7+ ♔xf7 16 ♕h5+ ♔f8 17 ♗xg7+ ♔xg7 18 ♘f5+ with a large advantage.

11 ...   a6?!

Black misses his chance. 11 ... ♘e5 would have forced White's bishop to abandon the active b3–g8 diagonal and after 12 ♗e2 ♘c6 13 ♕d2 a6 the position would have been roughly level.

12   0-0-0

Now White can set up the type of position he is aiming for.

12 ...   b5
13   ♗b3   ♘c5
14   f4

Defending g5 in preparation for h5–h6.

14 ...   ♕a5

Black intends to meet the advance of the h-pawn by ... e5, relying on a tactical point to secure the e5 square, but unfortunately White has a tactical counterpoint!

15   h5   b4
16   h6   e5 *(34)*

White cannot take twice on e5 because of the discovered attack along the 5th rank, but by means of a queen sacrifice White can convert his lead in development

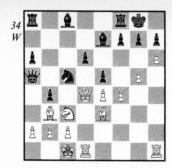

into a crushing attack against Black's king.

17 ♘d5! ♘xb3+

Black must remove one attacking piece. The immediate capture of the queen leads to mate after 17 ... exd4 18 ♘xe7+ ♔h8 19 hxg7+ ♔xg7 20 ♗xd4+ f6 21 gxf6+ ♖xf6 22 ♖dg1+ ♔f8 23 ♖g8+ ♔xe7 24 ♖xh7+ ♖f7 25 ♖xf7.

18 axb3 ♗xg5

Black decides to decline the offered queen. After 18 ... exd4 19 ♘xe7+ ♔h8 20 ♗xd4 f6 (20 ... ♖g8 21 hxg7+ ♖xg7 22 ♖xh7+ mates) 21 g6! Black is strangely helpless against the threat of 22 hxg7+ ♔xg7 23 ♖xh7 mate, for example 21 ... ♖g8 (**21 ... gxh6** 22 ♖xh6, **21 ... hxg6** 22 ♘xg6+ ♔g8 23 h7+ ♔f7 24 ♘xf8 and **21 ... ♕a1+** 22 ♔d2 ♕xd1+ 23 ♔xd1 ♗g4+ 24 ♔d2 hxg6 25 ♘xg6+ ♔h7 26 ♘xf8+ ♖xf8 27 hxg7+ ♔xg7 28

♖g1 are no better) 22 hxg7+ ♔xg7 (22 ... ♖xg7 23 ♖xh7+ ♖xh7 24 ♗xf6+ ♖g7 25 ♖h1+ mates) 23 ♖xh7+ ♔f8 24 ♖f7+ ♔e8 25 ♘xg8 ♗e6 26 ♘xf6+ ♔d8 27 ♖f8+ and in return for the queen White wins almost all Black's pieces.

19 fxe5

White must not repeat the offer because after 19 fxg5 exd4 20 ♘e7+ ♔h8 he cannot play 21 ♗xd4 due to 21 ... ♕xg5+.

19 ... ♗xe3+

After 19 ... dxe5 20 ♕xe5 ♗xe3+ 21 ♔b1 White will at the very least win Black's queen.

20 ♕xe3 g6

Or else hxg7 wins instantly.

21 ♕g5 f6

Black must jettison material to meet the threats of 22 ♘e7+ and 22 ♕f6.

22 ♘e7+

Even stronger than taking on f6. After 22 ... ♔h8 23 ♘xg6+ hxg6 24 ♕xg6 ♖a7 (or 24 ... ♖g8 25 ♕xf6+ ♔h7 26 ♕f7+ ♔h8 27 h7 ♕a1+ 28 ♔d2 ♖g2+ 29 ♔e3) 25 exf6 there is no defence to the threat of ♕g7+. Black has only one alternative, but then it is White who can exploit a line-up on the 5th rank.

22 ... ♔f7
23 e6+ Resigns

3   Classical Variation

In the first edition of this book I christened the line 1 e4 c5 2 ♘f3 ♘c6 3 d4 cxd4 4 ♘xd4 ♘f6 5 ♘c3 d6, which can also occur with the move order 2 ... d6 and 5 ... ♘c6, with the name 'Classical Variation'. This nomenclature seems to have caught on, so I will keep the name in this edition. The line I am recommending against the Classical is 6 ♗g5, called the Richter–Rauzer Attack even though the treatment used today doesn't seem to owe anything to Richter. This line is very common in practice, so there is a large body of theory. In general I will keep to the main lines in the proposed repertoire, but where there are interesting sidelines I will give them a brief mention.

The idea of 6 ♗g5 as it is played today is based on a quick ♕d2 and 0-0-0, exerting pressure down the d-file and restraining Black from active play in the centre. Black's most solid reply is the natural 6 ... e6 7 ♕d2 ♗e7 8 0-0-0 0-0, but despite its solid appearance it can often lead to sharp tactical play. This is covered in game 10. Sometimes Black players postpone ... 0-0 so as to delay exposing the king to a possible pawn storm. The line 6

... e6 7 ♕d2 a6 8 0-0-0 ♗d7 is the subject of game 11 while 6 ... e6 7 ♕d2 a6 0-0-0 h6 appears in game 12. Finally some players have experimented with the omission of 6 ... e6, not fearing the doubled pawns resulting from ♗xf6, and the most popular of these ideas, 6 ... ♗d7, forms the basis of game 13. Unusual lines involving ... e6 are dealt with in game 10, while the others are in game 13.

1	e4	c5
2	♘f3	d6
3	d4	cxd4
4	♘xd4	♘f6
5	♘c3	♘c6
6	♗g5	e6

Other moves are considered in game 13.

     7   ♕d2 *(35)*   ♗e7

7 ... a6 appears in games 11 and 12. There are two other alternatives:

(1) **7 ... h6** (7 ... ♗d7? 8 ♘db5 is just a mistake) 8 ♗xf6 gxf6 (8 ... ♕xf6 9 ♘db5 and 10 0-0-0 wins the d6 pawn) 9 0-0-0 (playing for 0-0 is also slightly better for

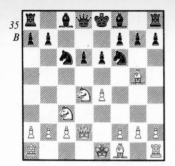

35
B

White, e.g. 9 ♖d1 a6 10 ♗e2 h5 11 0-0 ♗d7 12 ♘b3 ♕c7 13 ♔h1 0-0-0 14 f4, or 9 ♗e2 h5 10 0-0 a6 11 ♔h1! ♗d7 12 f4 ♕c7 13 ♖f3! ♘xd4 14 ♕xd4 ♗e7 15 ♖d1 h4 16 ♖fd3 ♖d8, van der Wiel–J. Piket, Leiden 1986, and now 17 ♗f3 gives White an edge) a6 10 f4 ♗d7 11 ♗e2 h5 (11 ... ♕b6 12 ♗h5 ♕xd4 13 ♕xd4 ♘xd4 14 ♖xd4 ♖g8 15 g3 ♗e7 16 ♖f1 ♗c6 17 f5 ♖g5 18 ♗e2 with advantage, Bondarevsky–Botvinnik, USSR Ch. 1951) 12 ♔b1 ♕c7 (or 12 ... ♕b6 13 ♘b3 0-0-0 14 ♖hf1 ♘a5 15 ♖f3 ♘xb3 16 axb3 ♔b8 17 ♘a4 ♕a7 18 f5 with a clear plus for White, Keres–Botvinnik, Moscow 1956) 13 ♖hf1 0-0-0 (13 ... ♗e7 14 ♖f3 ♘xd4 15 ♕xd4 ♕c5 16 ♕d2 ♗c6 17 ♖e3 ♕a5 18 a3 ♖d8 19 ♗c4 gives White an edge, Liberzon–Botvinnik, USSR 1967) 14 ♘b3 ♔b8 15 ♖f3 ♗e7 16 ♖h3 h4 17 ♕e1 and Black has not yet equalized, Vasyukov–Shamkovich, Dubna 1973.

(2) 7 ... ♘xd4 8 ♕xd4 ♗d7 9 0-0-0 ♕a5 10 ♗d2 a6 (10 ... ♕c5 11 ♕xc5 dxc5 12 ♘b5 is good for

White) 11 ♗e2! ♗c6 (11 ... ♕c5 is still bad, this time because after 12 ♕xc5 dxc5 13 e5 ♘d5 14 ♘xd5 exd5 15 ♗f3 ♗c6 16 ♗a5! White prevents ... ♖d8) 12 f3 ♕c7 13 g4 ♗e7 14 g5 ♘h5 15 ♕g1! (not 15 f4 at once because of 15 ... e5) and White's threat of f4 proved very hard to meet, Tal–Sosonko, Wijk aan Zee 1982.

8 0-0-0   0-0

Or 8 ... ♘xd4 9 ♕xd4 0-0 10 e5 dxe5 11 ♕xe5 *(36)* and now:

36
B

(1) **11 ... ♘d7** is bad after 12 ♗xe7 ♕xe7 13 ♕c7!

(2) **11 ... ♕b6** 12 ♗e3 ♘g4 gives White a favourable ending after 13 ♗xb6 ♘xe5 14 ♗c7 ♘g4 15 ♗g3 ♘f6 16 ♗b5! a6 17 ♗e2 b5 18 ♗f3 ♖a7 19 ♗d6, as in Vasyukov–Boleslavsky, USSR 1957.

(3) **11 ... ♗d7** 12 h4 ♖c8 (12 ... ♕e8 transposes to line 4) 13 ♖h3 (White's rook can come to d3 or g3) ♕c7 (13 ... ♖c5 14 ♕e3 ♕c8 15 ♖g3 ♔h8 16 ♔b1 followed by the push of the h-pawn gives White a dangerous attack) 14 ♕xc7 ♖xc7 15 ♘b5 ♗xb5 16

♗xb5 and White's two bishops give him an edge in this ending.

(4) **11 ...** ♕e8 12 h4 ♗d7 (12 ... a6?! 13 ♘e4 ♘d5 14 ♗xe7 ♘xe7 15 h5 ♘c6 16 ♕g3 ♕e7 17 h6 g6, Hubner–Timman, Belfort 1988, and now 18 ♗c4 is very good for White) 13 ♖h3 ♗c6 14 ♖g3 ♕b8 15 ♕e3 ♖d8, Tal–Timman, Brussels SWIFT 1988, and now 16 ♗d3! ♗d6 17 ♗xf6 ♗xg3 18 ♘e2! gxf6 19 ♘xg3 ♔f8 20 ♕h6+ ♔e7 21 ♖e1 ♖d5 22 ♘f5+ ♖xf5 23 ♗xf5 gives White the advantage according to Tal.

The position after 8 ... 0-0 is one of the most important in the whole Sicilian Defence and despite decades of practical experience no definite assessment can be given. Although 9 ♘b3 was often played in the late fifties and early sixties, it fell into disuse and 9 f4, which has always been regarded as the main line, became virtually universal. However 9 ♘b3 has been regaining popularity and now rivals 9 f4 for the distinction of being considered the 'main line'.

9   ♘b3   *(37)*

Notice that 9 ♗xf6? is bad since Black can play 9 ... ♗xf6 10 ♘xc6 bxc6 11 ♕xd6 ♕b6 when the threats to b2 and f2 are more than enough compensation for the pawn.

The main point of 9 ♘b3 is that it unveils an attack against the d6 pawn and so prepares ♗xf6. Black has four main methods of countering White's plan. The first

is to sacrifice the d-pawn, for example by 9 ... h6 10 ♗xf6 ♗xf6, but a number of games prove that White can gain an advantage. A second plan is to allow ♗xf6 and then recapture with the pawn. This leaves Black's king somewhat exposed, but White has no immediate method of launching an attack. More serious is that Black's central pawns are inflexible and White may have enough time to start a kingside pawn storm. The assessment of this line depends on the speed of the respective attacks. Black's third plan is to counter White's pressure on d6 directly by playing 9 ... a5 10 a4 d5 (moreover the immediate 9 ... d5 is just about possible). The final plan is to counterattack f2 by 9 ... ♕b6, gaining enough time to defend d6 by ... ♖d8. Apart from the first plan all these lines are playable.

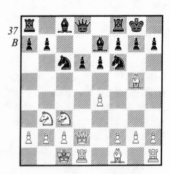

37
B

9   ...   a5

Apart from the two major alternatives of 9 ... a6 and 9 ... ♕b6, there are a number of less common ideas:

(1) **9 ... d5** 10 ♘xf6 ♗xf6 11 exd5 ♗xc3 (11 ... ♘b4 12 a3 ♘xd5 13 ♘xd5 exd5 14 ♕xd5 is slightly better for White since although Black has the two bishops it is not easy for him to avoid the exchange of queens) 12 ♕xc3 exd5 and now:

(1a) **13 g3** ♗g4 14 ♖d2 ♕e7 15 ♗g2 ♖fe8 16 ♔b1 ♖ac8 17 ♕c5! ♘b4? (17 ... ♗f5 is better) 18 ♕xe7 ♖xe7 19 ♖c1 with the superior ending for White, Psakhis–Aseev, Sevastopol 1986.

(1b) **13 ♘d4** should give White a small but safe advantage.

(1c) **13 ♗b5!?** ♕g5+ and now both 14 ♕d2 ♕xg2 15 ♖hg1 and 14 ♔b1 d4 15 ♕c5 ♕xg2 give White an attack in return for the pawn.

(2) **9 ... ♘a5** 10 ♔b1 ♘xb3 11 cxb3 a6 12 f4 b5 13 ♗xf6 gxf6 14 ♗d3 ♔h8 15 f5 b4 16 ♘e2 e5 17 ♗c4, Anand–Mateo, Dubai Ol. 1986, is worth mentioning because it is a perfect example of what Black should avoid. His king position has been weakened without any compensating queenside attack and Black has played ... e5 at a moment when White can reply ♗c4 to gain control of d5.

(3) **9 ... h6** (it now seems established that this line is good for White) 10 ♗xf6 ♗xf6 11 ♕xd6 ♗xc3 (11 ... ♕b6 12 ♕c5 ♕c7 13 g3 ♗e7 14 ♕e3 a6 15 f4 b5 16 ♗g2 ♘e5 17 ♕e2 was also good for White in Marjanovic–Barlov, Yugoslav Ch. 1985) 12 bxc3 ♕h4

13 g3 ♕f6 (not 13 ... ♕xe4? 14 ♗d3 and ♗h7+) 14 ♕c5 e5 15 ♗c4 ♗e6 (or 15 ... ♗g4 16 ♖d6 ♕g5+ 17 ♔b2 ♗f3 18 ♖e1 ♖ac8 19 h4 ♕g4 20 ♕e3 ♖fd8 21 ♖xd8+ ♖xd8 22 ♗d5 ♗g2 23 ♖g1 ♕f3 24 g4 with advantage to White, Lobron–Kunsztowicz, Bad Neuenahr 1984) 16 ♗xe6 ♕xe6 17 ♖d6 ♕h3 18 ♕e3 ♖fd8 19 ♖d5 and now both **19 ... ♖dc8** 20 ♖hd1 ♖c7 21 f4 exf4 22 ♕xf4 ♖e7 23 ♘c5, Chandler–Torre, London 1984 and **19 ... ♕g2** 20 ♖hd1 ♕xh2 21 ♘c5, Klovan–Tal, Jurmala 1983, were good for White.

We now move on the major lines:

(4) **9 ... a6** 10 ♗xf6 and now:

(4a) **10 ... ♗xf6** (this is dubious) 11 ♕xd6 ♗xc3 (or 11 ... ♕b6 12 f4 ♗e7 13 ♕d2 a5 14 a4 ♖d8 15 ♗d3 with advantage to White, Shaposhnikov–Boleslavsky, USSR 1950; as usual 12 ... ♗xc3 13 bxc3 ♕e3+ 14 ♔b2 ♕xe4 loses to 15 ♗d3 and 16 ♗xh7+) 12 bxc3 (the position is the same as after 9 ... h6, except that Black has played ... a6 instead; the verdict is unchanged) ♕f6 (12 ... ♕h4 13 g3 ♕f6 14 ♕c5 e5 15 ♗c4 ♗g4 16 ♖d6 ♕g5+ 17 f4 and White was clearly better in Ivanovic–Popovic, Novi Sad 1984) 13 ♕g3 e5 14 ♗c4 ♗e6 15 ♗xe6 ♕xe6 16 ♖d5 and again White had won the opening battle, Benjamin–Christiansen, USA 1984.

(4b) **10 ... gxf6** 11 ♕h6

(although this line had not been played very often, in my opinion it offers White the best chances; the plan is a general kingside pawn advance by g4, f4, h4 and g5) ♔h8 12 ♕h5 (Black is now virtually forced to lose time with his queen because he must free the f8 rook to defend h7 by ... ♖g8–g7) ♕e8 (12 ... ♖g8?, Ernst–Chandler, London 1988, and now 13 ♕xf7! ♖g6 14 f4 ♗d7 15 ♖d3 e5 16 ♖g3! ♗e8 17 ♕d5 exf4 18 ♖xg6 hxg6 19 ♕d2 g5 20 ♘d4 ♘xd4 21 ♕xd4 is good for White) 13 f4 b5 (in view of the note to White's 15th move it might be more accurate to play 13 ... ♖g8) 14 ♗d3 ♖g8 15 g4 (Tisdall points out the possibility of 15 ♘d5, based on the tactical point 15 ... exd5 16 exd5 ♗g7 17 dxc6 ♗g4 18 ♕d5 ♗xd1 19 ♖xd1 with fantastic compensation for White's slight material deficit; of course Black should play 15 ... ♗b7 16 ♘xe7 ♕xe7 and it is far from certain that the exchange of minor pieces favours White, especially as he has spent two tempi achieving it) ♗g7 (15 ... b4 16 e5 clears e4 for the knight with gain of tempo) 16 h4 b4 17 ♘e2 a5 18 g5 a4 19 ♘bd4 and now:

(4b1) **19 ... ♘xd4** 20 ♘xd4 ♗d7 21 gxf6 ♗xf6 22 e5 dxe5 23 ♖hg1 ♕g8, Arnason–Inkiov, Plovdiv 1986, and now Inkiov gives 24 ♘f3! ♗e8 (24 ... exf4 25 ♖xg7 ♗xg7 26 ♘g5 wins) 25 ♗e4 (25 fxe5 looks even better to me) as good for White.

(4b2) **19 ... b3!?** 20 axb3 (20 cxb3 axb3 21 a3 is also possible, when 21 ... ♘xd4 22 ♘xd4 ♕a4 is unclear) axb3 21 ♘xb3 ♗b7 22 ♘c3 ♘b4 23 ♖hg1 ♕c6 24 ♖g3 ♕b6 25 ♕e2 d5 was played in Psakhis–Kotronias, Dortmund 1989, and now the best move is 26 ♕e3!, when Kotronias gives 26 ... ♘xd3+ 27 ♖xd3 ♕xe3+ 28 ♖dxe3 ♗d6 29 e5 fxe5 30 fxe5 ♗e7 intending ... h6 as unclear. However after 31 ♘b5! I doubt if Black has enough for the pawn, e.g. 31 ... h6 32 gxh6 ♖xg3 33 ♖xg3 ♗xh4 34 ♖g7 intending ♘d6.

(5) **9 ... ♕b6** (the counterattack against f2 nullifies White's threat to take on f6, so Black gets time to support his d-pawn by ... ♖d8; White's usual reaction has been to start a kingside pawn storm, but he must be careful because too many pawn moves might encourage Black to open up the centre by ... d5) 10 f3 *(38)* and now:

(5a) **10 ... a6** 11 h4! (this is the move which has put 10 ... a6 out of favour) ♖d8 12 h5 ♕c7 (when the pawn reaches h5 Black faces a tricky problem—is he willing to let his black squares be weakened by allowing h6, or should be play ... h6 himself, even though this makes the subsequent advances of White's g-pawn very strong? After 12 ... h6 13 ♗e3 ♕c7 14 ♕f2 ♘d7 15 g4 ♘ce5 16 ♖g1 b5 17 g5 White had a very dangerous attack in Hellers–J. Piket, Amsterdam II 1985) 13 g4 (or 13 h6 g6 14 ♕f4 ♘e8 15 ♗xe7 ♕xe7 16 ♕e3 b5 17 ♗e2 ♖b8, Martinovic–Popovic, Yugoslav Ch. 1986, and now 18 ♖d2 followed by ♖hd1 is slightly better for White according to Martinovic) b5 14 ♗e3 ♘d7 15 g5 ♘ce5 16 g6! b4 (16 ... fxg6 17 f4! ♘c4 18 ♗xc4 bxc4 19 ♘d5! exd5 20 ♕xd5+ ♔h8 21 hxg6 ♘f6 22 ♖xh7+ ♘xh7 23 ♖h1 wins) 17 gxf7+ ♔xf7 18 ♘d5! exd5 19 ♕xd5+ ♔f8 (19 ... ♔e8 20 h6 g6 21 f4 ♘g4 22 ♗c4 is also good for White) 20 ♕xa8! ♗b7 21 ♕a7 with advantage to White since 21 ... ♘c6 is met by 22 ♘d4, Serper–Brodsky, USSR 1986.

(5b) **10 ... ♖d8** 11 ♔b1 (a useful semi-waiting move; the reply 11 ... d5 is bad for tactical reasons, so Black normally plays 11 ... a6, when White can switch to his kingside attack plan without allowing ... d5) and now:

(5b1) **11 ... d5?!** 12 ♗xf6 ♗xf6 (Black should not play 12 ... dxe4? because of 13 ♗xe7! ♖xd2 14 ♘xd2! when 14 ... ♘xe7 15 ♘c4 ♕c7 16 ♘b5 wins the queen,

so Anand–Benjamin, Wijk aan Zee 1989 continued 14 ... exf3 and now 15 ♘c4 fxg2 16 ♗xg2 ♕c7 17 ♗d6 ♕d8 18 ♗g3 ♕e7 19 ♖he1 is crushing for White) 13 exd5 ♗xc3 (13 ... a5 14 ♘a4 ♕a7 15 d6 b6 16 ♕e3! ♖b8 17 ♗b5 was very good for White in Mokry–Conquest, Gausdal 1989) 14 ♕xc3 exd5 (14 ... ♘b4 is worse as 15 d6! ♖xd6 16 ♗c4 makes it hard for Black to complete his development) 15 ♕c5 followed by ♗b5, with advantage to White.

(5b2) **11 ... a6** 12 ♗e3 ♕c7 13 ♕f2 (thanks to the threat of ♗b6 Black has no time for ... d5) ♘d7 14 h4 b5 with a position similar to line 5a above. Admittedly White has spent a move on ♔b1, but this is certainly not a waste of tempo, and while White's chances are not quite as good as in line 5a he has fair attacking chances. In Sax–Wilder, Lugano 1989, White adopted the rather strange plan 15 h5 ♗b7 16 ♕g3 ♗f8 17 ♗g5 ♖e8 and now Black is at least equal, but the simple 15 g4 is better.

10   a4

This appears to be the best response to the advance of the a-pawn.

10   ...   d5
11   ♗b5 *(39)*

This move was introduced by Tal in his game against Sisniega in the 1985 Taxco Interzonal, although Vitolinsh was apparently the originator.

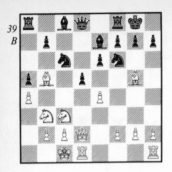

11 ... ♘b4

Or:

(1) **11 ... ♘xe4** 12 ♘xe4 dxe4 13 ♕xd8 ♖xd8 14 ♗xd8 ♘xd8 15 ♘c5 f5 (or 15 ... b6 16 ♘xe4 ♗b7 17 ♖he1 ♗d5 18 f3 ♖c8 19 ♘c3 ♗a8 20 ♗d7 ♖c7 21 ♘b5 ♖c5 22 ♖d6 ♘c6 23 ♘c3 with a slight plus for White, Rohde–Joshi, USA 1986) 16 ♖d6 ♔f7 17 ♖hd1 ♔e7 18 ♗d7 (Tal–Sisniega, Taxco 1985) and now **18 ... ♗xd7** was just slightly better for White according to Tal. In the game **18 ... ♖f7** 19 ♘xe6 ♗xd7 20 ♘c7 ♗xa4 21 ♘xa8 led to a quick White win.

(2) **11 ... dxe4** 12 ♕xd8 ♗xd8 13 ♖he1 ♘a7 (or 13 ... h6 14 ♗xf6 ♗xf6 15 ♘xe4 with an edge for White) 14 ♗c4 h6 15 ♗xf6 gxf6 16 ♘xe4 f5 17 ♘d6 ♗c7 18 g3 b6? (18 ... ♖d8 19 ♘b5 ♘xb5 20 ♗xb5 would have been slightly better for White according to Tal) 19 ♘xf5! and White won in the famous game Tal–Korchnoi, Montpellier 1985.

(3) **11 ... ♘a7** and now there are two tempting lines for White:

(3a) **12 ♗e2 ♗d7** (12 ... b5 13 exd5 bxa4 14 d6 axb3 15 dxe7 ♕xe7 16 cxb3 was unclear in Oll–Ryskin, USSR 1987, but 13 ♗xf6 ♗xf6 14 ♘xb5 is better according to Oll) 13 ♗xf6 ♗xf6 14 exd5 ♗xc3 15 ♕xc3 ♗xa4 16 dxe6 ♕e7 17 exf7+ ♔h8 (Black has some initiative for the two pawns, but not nearly enough) 18 ♗c4 ♖ac8 19 ♖he1 ♕g5+ 20 ♕d2 ♕g6 21 ♗e6 ♖c7 22 ♕d3 ♕xg2 23 ♕d6 and Black's counterattack has collapsed, Gelfand–Ryskin, Minsk 1986.

(3b) **12 ♗xf6 ♗xf6** 13 exd5 ♗xc3 14 ♕xc3 ♘xb5 15 axb5 a4?! (15 ... exd5 16 ♘d4 ♕b6 is relatively best, but still good for White after 17 ♖he1) 16 dxe6! ♕g5+ (the point is that 16 ... axb3 17 ♖xd8 ♖a1+ 18 ♔d2 ♖xd8+ 19 ♔e2 ♖xh1 fails to 20 ♕c7 ♖f8 21 e7 ♖e8 22 ♕d8) 17 ♕d2 ♕f6 18 ♘d4 and Black has very little for his minus pawn, Hoffman–Timoshchenko, Budapest Open 1989.

(4) **11 ... ♗b4** (an untested suggestion by Tal) 12 exd5 exd5 13 ♕f4 with an edge for White.

12 ♖he1 *(40)*

Or 12 e5 ♘d7 13 ♗xe7 ♕xe7 14 f4 (in this French Defence type of position, the exchange of black-squared bishops theoretically favours White, but with the kings castled on opposite sides of the board the game is more likely to be decided by the speed of the respective attacks rather than by the endgame advantage of the better bishop) ♘c5 (after 14 ...

b6 15 ♖he1 ♘c5 16 ♘d4 ♗d7 17 ♔b1 ♖ac8? 18 g4 ♖fd8 19 f5 ♘e4 20 ♘xe4 dxe4 21 c3 ♘d3 22 ♗xd3 exd3 23 ♕f4! ♗xa4 24 ♖xd3 White had an excellent position in Balashov–Khalifman, Minsk 1986, but 17 ... ♖fc8 intending ... ♗xb5 was better) 15 ♘xc5 ♕xc5 16 h4 (the idea is to bring the rook to g3, not only helping the kingside attack, but also providing useful defence along the third rank) b6 and now 17 h5 was quite unclear in Kinder-mann–Felsberger, Vienna 1986. Perhaps 17 ♖h3 was more accurate because in some lines the h-pawn plays no important role on h5, but in any case the position is very double-edged.

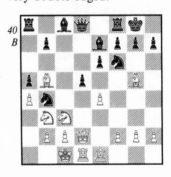

40
B

12 ...   dxe4

Or:

(1) **12 ... h6** and now:

(1a) **13 ♗xf6** ♗xf6 14 exd5 exd5 15 ♘xd5 ♗g4 16 f3 ♗g5 17 ♘e7+! (17 ♘e3 ♗f5 18 ♘d4 ♗g6 19 g3 ♗xe3 20 ♕xe3 ♖c8 gave Black enough for the pawn in Oll–Temirbaev, Kuibyshev 1986) ♕xe7 (17 ... ♗xe7 18

♕xd8 ♖fxd8 19 ♖xd8+ ♖xd8 20 ♖xe7 ♗e6 21 ♘d2 gives Black nothing for the pawn) 18 ♖xe7 ♗xe7 19 ♕e2 ♗g5+ 20 ♔b1 ♗f5 21 ♘d4 ♗g6 22 ♔a1! with excellent winning chances for White, Oll–Khalifman, USSR 1987.

(1b) **13 exd5!?** exd5 (13 ... hxg5 14 d6) 14 ♕e3 ♗e6 15 ♗f4 ♖c8 (Winsnes–Khalifman, Groningen 1985/6) and now 16 ♔b1 (intending ♘d4) ♘h5 17 ♗e5 ♘c6 18 ♗xc6 bxc6 19 ♗d4 is good for White according to Donaldson.

(1c) **13 ♗e3** ♕c7 14 ♗f4 e5 15 exd5 exf4 16 d6 gives White an edge, Andrijevic–Kapetanovic, Yugoslavia 1988.

(2) **12 ... ♗d7** (perhaps the most solid move) 13 e5 (13 exd5 ♗xb5 14 d6 ♕xd6 15 ♕xd6 ♗xd6 16 ♖xd6 ♗c6 gives White an edge, as does 13 ♗xd7 ♕xd7 14 e5 ♘e8 15 ♗xe7 ♕xe7 16 f4 ♘c7 17 ♘d4 ♘c6 18 ♘db5 ♘xb5 19 ♘xb5 ♖ac8 even though a draw was agreed here in Rachels–D. Gurevich, Boston 1988) ♘e8 14 h4 ♘c7 15 ♘d4 ♘c6 16 ♗xe7 ♕xe7 17 ♕g5 and again White has a small advantage, Wang Zili–D. Gurevich, Belgrade, 1988.

13 ♕xd8

White has a speculative alternative in 13 ♘xe4 ♘xe4 14 ♕xd8 ♗xg5+ 15 ♕xg5 ♘xg5 16 h4 e5 (16 ... h6 17 hxg5 hxg5 18 ♖d6 offers White reasonable play for the pawn as Black's development is very difficult) 17 hxg5 ♗f5 18 ♖d2 ♖fc8 (18 ... f6 was more cautious) 19 c3 &e6 20 ♘a1 ♖c5 21 &d7! with some advantage to White, Vitolinsh–Inkiov, Jurmala 1985.

| | **13** | **...** | **♖xd8** |

13 ... &xd8 14 ♘xe4 is good for White after 14 ... ♘xe4 15 &xd8 ♘xf2 16 ♖d2 or 14 ... &e7 15 ♘xf6+ &xf6 16 &xf6 gxf6 17 ♖d6.

| **14** | ♘xe4 | **♘bd5** |
| **15** | **c4!** | **♘c7** |

Or 15 ... ♘b4 16 ♖xd8+ &xd8 17 ♖d1 &e7 18 ♘d6 with a clear plus.

16	♖xd8+	**&xd8**
17	♖d1	**&e7**
18	♘xf6+	**gxf6**
19	&e3	**♘xb5**
20	**axb5** *(41)*

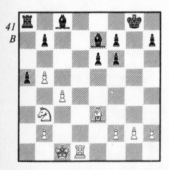

41
B

The liquidation has left White with a clear advantage. Black still has problems developing his pieces and White's queenside majority is ominously near to creating a passed pawn. True, Black has the two bishops, but White can always force an exchange (e.g. by &c5) if they show signs of becoming active.

| **20** | **...** | **f5** |

Black would like to play 20 ... e5 to free his white-squared bishop, but after 21 &c5 &xc5 22 ♘xc5 &g4 23 ♖d5 ♖c8 24 b3 Black's queenside pawns are in big trouble (24 ... ♖c7 25 b6 &e7 26 ♘e4). Black therefore prepares to duck the exchange of bishops after &c5 by ... &g5+.

| **21** | **♘c5** | **e5** |

In *Informator* Anand gives 21 ... f4 22 &d4 f6 (22 ... e5? 23 &xe5) as only slightly better for White. I find this assessment unduly modest, since after 23 ♘a4 e5 24 ♘b6 ♖b8 25 ♘d5! &d8 (25 ... ♔f7 26 ♘xe7 ♔xe7 27 &c5+ ♔e8 28 ♖d6 is also unpleasant) 26 &a7 ♖a8 27 &b6 Black is in serious trouble.

| **22** | ♘d7 | **f4** |
| **23** | &b6 | **f6** |

Practically the only legal move! Black intends ... ♔f7–e6.

| **24** | &c7 |

The threat of ♘b6 forces liquidation into a winning rook and pawn ending.

24	**...**	**&xd7**
25	♖xd7	**&c5**
26	&d6	**&xd6**

After 26 ... &xf2 27 ♖xb7 White's two connected passed pawns roll forwards.

| **27** | ♖xd6 | **♖c8** |

Black goes for counterplay, but he cannot repair the fundamental defects of his position. After 27 ... ♖f8 28 ♔c2 e4 29 ♖e6 f5 30 ♔c3 White's active king will decide the issue.

28	b3	a4
29	♔b2	axb3
30	♔xb3	♔f7

Black offers a pawn to get his own majority moving, but the two connected passed pawns outweigh anything Black can do with his e-pawn.

31	♖d7+	♔e6
32	♖xb7	e4
33	♖a7	e3
34	fxe3	fxe3
35	♖a2	♖d8

The immediate 35 ... ♔e5 is also met by 36 ♔c3, and if 36 ... ♔e4 then 37 b6.

| 36 | ♔c3 | ♔e5 |

Black could have quite reasonably resigned instead.

37	b6	♔e4
38	b7	♖d3+
39	♔b4	♖d2
40	b8 (♕)	♖xa2
41	♕b7+	♔d3
42	♕d5+	♔e2
43	c5	**Resigns**

Game 11
Ernst–Popovic
Subotica 1987

1	e4	c5
2	♘f3	♘c6
3	d4	cxd4
4	♘xd4	♘f6
5	♘c3	d6
6	♗g5	e6
7	♕d2	a6
8	0-0-0 *(42)*	♗d7

8 ... h6 is examined in game 12. Other ideas are dubious, e.g. 8 ...

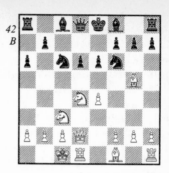

♗e7 (8 ... ♕b6 9 ♘b3 ♗d7 10 ♗e2 ♕c7 11 f4 h6 12 ♗xf6 gxf6 13 ♗h5 is good for White, Panchenko–Csom, Las Palmas 1978) 9 f4 ♕c7 (9 ... ♘xd4 10 ♕xd4 ♕a5 11 e5 dxe5 12 fxe5 ♘d5 13 ♗xe7 ♘xe7 14 ♗d3 ♘c6 15 ♕h4 ♘xe5 16 ♘e4 f6 17 ♖hf1 with a very dangerous attack for White, Adler–Bannik, USSR 1978) and now:

(1) 10 ♔b1 ♗d7 (10 ... 0-0 11 ♗e2 ♖d8 12 ♗f3 h6 13 h4 ♘xd4 14 ♕xd4 b5 15 ♕f2 ♗b7 16 g4 was good for White in Kavalek–Larsen, Montreal 1979) 11 ♘f3 ♖d8 12 ♗d3 b5 13 ♖he1 b4 14 ♘e2 a5 15 ♘g3 0-0 16 e5 ♘d5 17 ♕e2 was unclear in Przewoznik-Bielczyk, Katowice 1986.

(2) 10 ♗e2 ♘xd4 11 ♕xd4 b5 12 e5 dxe5 13 fxe5 ♘d5 14 ♗xe7 ♘xc3 15 ♗f3! ♘xd1 16 ♗d6! and White went on to win quickly in Tal–Larsen, Montreal 1979 after 16 ... ♕c4 17 ♕b6! ♘f2 18 ♗c6+ ♗d7 19 ♗xd7+ ♔xd7 20 ♕b7+ ♔d8 21 ♕xa8+ ♕c8 22 ♕a7 Resigns.

(3) 10 ♗xf6 gxf6 11 g3 ♗d7 12 f5 ♘xd4 13 ♕xd4 ♖c8?! (13 ...

0-0 and 13 ... b5 are possible improvements) 14 ♗b1 b5 15 ♕d2 ♕c5 16 ♗d3 h5? 17 fxe6 fxe6 18 ♘e2 intending ♘f4, Short–Larsen, London 1986, and White has the advantage.

9   f4   b5

Black has two major alternatives, 9 ... h6 and 9 ... ♗e7:

(1) **9 ... h6** (9 ... ♖c8 10 ♘f3 ♕a5 11 ♔b1 b5 12 e5 b4 13 exf6 bxc3 14 fxg7 ♗xg7 15 ♕xd6 ♖c7 16 ♘e5 ♗xe5 17 fxe5 ♖g8 18 h4 is good for White, Yanofsky–Olafsson, Dallas 1957) 10 ♗h4 *(43)* and now:

43
B

(1a) **10 ... ♗e7** (10 ... ♘xd4 11 ♕xd4 ♗c6 12 ♗c4 is clearly good for White, while **10 ... ♖c8** 11 ♘f3 ♕a5 is similar to the note to Black's 9th move) 11 ♘f3! b5 12 e5 (12 ♗xf6 ♗xf6 13 ♕xd6 ♖a7 14 e5 ♗e7 15 ♕d3! ♕a5 16 ♔b1 ♖c7 17 ♕e3! 0-0 18 ♕e4 was also good for White in Georgadze–Makarychev, Nikolaev 1983) b4 13 exf6 bxc3 14 ♕xc3 gxf6 15 f5 and White stands well, Thiemann–Reynolds, corr. 1966.

(1b) **10 ... ♘xe4** 11 ♕e1 ♘f6

(11 ... g5 12 ♘xe4 gxh4 13 ♕c3) 12 ♘f5 ♕a5 (**12 ... ♕b8** 13 ♗xf6 gxf6 14 ♘e4, **12 ... ♗e7** 13 ♘xd6+ ♔f8 14 ♘xb7 ♕c7 15 ♕d2 and **12 ... ♕c7** 13 ♗xf6 gxf6 14 ♘d5 ♕d8 15 ♕e3! are all very pleasant for White) 13 ♘xd6+ ♗xd6 14 ♖xd6 0-0-0 (**14 ... ♕c7** 15 ♖d2 is unsatisfactory after **15 ... 0-0-0** 16 ♕f2 ♘e7 17 ♗d3 ♗c6 18 f5 e5 19 ♖hd1 or **15 ... ♕xf4** 16 ♗e2 ♘e4 17 ♘xe4 ♕xe4 18 ♕f2, Gligoric–Barden, Bognor Regis 1957, while **14 ... ♘e7** 15 ♖d1 ♘g6 16 ♘e4! ♕xe1 17 ♘d6+ ♔e7 18 ♗xe1 ♘d5 19 ♘x7 ♗xf4 20 g3 ♘g6 21 ♗g2 and **14 ... ♘b4** 15 a3 ♘bd5 16 ♕e5 ♗c6 17 ♗c4! are both very good good for White) 15 ♖d1! ♕c7 (**15 ... ♘e7?** 16 ♘d5 wins, **15 ... g5** 16 fxg5 hxg5 17 ♗g3 gives White very strong pressure on the dark squares and **15 ... e5** 16 fxe5 ♖he8 17 ♗g3 ♘xe5 18 ♘b5 ♗g4 19 ♖xd8+ ♖xd8 20 ♘a7+ ♔b8 21 ♘c6+ bxc6 22 ♕xe5+ is a very good ending for White) 16 ♕f2 ♘e7 17 ♗d3 ♗c6 18 f5 e5 19 ♖he1 ♘ed5 20 ♘xd5 ♖xd5 (20 ... ♗xd5 21 ♕a7) 21 ♕g3 e4 22 ♕xc7+ ♔xc7 23 ♗xf6 exd3 24 ♗xg7 ♖hd8 25 ♗e5+ with good winning chances for White, Spassky–Rabar, Goteborg 1955.

(1c) **10 ... g5** 11 fxg5 ♘g4 and now:

(1c1) **12 ♘f3** hxg5 (12 ... ♗e7 13 g6! ♗xh4 14 gxf7+ ♔xf7 15 ♕f4+ is good for White, or **14 ... ♔f8** 15 ♕xd6+ ♗e7 16 ♕xd7 ♘f2 17 ♕xb7 ♘xd1 18 ♕xc6 and

White should win) 13 ♗g3 ♗e7 14 ♗e2 ♘ge5 and now:

(1c11) **15 ♔b1** b5 (15 ... f6 16 h4! gxh4 17 ♘xh4 ♕a5 18 ♘f5! ♖xh1 19 ♖xh1 exf5 20 ♖h8+ ♗f8 21 ♖xe5! ♖xe5 22 ♕xd6 is good for White, Mokry–Banas, Trnava 1986) 16 a3 ♖b8 17 ♘a2 a5 18 ♘c1 ♘xf3 19 gxf3 e5? (19 ... ♘e5! is unclear) 20 ♗f2 ♗e6 21 ♗e3 with an edge for White, Riemersma–A. Rodriguez, Dieren 1987.

(1c12) **15 ♖hf1** f6 (15 ... ♕a5 16 ♔b1 f6 17 ♕e1 b5 18 ♗d3 0-0-0 19 ♘d2 ♔b7 20 h3 ♔a8 21 ♗f2 was a little better for White, Vogt–Barczay, Zalakaros 1987) 16 ♘xe5 ♘xe5 17 ♗xe5 dxe5 18 ♖f3 ♕c7 19 ♖d3 ♖d8 20 h3 ♗c8 21 ♖xd8+ ♕xd8 22 ♕e3 ♕a5 (22 ... ♕c7 preventing ♗c4 appears better) 23 ♗c4 ♕c5 24 ♕e2 ♗d8, Vogt–Wirius, Zalakaros 1987, and now 25 ♔b1 gives White an edge.

(1c2) **12 ♘xc6** (this seems the better choice) ♗xc6 13 ♗e2 ♘e5 14 g3 ♘g6 15 ♔b1 h5 (15 ... ♗e7?! 16 gxh6 ♗xh4 17 gxh4 ♕xh4 18 ♕xd6 was good for White in Marjanovic–Popovic, Belgrade 1987) with a further branch:

(1c21) **16 ♕e3 ♗e7** (better than 16 ... ♗g7 17 ♘d5! exd5 18 exd5+ ♕e7 19 ♕xe7+ ♔xe7 20 dxc6 bxc6 21 c3 with an edge for White, Chandler–Bellin, Commonwealth Ch. 1985, or 16 ... ♕e7 17 ♖hf1 ♗g7 18 ♖f2 ♔f8 19 ♖df1, Mainka–Popovic, Dort-

mund 1988 and White is better) 17 ♖hf1 ♕c7 18 ♕f2 ♘e5 19 h3 0-0-0 20 g4 hxg4 21 ♗xg4 ♘xg4 22 hxg4 ♖h7 is unclear, Jansa–Banas, CSSR Ch. 1986.

(1c22) **16 ♖hf1** (16 ♖df1!? intending 17 ♕d1 attacking h5 is an interesting idea) ♕c7 (16 ... ♗g7!? is better) 17 e5! 0-0-0 18 ♗d3 ♘xh4 19 gxh4 ♗g7 20 ♕f2! and White stands well, Tseshkovsky–Fahnenschmidt, Baden-Baden 1988.

(1d) **10 ... b5** 11 ♗xf6 ♕xf6!? 12 e5 (12 ♗xb5 axb5 13 ♘dxb5 ♕d8 14 ♘xd6+ ♗xd6 15 ♕xd6 ♕e7 16 e5 ♕xd6 17 ♖xd6 ♔e7 is unconvincing) dxe5 13 ♘dxb5 ♕d8 14 ♘d6+ ♗xd6 15 ♕xd6 exf4 16 ♘e4! ♕e7 17 ♕c7 ♖a7 18 ♘d6+ ♔f8 19 ♕b6 and White is at least slightly better, Sobura–Berebora, Poland 1988.

(2) **9 ... ♗e7** 10 ♘f3 b5 (other moves are inconsistent, e.g. 10 ... ♕c7 11 e5 dxe5 12 fxe5 ♘d5 13 ♘xd5 exd5 14 ♗xe7 ♘xe7 15 ♗d3 0-0 16 ♕g5 ♘c6 17 ♕h5 or 10 ... h6 11 ♗xf6 gxf6 12 f5 ♕c7 13 ♔b1 0-0-0 14 ♗c4 with a clear plus for White in both cases) 11 e5 b4 (not 11 ... dxe5 12 fxe5 b4 13 exf6 bxc3 14 ♕xd7+ and White wins) 12 exf6 bxc3 13 ♕xc3 gxf6 14 ♗h4 *(44)* and now:

(2a) **14 ... a5** (14 ... ♕a5 15 ♗xf6 ♖b4 16 ♗c4 ♖c8 17 a3 is good for White) 15 ♔b1 ♘b4 (15 ... ♖b8 16 g4 ♘b4 17 a3 ♖c8 18 ♕b3 ♘d5 19 ♖xd5 with an excellent position for White, Gligoric–Conrady, Dublin 1957) 16 a3 ♖c8

17 ♛b3 ♞d5 18 ♖xd5 exd5 and now either 19 ♞d4 or 19 ♛xd5, with very good compensation for the exchange.

(2b) **14 ... d5** 15 ♚b1 with a further branch:

(2b1) **15 ... a5** 16 ♗b5 ♖c8 17 ♞d4 ♞xd4 18 ♗xd7+ ♛xd7 19 ♛xd4 ♖g8 20 g3 ♛b5 21 ♖he1 is good for White.

(2b2) **15 ... ♞b4** 16 ♞d4 ♛a5 (16 ... ♖c8 17 ♛b3 ♛a5 18 ♗e1! ♗a4 19 ♛a3 with a clear plus for White, Matanovic–Jansa, Lugano 1968) 17 a3 ♞c6 18 ♛g3 ♞xd4 19 ♖xd4 ♖b8 20 ♖d3 ♚f8 21 ♗e2 with a small plus for White according to Lukin.

(2b3) **15 ... ♞a5** 16 f5 ♖c8 17 ♛d2 ♛c7 18 fxe6 fxe6 19 ♗d3! ♞c4 20 ♗xc4 ♛xc4 21 ♖he1 ♖g8 (21 ... 0-0 is most simply met by 22 g4!) 22 h3 ♖b8 23 ♚a1 h5 24 g3 with a small advantage for White, Tseshkovshy–Lukin, USSR 1982.

10	♗xf6	gxf6
11	♞xc6	♗xc6

White's chances lie in the fact that Black's king has no really safe spot, and in an attack against the weak e6 square by f5, ♗d3 and ♞e2–f4. Black must be careful about playing ... b4; he may gain time by driving the knight away, but he may also allow the bishop to become active at c4. In general the exchange of queens favours Black, so White must make sure he avoids this.

12   ♛e1 *(45)*

Probably the most accurate move. Black's immediate ambition is to bring his queen to an active square, so White often plays 12 ♛e3 to prevent ... ♛b6, but after ... ♛e7–a7 White has to waste time avoiding the queen swap. 12 ♛e1 also prevents 12 ... ♛b6 because of 13 ♞d5, but it also tucks the queen away from the unwelcome attentions of her opposite number.

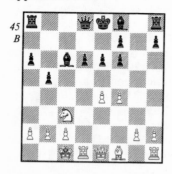

12   ...   ♗e7

Or:

(1) **12 ... b4** 13 ♞d5 a5, A. Ivanov–Ermolinsky, USSR 1981, and now 14 ♖d4! intending ♖c4 is good for White.

(2) **12 ... ♛a5** 13 ♚b1 0-0-0 14 ♗d3 ♚b8 15 ♛h4 ♛c7 16 f5 was

promising for White in Kuzmin–
Tukmakov, USSR ch. 1977.

(3) **12 ... ♛e7 13 ♗d3 ♗g7** (13
... ♗b7 14 ♚b1 0-0-0 15 a4 b4 16
♘a2 a5 17 c3 d5 18 cxb4 axb4 19
exd5 ♖xd5 20 ♛e3 ♛d7 21
♖c1+ ♚b8 22 ♗e4 with some
advantage for White, Spraggett–
Mednis, Lugano 1985) **14 ♛g3** (I
prefer 14 ♚b1 intending f5) **♖g8
15 ♖he1 ♚f8 16 ♛h4 f5 17
♛xe7+ ♚xe7 18 exf5 ♗xc3 19
bxc3 ♖xg2** with equality, Kudrin–Christiansen, USA Ch. 1986.

13   ♗d3   ♛b6
14   ♚b1

Safer than 14 ♛g3 b4 15 ♘e2
♚d7 16 f5 e5 17 ♛f3 ♛c5, Menc-
inger–Damljanovic, Bled 1984,
with an unclear position.

14   ...   b4

The alternative is 14 ... h5 15
f5 b4 (after 15 ... ♛c5 White is a
little better after the solid 16
♖f1!?, but 16 ♛g3 ♚d7 17 ♛h3
♖ag8 18 ♖he1 ♖g5, Hellers–van
der Wiel, Amsterdam 1986, is also
possible, when 19 g3 gives White
an edge) 16 ♘e2 e5 17 ♛g3 (17
♘g3 a5 18 ♛e2 h4 19 ♘f1 was
unclear in Watson–Yrjola, Kecs-
kemet 1988) ♗f8? 18 ♛f3! and
White stands well, A. Ivanov–
Anikaev, USSR 1979. *ECO*
suggests 17 ... d5, but 18 ♛f3
looks good in this case too.

15   ♘e2   a5
16   f5!

More active than 16 ♛g3, as
played hitherto. White threatens
17 fxe6 fxe6 18 ♘f4, so Black's
reply is virtually forced.

16   ...   e5
17   ♘g3 *(46)*

With the simple plan of ♗c4–
d5.

17   ...   ♛c5
18   ♛e2   a4

There is nothing more Black
can do to prevent White's bishop
manoeuvre, so his only chance is
to aim for queenside counterplay

19   ♗c4   0-0

Black needs his other rook if
this queenside play is to genuinely
worry White, but there is an
obvious danger to his king after
... 0-0.

20   ♘h5   ♚h8
21   ♖hf1   a3?

Overlooking that White has an
immediate mating threat, but
even the best line 21 ... ♖fc8 22
b3 ♖a7 23 ♖f3 axb3 24 ♗xb3 is
very unpleasant for Black.

22   ♖f3

White can afford to abandon
the queenside since he has a
forced win on the other flank.

22   ...   axb2
23   ♖h3

Intending 24 ♘xf6 ♗xf6 25 ♕h5.

23	**...**	**♖g8**
24	**♘xf6**	**Resigns**

After 24 ... ♗xf6 25 ♖xh7+ ♚xh7 26 ♕h5+ ♚g7 27 ♕xf7+ ♚h6 (27 ... ♚h8 28 ♕h5+ ♚g7 29 ♕g6+ and mate next move) 28 ♕xf6+ ♚h7 29 ♕h4+ ♚g7 30 ♕g5+ the rook is the first of many Black pieces to disappear.

Game 12
Short–Ljubojevic
Amsterdam (Euwe Memorial) 1988

1	**e4**	**c5**
2	**♘f3**	**d6**
3	**d4**	**cxd4**
4	**♘xd4**	**♘f6**
5	**♘c3**	**♘c6**
6	**♗g5**	**e6**
7	**♕d2**	**a6**
8	**0-0-0**	**h6**

Black once again aims to further his queenside ambitions by ... ♗d7 and ... b5 before committing his king, but in this line he first of all forces White to decide where to put his bishop.

9 ♗e3 *(47)*

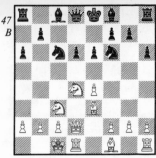

This move is currently thought best. White intends to play f4 and develop his king's bishop to e2 or d3. If Black castles kingside then White can launch a direct attack by h3 and g4–g5.

9 ... ♗d7

Black has a number of possible moves, but the basic rule is 'f4 against anything'. The alternatives are:

(1) **9 ... ♕c7** (9 ... ♘g4 10 ♘xc6 bxc6 11 ♗c5 is good for White) 10 f4 ♗e7 11 ♗e2 ♗d7 (or 11 ... ♘a5 12 e5! dxe5 13 fxe5 ♕xe5 14 ♗f4 ♕c5 15 ♘a4 ♕d5 16 ♚b1! with a very strong attack for the sacrificed pawn) 12 ♘b3 ♘a5 13 ♘xa5 ♕xa5 14 ♚b1 ♗c6 15 ♗f3 ♕c7 16 ♖he1 (the immediate 16 g4 may be even better) ♖c8 17 g4 with advantage to White, Chiburdanidze–Lanka, USSR 1980.

(2) **9 ... ♗e7** 10 f4 ♘xd4 11 ♗xd4 b5 12 ♗e2 transposes to line 3.

(3) **9 ... ♘xd4** 10 ♗xd4 b5 11 f4 ♗e7 (**11 ... b4** 12 ♗xf6 ♕xf6 13 ♘e2 ♖b8 14 ♘d4 ♖b6 15 ♗c4, Tal–Radulov, Malta Ol. 1980 and **11 ... ♗b7** 12 ♗xf6 gxf6 13 ♗d3 ♕b6 14 ♚b1 ♗e7 15 f5 e5 16 ♗e2 followed by ♗f3, Jansa–Spassov, Sochi 1980, were both slightly better for White) 12 ♗e2 (a promising pawn sacrifice) b4 (12 ... ♗b7 13 ♗f3 b4 14 ♗xf6 ♗xf6 15 ♘e2 ♕a5 16 a3 is good for White) 13 ♘a4 ♘xe4 14 ♕e3 ♘f6 15 ♗f3 and now:

(3a) **15 ... d5** 16 ♚b1 (this has

been played in practice, but in fact 16 g4 0-0 17 ♘b6 ♖b8 18 ♔b1 may be more accurate, transposing into Short–A. Rodriguez below but without allowing Black so much choice) 0-0 (16 ... ♗d7 17 ♘b6 ♖b8 18 g4 ♗b5 19 h4 ♔f8 20 g5 ♘e8 21 f5 was also dangerous for Black in Chandler–Kosten, Hastings 1988/9) 17 ♘b6 ♖b8 18 g4 ♗d6?! (18 ... ♘d7 19 ♘xd7 ♗xd7 20 h4 ♗f6 21 g5 ♗xd4 22 ♖xd4 was better, even though White still has a dangerous attack) 19 g5 hxg5 20 fxg5 ♘d7 21 ♘xc8 ♖xc8 22 g6 with a clear plus for White, Short–A. Rodriguez, Subotica 1987.

(3b) **15 ...** **♖b8** 16 ♗a7 ♗d7! (not 16 ... ♖b5 17 ♗b6 ♕d7 18 ♘c5 and White wins, Balashov–Tukmakov, Sverdlovsk 1987) 17 ♘b6 ♗b5 18 ♔b1!? (after 18 g4 0-0 19 ♗xb8 ♕xb8 20 g5 hxg5 21 fxg5 ♗d8! 22 gxf6 ♕xb6 23 ♕xb6 ♗xb6 Black had sufficient compensation in Khalifman–Ionov, USSR 1988) 0-0 19 f5 ♕c7 (the only move) 20 ♗xb8 ♖xb8 21 ♘a8! ♕d8! (not 21 ... ♕c8? 22 ♕a7 ♗f8 23 fxe6 fxe6 24 ♘c7 and the knight excapes, nor 21 ... ♕d7 22 fxe6 fxe6 23 Rhe1 d5 24 ♘b6, followed by taking on e6) 22 ♕a7! (after 22 fxe6 ♖xa8 23 exf7+ ♔xf7 24 ♗xa8 ♕xa8 25 ♖he1 ♕b7 Black's active minor pieces are at least as valuable as White's rooks) d5! (22 ... exf5 23 ♖he1 ♘e4 24 ♗xe4 fxe4 25 ♖xe4 ♗f6 26 ♘c7 and 22 ... e5 23 ♖he1! ♗d7 24 ♘c7 ♗xf5 25

♘xa6 are good for White) 23 ♘c7 ♗c6 (threatening 24 ... ♖b7, and if 24 ♘xa6 then 24 ... ♖a8 wins) 24 fxe6 ♖b7 25 ♘xd5! ♖xa7 (not 25 ... ♘xd5 26 exf7+ ♔f8 27 ♕xa6 ♖c7 28 ♕d3 ♖d7 29 ♕h7 ♘f6 30 ♕h8+ ♔xf7 31 ♕xd8 and wins) 26 ♘xf6+ ♗xf6 27 ♖xd8+ ♗xd8 28 exf7+ ♔xf7 29 ♗xc6 (normally an extra pawn offers some winning chances in a rook and opposite bishop ending, but White must overcome the problem of his inactive king) ♗f6 30 ♖d1 ♖c7 31 ♗f3 ♗e7, Nunn–van der Wiel, Lucerne 1989, and now 32 ♖d5! ♖c5 33 ♖d3 leads to an ending in which Nigel Short believes White has significant winning chances. The plan is a3 or c3, followed by advancing the king to attack Black's remaining queenside pawn. Certainly Black will be tortured for a long time.

10 f4 b5

Against other moves White adopts the same general plan of ♗d3, ♔b1, and then a kingside pawn advance, but he has to be careful against 10 ... ♗e7, because 11 ♗d3 allows the awkward 11 ... ♘g4! Therefore the best answer to 10 ... ♗e7 is 11 h3 b5 12 ♗d3, transposing into the note to White's 12th move.

11 ♗d3 ♗e7(48)

Two alternatives are **11 ...** **♖c8** 12 ♔b1 ♘a5?! 13 e5! b4! 14 ♘ce2 dxe5 15 fxe5 ♘d5 16 ♖hf1 ♘c4 17 ♗xc4 ♖xc4 18 ♘f4 ♘xe3 19 ♕xe3 ♗c5 20 ♘g6!, Hazai–Szabo, Hungary 1983, and **11 ...**

&xd4 12 &xd4 b4 13 &e2 &a5
14 &xf6 gxf6 15 &b1, Psakhis–
Ivanovic, Sochi 1979, with a clear
plus for White in both cases.
Against other moves, such as **11
... &a5** or **11 ... &c7**, White
proceeds with his plan by 12 &b1.

48
W

12 &b1
12 &b1 has been played a
number of times recently, but
there is a strong argument for the
immediate 12 h3, e.g. 12 ... &xd4
13 &xd4 &c6 (13 ... b4 14 &e2
a5 15 g4 &c6 16 &g3 d5 17 &e2
&b8 18 &hf1 b3 19 cxb3 a4 20
&b1 axb3 21 a3 gives White a
modest advantage, Murei–
Lobron, Lyons 1988) 14 &e3 (14
&del 0-0 15 &b1 &d7 16 g4 was
slightly better for White in
Timoshchenko–Tukmakov,
USSR Ch. 1978) b4 15 &e2 &c7
16 e5 dxe5 17 &xe5 &b7 18 f5
&d5 19 &g3 with dangerous
threats for White, Timoshchenko–Sirov, Moscow GMA
1989.
12 ... b4
This move has been criticised,
but it isn't clear that the alterna-

tives are better, for example **12 ...
&c7** 13 h3 &a5 (13 ... &xd4 14
&xd4 &c6 is probably the most
sensible, but even here White has
an edge) 14 g b4 15 &ce2 &c4 16
&xc4 &xc4 17 &g3 a5 18 &hf1
&a6 19 g5 with advantage, Hodg-
son–Csom, Tel Aviv 1988, or **12
... &xd4** 13 &xd4 b4 14 &e2
&b8 15 &g3 (15 h3 is more consistent) 0-0?! (15 ... e5 is better)
16 e5! &d5 17 &e4 &d8 18 &f2
dxe5 19 fxe5 &e8 20 &hf1 and
White is better, Hazai–Lobron,
Rotterdam 1988.
13 &ce2 0-0
14 h3
Black's problem is that White
has an automatic attack by h3, g4,
&g3 and g5 while Black has to
struggle to create any counter-
chances at all. It is curious that
Black's troubles stem from the
apparently innocuous 8 ... h6,
which in this type of position
creates a fatal kingside weakness.
14 ... &c7
15 g4 &b7
16 &g3 &xd4
17 &xd4 &c6
All Black has achieved is to
create a threat to e4, which delays
White's attack by precisely one
move.
18 &he1 &fe8?
This doesn't help the belea-
guered kingside. The last chance
was to play 18 ... &d7 intending
... e5 to block the deadly long
diagonal, but in this case Short
gives the line 19 g5 hxg5 20 &g1
(threat &h5) e5 21 &f5 &fe8 22

fxe5 ♘xe5 23 ♗xe5 dxe5 24 ♖xg5! ♗xg5 25 ♕xg5 f6 26 ♗c4+ ♚f8 27 ♕h5 and mate at h8.

| 19 | g5 | hxg5 |
| 20 | fxg5 | ♘d7 *(49)* |

After this we are treated to a king-hunt in the style of the 19th century. 20 ... ♘h7 was objectively better (anything is better than being mated), but 21 h4 locking the knight out of play is very good for White.

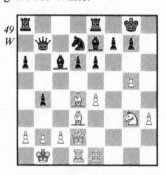

49
W

| 21 | ♗xg7! | ♚xg7 |
| 22 | ♘h5+ | ♚g6 |

There is no choice as 22 ... ♚g8 23 g6 fxg6 24 ♕h6, 22 ... ♚f8 23 g6 ♗f6 24 ♘xf6 ♘xf6 25 ♖f1 ♚e7 26 ♕g5 and 22 ... ♚h8 23 g6 ♗f8 24 ♖g1 fxg6 25 ♖xg6 ♘e5 26 ♖h6+! all lead to disaster.

| 23 | e5+ | ♚xh5 |
| 24 | ♕f4 | ♗xg5 |

All Black's moves are forced.

| 25 | ♕xf7+ | ♚h4 |
| 26 | ♕h7+ | ♚g3 |

The main problem when playing such positions with White is trying to keep a broad grin off

your face. The main problem when playing such positions with Black is to avoid looking at the broad grin on your opponent's face.

| 27 | ♕h5 | ♚h2 |

Or 27 ... ♖g8 28 ♕g4+ ♚h2 29 ♕g1+ ♚xh3 30 ♗f1+ ♚h4 (30 ... ♗g2 31 ♖d3+ and 32 ♗xg2) 31 ♕h2+ ♚g4 32 ♖d4+ ♚f5 33 ♕h7+ ♖g6 34 ♗h3 mate is a nice line given by Short.

| 28 | ♕xg5 |

In fact White could have forced mate by 28 ♕e2+ ♚xh3 (28 ... ♗g2 29 ♖h1+ ♚g3 30 ♕g4+ ♚f2 31 ♖hf1+ ♗xf1 32 ♖xf1+ ♚e3 33 ♖e1+ ♚f2 34 ♕g1+ ♚f3 35 ♖f1 mate) 29 ♕h5+ ♗h4 30 ♖e3+ ♖f3 (30 ... ♚g2 31 ♕xh4 or 30 ... ♗f3 31 ♖h1+ ♚g2 32 ♕xh4) 31 ♖h1+ ♚g2 32 ♕xh4 etc., but there is nothing wrong with winning Black's queen (and having his king on h2).

28	...	♖g8
29	♖d2+	♗g2
30	♕f4+	♖g3
31	♗e4	♕xe4
32	♕xe4	**Resigns**

Game 13
Kupreichik–Kuzmin
Minsk 1982

1	e4	c5
2	♘f3	♘c6
3	d4	cxd4
4	♘xd4	♘f6
5	♘c3	d6
6	♗g5 *(50)*

50
B

6 ...   ♗d7

This is the most popular alternative to 6 ... e6, but there are other moves:

(1) **6 ... g6** (this appears to be an underrated move) 7 ♗xf6 exf6 8 ♗c4 (if Stoica's recommendation below is effective, White should prefer 8 ♗b5 ♗d7 9 0-0 ♗g7 10 ♘de2 with a slight plus) ♗g7 (after this Black must sacrifice a pawn, but 8 ... ♗e7 9 ♕d2 followed by 0-0-0 is depressing for Black) 9 ♘db5 0-0 10 ♕xd6 f5 11 0-0-0 ♕a5 (11 ... ♕g5+ 12 f4 ♕xg2 13 e5 is given as good for White by theory, but Stoica suggests 13 ... ♕g4!, threatening both ... ♕xf4+ and ... ♘xe5; at the moment I can't see a good reply for White) 12 ♕c7 a6 (the lines **12 ... ♗xc3** 13 bxc3 ♕a4 14 ♘d6, **12 ... ♕b4** 13 ♘d6 ♗xc3 14 bxc3 ♕xc3 15 ♗xf7+ ♔h8 16 ♔b1 and **12 ... fxe4** 13 ♕xa5 ♘xa5 14 ♗d5 ♗h6+ 15 ♔b1 are all good for White) 13 ♕xa5 ♘xa5 14 ♘c7 ♖a7 15 ♗b3 ♗xc3 16 bxc3 fxe4 (Kholmov–Chernikov, USSR 1982) and now 17

♘d5! is good for White according to Kholmov.

(2) **6 ... ♕a5** ♗xf6 gxf6 8 ♗b5 ♗d7 9 ♘b3 ♕c7 10 ♘d5 ♕d8 11 ♕h5 e6 12 ♘e3 a6 13 ♗e2 ♕c7 14 0-0-0 ♗e7 15 ♔b1 0-0-0 16 f4 was good for White in S. Nikolic-Gufeld, Kislovodsk 1968.

(3) **6 ... a6** 7 ♕d2 ♘xd4 (other moves transpose to the main variations) 8 ♕xd4 e5 9 ♕a4+ (White has no trouble keeping a slight advantage by 9 ♕d3 ♗e6 10 0-0-0 ♖c8 11 ♘d5 ♗xd5 12 ♗xf6, but with ♕a4+ he is playing for more) ♗d7 10 ♕b3 b5 11 ♗xf6 gxf6 12 ♗e2 ♗e6 13 ♘d5 ♗h6 14 a4 with some advantage for White, Marjanovic–Stoica, Istanbul 1988.

(4) **6 ... ♕b6** (this has become popular recently) 7 ♘b3 (7 ♗e3!? is interesting, e.g. 7 ... ♕xb2 8 ♘db5 ♕b4 9 ♗d2 ♕c5! 10 ♗e2!? ♕b6 11 ♖b1 ♘e5? 12 ♗e3 ♕a5 13 ♖b3 g6 14 ♖a3 ♕d8 15 ♗xa7 ♘ed7 16 f4! and White stands well, Balashov–Petrienko, Voronezh 1987, but 11 ... ♕d8 was the critical test) e6 and now:

(4a) **8 ♗f4** ♘e5 9 ♗e3 ♕c7 10 f4 ♘g6 11 ♕f3 ♗d7 12 ♗d3 ♗e7 13 0-0-0 ♗c6 14 ♘d4 was good for White in Greenfield–Schrenzel, Israel 1983, but 8 ... e5 may be better.

(4b) **8 ♕d2** a6 9 0-0-0 ♗e7 (9 ... ♗d7 10 f4 ♕c7 11 ♗e2 b5 12 ♗xf6 gxf6 13 ♗h5 ♗h6 14 ♖hf1 was a little better for White, Kholmov–Petrienko, USSR 1980, while 9 ... ♕c7 10 ♔b1 b5 11

♛f4! ♘d7 12 ♗xb5 axb5 13 ♘xb5 ♛b8 14 ♘xd6+ ♗xd6 15 ♛xd6 ♛xd6 16 ♖xd6 ♘ce5 was unclear in van der Wiel–Spraggett, Wijk aan Zee 1985) 10 ♔b1 (10 h4 is a promising alternative which anticipates Black's ... 0-0) ♛c7 11 f4 ♗d7?! (Black allows a central breakthrough) 12 e5 dxe5 13 fxe5 ♘d5 (13 ... ♘xe5 14 ♗f4 ♗c6 15 ♛e1 is very good for White) 14 ♘xd5 exd5 15 ♗xe7 ♘xe7 16 ♛g5 ♗f5 17 ♘d4 ♗g6 18 ♗d3 and White has a dangerous lead in development, Ivanovic–Popovic, Vinkovci 1982.

(4c) **8 ♗d3** (aiming for 0-0 has been the most popular reply, and it has also scored well) ♗e7 9 0-0 a6 10 a4 (10 ♔h1 ♛c7 is also possible, e.g. **11 a4** b6?! 12 f4 ♗b7 13 f5 ♘e5?! 14 ♘d4, Kindermann–Liberzon, Beersheva 1984 or **11 f4** ♗d7 12 ♛e2! h6 13 ♗h4 g5?! 14 ♗g3, Byrne–J. Benjamin, USA Ch. 1984 with advantage to White in both cases although Black's play was doubtful in these examples) ♘a5 11 ♘xa5 (11 ♗e3 ♛c7 12 ♘xa5 ♛xa5 13 h3 ♗d7 14 f4 ♖c8 15 ♛d2 ♗c6 16 f5 e5 17 b4 ♛c7 18 b5 gave White some advantage, Grunfeld–Ivanov, Toronto 1984) ♛xa5 12 ♗d2 ♛h5 13 ♛e1 ♘g4 14 h3 ♘e5 15 ♗e2 ♛h4 16 ♛d1 g5 17 f4 gxf4 18 ♖xf4 ♛g3 19 ♗g4 ♘g6 20 ♘e2 ♛h4 21 g3 and White wins, Ivanovic–Plachetka, Stara Pazova 1988.

7 ♗e2 *(51)*

White usually plays 7 ♛d2 when Black continues 7 ... ♘xd4 8 ♛xd4 ♛a5. The move ♗e2 is well motivated since if Black exchanges on d4 he has lost a tempo over the usual line, so he has to change his plan.

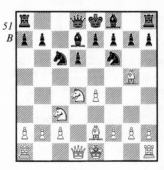

51
B

7 ... a6

A flexible reply, but 7 ... ♛a5 may be better. This and other options:

(1) **7 ... ♛b6** 8 ♘db5 (threatening 9 ♗xf6 and 10 ♘d5, while at the same time preventing ... e6) ♖c8 9 0-0 a6 10 ♗xf6 gxf6 11 ♘d5 ♛d8 12 ♘bc3 e6 13 ♘e3 and White's knights proved well-placed in Vogt–Mascarinas, Polanica Zdroj 1977.

(2) **7 ... e6** 8 ♘db5 ♛b8 9 a4 ♗e7 10 ♛d2 a6 11 ♘a3 ♛c7 12 ♖d1 ♖d8 13 ♘c4 ♗c8 14 ♗e3 ♛b8 15 ♘b6 with an edge for White, Spassky–Hort, Moscow 1971.

(3) **7 ... ♛a5** 8 ♗xf6 gxf6 9 0-0!? and now:

3a) **9 ... ♛g5** 10 ♘f5! ♖g8 (10 ... ♗xf5 11 f4 ♛g6 12 ♗h5 is good for White) 11 ♘g3 with an edge for White.

(3b) **9 ... ♕e5** (too ambitious) 10 ♘f3 ♕c5 (10 ... ♕a5 is better even though this is an admission that Black's last move was a mistake) 11 ♘d5 ♖c8 12 c3 a6 13 ♘d4 ♗g7 14 b4 ♕a7 15 ♗h5 with advantage to White, Stoica–Kotronias, Istanbul 1988.

(3c) **9 ... ♘xd4** 10 ♕xd4 ♕c5 (this is Black's best; 10 ... ♖c8 11 ♘d5 ♕c5 12 ♕d2 ♕xc2 13 ♕e3 ♕c4 14 ♕f4 gives White a strong initiative in return for the pawn) and now Stoica gives 11 ♕xc5 dxc5 12 ♗c4 as slightly better for White. I cannot see any White advantage after 12 ... e6, so I prefer 12 ♘d5 ♖c8 (12 ... 0-0-0 13 ♗h5 and now **13 ... ♗e6** 14 ♘f4 and **13 ... ♗e8** 14 ♖ad1 are good for White) 13 ♖ad1 and White probably does have an edge. White can also consider 11 ♕d3 intending ♔h1 and f4.

| **8** | **♗xf6** | **gxf6** |
| **9** | **0-0** | |

There is a second possibility which, like the main line, is based on the move ♘f5, namely 9 ♘f5 ♕a5 10 0-0 ♖c8 11 ♘d5 ♕d8 12 ♘de3! ♘e5 13 f4 ♘g6 14 ♕d3! h5 15 ♖ad1 b5 16 a4 and White is better, Sznapik–Hawelko, Poland 1984.

| **9** | **...** | **♕b6** |

9 ... e6 10 ♔h1 ♗e7 11 f4 ♘xd4 12 ♕xd4 ♕a5 13 ♖ad1 is clearly good for White, Geller–Hort, Palma de Mallorca 1970.

| **10** | **♘f5!** *(52)* | |

Many players would have automatically retreated the knight to b3 but Kupreichik realizes that he can afford to give up his b-pawn. Although Black can organize ... e6 to expel the knight we have already seen in Vogt–Mascarinas above that knights on c3 and e3 can be well placed.

| **10** | **...** | **0-0-0?!** |

Black prepares ... e6 but it turns out that this is too slow. He should have tried 10 ... e6 (10 ... ♕xb2? at once fails to 11 ♘d5 and 12 ♖b1) 11 ♘xd6+ ♗xd6 12 ♕xd6 ♕xb2 13 ♖fd1 and now:

(1) **13 ... ♘e5** 14 ♘d5! exd5 15 ♕xf6 ♘c4 (15 ... ♖g8 16 ♖ab1 ♕c3 17 ♖xd5 loses at once) 16 c3 ♖f8 (16 ... ♖g8 17 ♗h5) 17 ♖ab1 ♕xe2 18 ♖e1 followed by exd5+ forcing Black to play ... ♗e6, when White continues dxe6 with a winning attack.

(2) **13 ... 0-0-0** 14 ♘d5! exd5 15 exd5 ♕c3 (15 ... ♕e5 16 dxc6 ♕xd6 17 ♖xd6 ♗xc6 18 ♖xf6 wins a pawn) 16 dxc6 ♕xc6 17 ♕f4 followed by ♗f3 when Black has problems with his exposed king and his weak f-pawns.

(3) **13 ... ♖d8!** 14 ♕g3 (the

sacrifice 14 ♖ab1 ♕xc3 15 ♖xb7 flops after 15 ... ♗c8 16 ♖e7+ ♔f8) ♕a3 15 ♗h5 and White still has some pressure although far less than in the game.

11   a4

11 ♘d5 ♕a7 only leaves White with the problem of meeting ... e6.

11   ...   ♘b4

In the Sicilian, Black can normally only contemplate castling queenside when White has also played 0-0-0, since in a race between attacks on opposite wings the missing Black c-pawn gives White a large head start.

12   a5   ♕c7
13   ♘a4

Black's ... ♘b4 has stopped ♘d5 by White but there are other ways to reach b6.

13   ...   e6

13 ... ♕xa5 14 c3 ♘c6 15 b4 ♕c7 16 ♕b3 gives White two free tempi and an open a-file for his attack.

14   ♘d4   ♗xa4

White could not prevent this exchange by playing 14 ♘b6+ ♔b8 15 ♘d4 as then 15 ... e5 followed by ... ♕xc2 would confuse the issue.

15   ♖xa4   d5

Black's only chance is to find some counterplay quickly, or else he will be crushed by c3 followed by b4–b5.

16   c3   ♘c6

Naturally not 16 ... dxe4 17 cxb4 e5 when 18 ♕b1 threatening ♖c1 wins.

17   exd5   ♖xd5
18   ♗f3   ♖d6

18 ... ♖xa5 19 ♘xc6 ♖xa4 20 ♕xa4 bxc6 21 ♗xc6 is one of those positions in which the opposite-coloured bishops increase the strength of an attack to alarming proportions.

19   ♖c4   ♖g8?

Black overlooks the threat. 19 ... e5 was necessary but even then 20 ♘xc6 ♖xd1 21 ♖xd1 bxc6 22 ♖xc6 gives White an ending with an extra pawn and the better position, while some players might prefer 20 ♗xc6 bxc6 21 ♕g4+ and 22 ♘f5.

20   ♕a4

So simple; c6 collapses and with it Black's position.

20   ...   ♖g5
21   ♗xc6   bxc6
22   ♘xc6   Resigns

4 Pelikan Variation

This line arises after 1 e4 c5 2 ♘f3 ♘c6 3 d4 cxd4 4 ♘xd4 ♘f6 5 ♘c3 e5. Black is willing to accept a backward d-pawn in return for active piece play and, in some variations, the two bishops. The historical background to this line is rather obscure since many players have adopted it over the years with different ideas in mind. The names of Lasker and Pelikan are associated with it, but the modern handling probably owes most to the Soviet Grandmaster Sveshnikov. We have given Pelikan's name to the whole system with 6 ... e5, reserving that of Sveshnikov for the 8 ... b5 variation, today considered the main line. It has gained many other adherents in recent years and is regarded as an excellent way to play for a win with Black, since unbalanced positions arise in almost every line. Very recently it has suffered a decline, probably more because of changing fashions than for any clear objective reason.

There is a second move order by which the Pelikan can arise, namely 1 e4 c5 2 ♘f3 ♘c6 3 d4 cxd4 4 ♘xd4 ♘f6 5 ♘c3 e6 (or 2 ... e6 and 5 ... ♘c6) 6 ♘db5 d6 7 ♗f4 e5 8 ♗g5, reaching the same position as after 1 e4 c5 2 ♘f3 ♘c6 3 d4 cxd4 4 ♘xd4 ♘f6 5 ♘c3 e5 6 ♘db5 d6 7 ♗g5, but in one extra move. To avoid the confusion of having two different move numbers in each position I will take the 5 ... e5 order as standard, although in practice the two move orders are equally common.

Since Black is incurring strategic weaknesses White's most logical (and best) lines are those in which he limits his immediate ambitions to nullifying Black's piece play and only later turns his mind to the exploitation of his long-term advantage. Our recommendation for White runs 6 ♘db5 d6 7 ♗g5 a6 8 ♘a3 b5 (the less common line 8 ... ♗e6 is considered in game 14) 9 ♗xf6 gxf6 10 ♘d5 f5 (10 ... ♗g7 is an important alternative) 11 ♗d3. In this unbalanced position Black pits his two bishops and central pawn majority against White's control of d5 and superior pawn structure. The offside knight on a3 can be an important factor, and White usually aims to bring the knight back into the game by playing c4. All the lines of the Sveshnikov are covered in game 15.

Game 14
Karpov–Nunn
London 1982

1	e4	c5
2	♘f3	♘c6
3	d4	cxd4
4	♘xd4	♘f6
5	♘c3	e5
6	♘db5	*(53)*

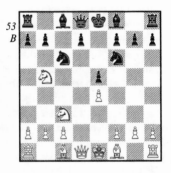

53
B

6 ... d6

All Black's 6th move alternatives give White a clear plus:

(1) **6 ... a6** 7 ♘d6+ ♗xd6 8 ♕xd6 ♕e7 9 ♕xe7+ ♘xe7 (9 ... ♔xe7 10 ♗g5 ♘b4 11 0-0-0 is similar) 10 ♗g5 and White has undisputed control of d5.

(2) **6 ... ♗c5** 7 ♗e3!? (7 ♘d6+ is also good) ♗xe3 8 ♘d6+ ♔f8 9 fxe3 ♕b6 10 ♘c4 ♕c5 11 ♕d6+ ♕xd6 12 ♘xd6 and f7 is about to come under heavy attack by ♗c4.

(3) **6 ... ♗b4** 7 a3 ♗xc3+ 8 ♘xc3 d6 9 ♗g5 h6 (9 ... a6 10 ♘d5 is also very pleasant for White) 10 ♗xf6 ♕xf6 11 ♘b5 and Black will lose his d-pawn for insufficient compensation.

(4) **6 ... h6** (by preventing ♗g5 Black avoids the loss of control of d5 as in line 1, but the move is really just too slow) 7 ♘d6+ ♗xd6 8 ♕xd6 ♕e7 9 ♘b5 (Spassky introduced this pawn sacrifice—the older lines 9 ♕xe7+ ♔xe7 10 b3 and 10 ♗e3 also give White a favourable ending) ♕xd6 (9 ... 0-0 10 ♕xe7 ♘xe7 11 ♘d6 or 10 b3 ♘xe4 11 ♕xe7 ♘xe7 12 ♗a3) 10 ♘xd6+ ♔e7 11 ♘f5+ ♔f8 12 b3 d5 (12 ... ♘xe4 13 ♗a3+ ♔g8 and now 14 f3 or 14 ♘d6) 13 ♗a3+ ♔g8 14 exd5 ♘xd5 15 ♘d6 ♖b8 16 ♗c4 ♗e6 17 0-0-0 and White has a very pleasant position, Spassky–Gheorghiu, Bath 1973.

7 ♗g5 a6

Black must meet the threat of ♘d5 so the only other move is 7 ... ♗e6, but then White does not need to retreat his b5 knight to the bad square a3 and can gain the advantage by 8 ♘d5 ♖c8 (8 ... ♗xd5 9 exd5 ♘e7 is good for White after 10 ♕f3 or 10 c3 a6 11 ♕a4) 9 c3 a6 10 ♘a3 ♗xd5 11 ♗xf6 gxf6 12 ♕xd5 ♕a5 13 ♗c4, Jansa–Danek, CSSR Ch. 1982, with a firm hold on d5 in both cases.

8 ♘a3 ♗e6

8 ... b5 is the line popularized by Sveshnikov and is examined in game 15. Other moves are definitely inferior:

(1) **8 ... ♗e7** (Black commits the bishop too soon) 9 ♘c4 ♗e6 (9 ... ♘d4 10 ♗xf6 ♗xf6 11 ♘d5 b5 12 ♘cb6 ♖b8 13 ♘xc8 ♖xc8

14 c3 ♘e6 15 a4! is very good for White, Averbakh–Korchnoi, semi-final USSR. Ch. 1950, 9 ... 0-0 10 ♗xf6 ♗xf6 11 ♕xd6 doesn't give Black enough for the pawn and 9 ... b5 10 ♗xf6 gxf6 11 ♘e3 gives White a crushing bind) 10 ♗xf6 gxf6 11 ♘e3 (thanks to Black's ... ♗e7 he cannot now dislodge the knight by ... ♗h6) ♕d7 12 ♘cd5 followed by ♗d3 and ♕h5, once again with a total white-squared bind.

(2) **8 ... d5** (not correct) 9 ♘xd5 ♗xa3 10 bxa3 ♕a5+ 11 ♕d2 ♕xd2+ 12 ♗xd2 ♘xd5 13 exd5 ♘d4 14 ♗d3 followed by 0-0 and f4, when White has two bishops in an open position and a moderately relevant extra pawn.

9 ♘c4 ♖c8 *(54)*

9 ... ♗e7 transposes to line 1 of the last note, while the alternative **9 ... ♘d4** (9 ... b5 10 ♗xf6 ♕xf6 11 ♘e3 and 12 ♘cd5 is very good for White) often leads to the knight being driven back with loss of time, e.g. 9 ... ♘d4 10 ♗xf6 gxf6 (10 ... ♕xf6 11 ♘b6 ♖b8 12

54
W

♘cd5 ♕d8 13 c3 leaves Black a tempo down on Karpov–Nunn) 11 ♘e3 ♖c8 12 ♗d3 ♗h6 (12 ... h5 13 0-0 h4 14 ♘cd5 ♗g7 15 c3 ♘c6 16 ♕f3 is excellent for White, Bronstein–Pilnik, Moscow 1956) 13 0-0 0-0 14 ♘cd5 and again Black's knight is expelled by c3, Dely–Flesch, Hungary Ch. 1965.

10 ♗xf6 ♕xf6

With this move Black accepts a loss of time to prevent his pawn structure being damaged but as a result he is driven into a passive position. The important alternative 10 ... gxf6 is met by 11 ♗d3 ♘e7 (**11 ... ♘d4** 12 ♘e3 transposes to the last note while **11 ... ♖g8?!** 12 0-0 ♗h6 13 ♘d5 f5 14 ♕h5! ♗f8 15 ♘cb6 f4 16 ♘xc8 ♗g4 17 ♕xh7 ♖g7 18 ♕xg7! ♗xg7 19 ♘cb6 gave White too much for the queen in Matulović–Arnason, Zeman 1983) 12 ♘e3 ♗h6 (12 ... ♕b6 13 0-0! ♕xb2 14 ♘cd5 ♗xd5 15 ♘xd5 ♘xd5 16 exd5 ♕d4 17 ♕f3 ♔e7 18 a4! ♖c7 19 ♖fd1 ♕c3 20 ♖ab1 ♕a5 21 ♕e4 gave White more than enough for the pawn in Mednis–Lombardy, USA Ch. 1978—this type of pawn sacrifice in return for white-squared pressure and attacking chances occurs frequently in the 10 ... gxf6 line) 13 0-0 ♗xe3 14 fxe3 ♕b6 15 ♕f3 h5 (15 ... ♕xb2? 16 ♘d5 ♗xd5 17 exd5 is bad for Black) 16 ♘d5 ♗xd5 17 exd5 ♖h6 18 ♖ab1 ♕a5!? (18 ... ♖c7 19 c4 was good for White in Tseshkovsky–

Chandler, Minsk 1982) 19 e4 f5 (19 ... ♛xa2? 20 ♕e3 ♖h8 21 ♕b6 wins) and there is no doubt that White is better, although it is not clear by how much. In de Firmian–Matulovic, Vrnjacka Banja 1983 White played 20 a3 ♗f8 and now 21 c4 or 21 exf5 is good for White, but in Kolosovskaia–Suspanova, corr. 1986 Black muddied the waters by 20 a3 f4!? 21 c4 ♘g6 22 ♖fc1 ♕d8 23 b4 ♘h4. Therefore the simple 20 exf5 may be stronger, when White's effective bishop and Black's misplaced rook on h6 guarantee White at least a slight advantage.

11 ♘b6

It is very dangerous for White to take the pawn by 11 ♘xd6+ ♗xd6 12 ♕xd6 when 12 ... ♖d8! 13 ♕c5 ♘d4 14 ♗d3 ♕g5 15 ♔f1 ♖c8 16 ♕b4 b5 gives Black adequate compensation.

11 ... ♖b8
12 ♘cd5 ♕d8

12 ... ♕g6 13 ♕d3 ♗e7 14 ♘c7+ ♔d8 15 ♘cd5 followed by 0-0-0 gives White a dangerous attack.

13 c3 ♗e7

Attempting to develop the bishop more actively runs into trouble after 13 ... g6 14 ♕a4! ♗xd5 15 ♘xd5 ♗g7 16 ♗xa6 ♖a8 17 ♗xb7 ♖xa4 18 ♗xc6+ with a clear plus for White.

14 ♗c4

Karpov correctly steers clear of the complications resulting from the win of a pawn by 14 ♘c4 0-0 15 ♘xe7+ ♕xe7 16 ♕xd6 ♕h4,

and quietly consolidates his grip on d5. White's knights are rather clumsily placed but Black's possibilities for active play are very limited and aiming for ... f5 is his only constructive plan.

14 ... 0-0
15 0-0 ♗g5
16 a4 ♔h8

Chekhov suggests the imaginative 16 ... ♕e8 intending 17 ... ♗d8, but after 17 a5 (with the queen on e8 Black can no longer meet this move by ... ♘xa5) ♗d8 18 b4 ♔h8 19 ♖a2 f5 20 exf5 ♗xf5 21 ♘e3 White has the better chances.

17 ♕e2 *(55)*

This move and the next are evidence of Karpov's understanding of the position. White would like to play 17 a5 defending the b6 knight and thereby freeing the tangle of minor pieces, but at the moment it just allows 17 ... ♘xa5! 18 ♖xa5 ♗xd5. It seems natural, therefore, to prepare a5 with 17 b4 but in Sznapik–Simic, Smederevo 1981, Black obtained active play by 17 b4 f5 18 b5 ♘a5 19 ♗d3 g6 and equalized comfortably.

Karpov's first concern is to take the sting out of ... f5 by preparing to answer it with exf5 and f4. For this purpose ♕e2, which pins the e-pawn against the loose bishop on e6, and his next move ♔h1 removing the king from the vulnerable diagonal are excellent preparation. Only when Black's counterplay is completely neutralized does White return to the exploitation of his queenside space advantage and d5 control.

55
B

17 ... g6

I made use of Karpov's chess lesson five years later in the game Nunn–Manor, London (Lloyds Bank) 1987, which continued 17 ... a5!? 18 ♖ad1 ♗h6 (after 18 ... g6 19 ♗a2! Black should avoid 19 ... ♘e7 20 ♕b5 and 19 ... ♗h6 20 ♘c4 f5 21 exf5 gxf5 22 ♘db6 with a clear plus for White, but even his best line 19 ... f5 20 exf5 gxf5 21 ♘c4 f4 22 f3 is slightly better for White) 19 ♔h1 ♘e7?! (19 ... g6 was more solid, as in Karpov–Nunn) 20 ♘xe7 ♕xb6 (20 ... ♕xe7 21 ♗xe6 fxe6 22 ♕b5 is very bad) 21 ♘f5 and Black has no compensation for his serious weaknesses. White went on to win.

18 ♔h1 ♗h6
19 b4?!

Afterwards Karpov thought that this was still too soon and that 19 ♖ad1 or ♖ae1 would have been better.

19 ... f5
20 exf5 gxf5

21 f4 ♗xd5

Black hopes for salvation in the opposite-coloured bishops, but White's bishop has a fine outpost at d5 whereas Black's is rather useless.

22 ♘xd5 e4?!

22 ... ♘e7 at once is more logical, based on the fact that White cannot win a pawn by 23 fxe5 ♘xd5 24 ♗xd5 dxe5 25 ♕xe5+ because of 25 ... ♗g7 26 ♕e6 ♖f6.

23	a5	♗g7
24	♖ac1	♘e7
25	♖fd1	♘xd5
26	♗xd5	♕c7
27	♖c2	♕e7
28	♕e3	♖bc8
29	c4	♖c7

White has two ways of making further progress. He can either play b5 to leave Black with an isolated pawn on the queenside, which will be hard to defend when his bishop is operating only on the kingside, or he can prepare g4 to attack Black's king. For the moment White is not sure which plan offers the best chances.

30	g3	♖e8
31	♖g2	♕f6 *(56)*
32	g4	

This doesn't have the desired effect and it would probably have been better to try the other plan. If Black moved his forces to the queenside White could then have contemplated g4 later.

32	...	fxg4
33	♖xg4	♕c3
34	♖g3	♕xb4

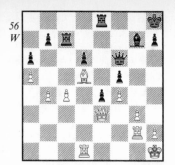

56
W

If Black swaps queens Karpov gives the line 34 ... ♕xe3 35 ♖xe3 ♖ce7 36 b5! ♗h6 37 ♖f1 ♖f8 38 ♖xe4 ♖xe4 39 ♗xe4 ♖xf4 40 ♖xf4 ♗xf4 41 ♗xb7 and wins.

| 35 | ♖dg1 | ♕b2 |

Stopping White's threat of ♕d4.

36	♖g5	♕f6
37	♖1g4	♕a1+
38	♔g2	♕b2+
39	♔h3	♖ce7
40	f5	♕f6?

This was the sealed move (move 41 in the game, which started with the 2 ... e6 move order) and, as so often happens, after a long period of difficult defence a player's relief at reaching the time control results in a casual sealed move. White obviously has considerable pressure for the pawn but after 40 ... ♖f8 (Karpov also suggests 40 ... ♕a1 threatening ... ♕f1+) it is likely that Black can draw. Black's passive queen move gives White the freedom of action he needs to mount the decisive assault.

| 41 | ♖h5 | ♖f8 |

| 42 | ♖gh4 | h6 |

White cannot now play 43 ♖xh6+ ♗xh6 44 ♖xh6+ due to 44 ... ♕xh6+ 45 ♕xh6+ ♖h7.

| 43 | ♖g4 | ♖e5 |

Forced in order to meet 44 ♖g6 by 44 ... ♕xg6.

| 44 | ♖gg5 | ♖c8 *(57)* |

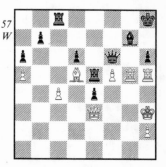

57
W

There isn't much Black can do to meet the threat of ♔g4 followed by ♖g6.

| 45 | ♔g4! | ♔h7? |

Going under without a fight. I should have tried 45 ... ♖xd5 46 cxd5 ♖c2 although White is still winning even after this.

| 46 | ♖g6 | ♕f8 |
| 47 | ♕g5 | ♕xf5+ |

Or else 48 ♖gxh6+ ♗xh6 49 ♕g6+ is the end.

48	♕xf5	♖xf5
49	♖xg7+	♔xg7
50	♖xf5	**Resigns**

Game 17
Short–Sax
Candidates' Match
Saint John 1988

| 1 | e4 | c5 |
| 2 | ♘f3 | ♘c6 |

3	**d4**	**cxd4**
4	♘xd4	♘f6
5	♘c3	e5
6	♘db5	d6
7	♗g5	a6
8	♘a3	b5
9	♗xf6	gxf6

9 ... ♕xf6 10 ♘d5 ♕d8 11 c4
♘e7 (11 ... b4 12 ♕a4 ♗d7 13
♘b5! axb5 14 ♕xa8 ♕xa8 15
♘c7+ wins material) 12 cxb5
♘xd5 13 ♕xd5 (13 exd5 is also
safe and good) ♗e6 14 ♕d2 d5 15
bxa6 ♗xa3 16 ♗b5+! gives
White a clear advantage.

| 10 | ♘d5 *(58)* | |

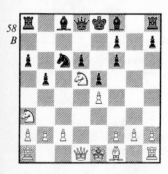

58
B

| 10 | ... | f5 |

This is an already an important
moment for Black. At one time 10
... f5 was the only move played in
this position, but recently the
alternative 10 ... ♗g7 has
become popular. The idea behind
this move is to delay Black's thematic break ... f5, giving first
priority to removing the powerful
knight from d5 by ... ♘e7.
Theory gives no clear-cut recommendation against this new plan,
so we give a more detailed cover-

age than usual: 10 ... ♗g7 (10
... ♗e6 11 c3 ♗g7 12 ♘c2 f5 13
exf5 ♗xf5 14 ♘e3 leaves Black a
tempo down over a standard line
and after **14 ... ♗e6** 15 ♕f3 0-0
16 ♗d3 or **14 ... ♗g6** 15 a4
White has good chances) and
now:

(1) **11 ♕h5** (11 ♘e3 ♘e7 12
♕h5 is the same, while 11 c4 0-0
12 cxb5 ♘d4 is very risky) ♘e7
(better than 11 ... f5 12 exf5
♕a5+ 13 c3 b4 14 ♕g5! ♕xd5 15
♕xg7 bxa3 16 ♕xh8+ ♔d7 17
b3 with advantage to White, Sir-
ias–Ochoa de Echaguen, Havana
1984) 12 ♘e3 f5! 13 exf5 e4 14
0-0-0 0-0 and now:

(1a) **15 f3?!** ♕b6 16 ♗g5 d5 17
♘xd5? (17 f6 ♕xf6 18 ♕xf6 ♗xf6
19 ♘xd5 ♘xd5 20 ♖xd5 ♗e6
was an improvement, but Black is
at least equal) ♘xd5 18 ♖xd5
♔h8! and Black is better,
Klinger–Vaiser, Szirak 1985.

(1b) **15 h4** (15 g4!? is untested)
d5!? 16 ♖h3 ♕d6 17 ♖g3 ♕e5 18
c3 b4 19 ♘ac2 bxc3 20 bxc3 ♖b8!
(not **20 ... ♕xc3?** 21 ♖d4!, nor
20 ... ♘xf5? 21 ♖xg7+!) 21
♘d4 ♗d7 22 ♖d2, Vakhnov–
Shipkov, USSR 1987 and now 22
... ♔h8 23 ♘g4 ♕f4 24 f6! ♗xf6
25 ♘xf6 ♕xf6 26 ♕g5 ♕xg5 27
hxg5 ♖b6 is roughly equal. This
murky variation must be a good
place to look for a White improvement!

(2) **11 ♗d3** ♘e7 12 ♘xe7 (not
12 ♘e3 f5! 13 ♕h5 d5!) ♕xe7
(59) with a branch:

(2a) **13 c3** f5 14 ♘c2 0-0 (**14 ...**

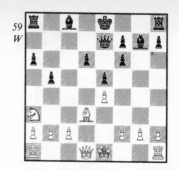

59
W

d5?! 15 exf5 e4 16 ♗e2 and **14 …** ♗b7 15 ♘e3 fxe4 16 ♘f5 ♕f6 17 ♗xe4 d5 18 ♗xd5 ♖d8 19 ♕g4 ♗xd5 20 ♘xg7+ ♔f8 21 ♘h5 are good for White, but **14 …** ♕g5 15 0-0 ♗b7 16 f3 0-0 17 exf5 d5 was unclear in Feigelson–Malyshev, USSR 1988) 15 0-0 d5! (not **15 … fxe4?!** 16 ♗xe4 ♖b8 17 ♘b4, while **15 … ♖b8** 16 exf5! e4 17 ♖e1 ♗xf5 18 ♘e3 ♗g6 19 ♘d5 ♕e5 20 ♗c2 f5 21 f4 ♕e8 22 ♘c7 ♕c6 23 ♘e6 led to a slight plus for White, Dolmatov–Simic, Belgrade 1988) 16 exf5 e4 17 ♗e2 ♖d8 18 ♘d4 ♗xd4 19 cxd4 ♗xf5 20 ♕d2 ♗e6 21 f4 f5 Draw, Psakhis–Dolmatov, Klaipeda 1988.

(2b) **13 c4** f5 14 0-0 (not 14 ♕d2?! ♗b7 15 exf5 e4 16 ♗e2, Hardicsay–Vaiser, Berlin 1988 and now 16 … e3! 17 fxe3 ♗xg2 18 ♖g1 ♕h4+ 19 ♔d1 ♕xh2 20 ♔c2 ♗e4+ 21 ♔b3 bxc4+ 22 ♘xc4 ♖b8+ 23 ♔a3 ♗f8 wins for Black) 0-0 (14 … ♗b7!? is interesting, e.g. 15 cxb5 fxe4 16 bxa6 exd3 17 axb7 ♕xb7 18 ♕xd3 d5 19 ♖ad1 and now **19 … 0-0** 20 ♕xd5 ♕xb2 21 ♘c4 ♕xa2 22 ♘xe5 ♕xd5 23 ♖xd5 ♗xe5

should be a draw, while after **19 … ♕xb2** 20 ♖b1 ♕xa3 21 ♖b8+ ♔e7 22 ♖b7+ ♔e6 23 ♖b6+ ♔e7 White unwisely declined the draw by repetition and lost in Solozhenkin–Skvortsov, Berdiansk 1987; 15 ♕f3! is probably the best reply) with a wide choice for White:

(2b1) **15 cxb5?!** d5 and 15 ♕e2 ♗b7! 16 ♖ad1 ♖fd8 17 cxb5 (17 exf5?! bxc4 18 ♘xc4 d5 19 ♘e3 e4 20 ♗b1 ♕f6 is also good for Black) fxe4 18 ♗xe4 d5 19 bxa6 ♗xa6 20 ♗d3 ♗b7! and Black has very good compensation for the pawn.

(2b2) **15 ♕h5!?** ♖b8 (**15 … bxc4** 16 ♘xc4 d5 17 exd5 e4 18 ♗e2 and **15 … ♕b7** 16 ♖fe1 d5 17 exd5! e4 18 ♗f1 ♗xb2 19 ♖ab1, Vogt–Chekhov, Berlin 1988, are good for White) 16 exf5 e4 17 ♖ae1 ♗b7 and now:

(2b21) **18 ♖e3** bxc4 19 ♗xc4 (19 ♖h3 h6 20 ♗xc4 d5 21 ♗xd5 ♗xd5 22 f6 ♕xf6 23 ♕xd5 ♖xb2 24 ♕xe4 ♖xa2 25 ♘c4 ♕e6 26 ♕d3 ♕e2 27 ♕d5 ♕e6 28 ♕d3 ♕e2 29 ♕d5 ♕e6 Draw, Smagin–Vaiser, Sochi 1988) d5 20 ♗xd5 ♗xd5 21 f6 ♕xf6 22 ♕xd5 ♖xb2 23 ♖xe4 ♖d8 24 ♕c4 ♕c3 25 ♕xa6 ♕c5 26 ♖c4 ♕f5 was unclear in Hjartarson–Yusupov, Munich 1988.

(2b22) **18 ♕g4** ♖fe8 19 cxb5 (19 f3 bxc4 20 ♗xe4 ♕f6 was also good for Black in Kuijf–Schmitt-diel, Luxembourg 1988) d5 20 bxa6 ♗c6 21 a7 ♖xb2 22 ♖c1 ♗d7! 23 ♗b5 h5! 24 f6 hxg4 25 fxe7 ♗xb5 and Black is better, Bosboom–van der Wiel, Netherlands Ch. 1988.

(2b23) **18 cxb5** d5! 19 bxa6 ♗c6 20 ♖e3 ♖xb2 21 ♗b1 ♖fb8 with a clear plus for Black, Kolotilin–Shipkov, USSR 1984.

(2b3) **15 ♖e1** fxe4 (15 ... ♗b7 16 exf5 e4 17 ♕g4 ♖fe8 18 cxb5 d5 19 bxa6 ♗xa6 20 ♗xa6 ♖xa6 21 ♘b5 was good for White in Ivanovic–Ivanov, Belgrade 1988) 16 ♗xe4 ♖b8 17 cxb5 axb5 and now **18 ♕b3** ♗e6 19 ♗d5 ♖fc8 20 ♖ad1 ♗f5! 21 ♗e4?! (21 ♖c1 would have been equal) ♗xe4 22 ♖xe4 ♕e6 gave Black some advantage in Klovans–Ivanchuk, Frunze 1988. However **18 ♕d3!?** is interesting (18 ♘c2 f5 19 ♗d5+ ♗e6 20 ♘b4 is also possible), when Nunn–Kosten, British ½-hour Ch., continued 18 ... f5 19 ♗d5+ ♔h8 20 ♘xb5 e4 21 ♕b3 ♕e5 22 a4 ♗d7 23 ♖e2 ♖fc8 24 ♖d1 ♖c5 25 ♗c4 f4? 26 ♘xd6! and wins. Slim evidence, but there are unexplored ideas in this line.

At the moment Black's chances in the 10 ... ♗g7 line appear quite good, but a number of lines above, such as 1b and 2b3, deserve further investigation by White players.

11   ♗d3   ♗e6

11 ... ♕g5 (11 ... f4 12 g3! is also good for White) 12 g4! ♔d8 13 gxf5 ♗xf5 14 ♘e3 ♗e6 15 ♕d2 gives White a positional advantage.

12   0-0 *(60)*

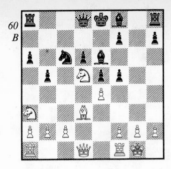

12   ...   ♗g7

Or 12 ... ♗xd5 (12 ... f4?! 13 c4! is very good for White after **13 ... bxc4** 14 ♗c2! ♗g7 15 ♗a4 ♖c8 16 ♘xc4 or **13 ... b4** 14 ♕a4! ♗d7 15 ♘b5) 13 exd5 ♘e7 14 ♘xb5 ♗g7 15 ♘c3 e4 16 ♗c4 ♕a5 (16 ... ♕c7 17 ♕e2! puts pressure on the a6 pawn) and now:

(1) **17 ♕d2** ♖c8 18 ♗b3 (not 18 ♘xe4? ♕b6 19 ♕g5 ♖g8 20 ♘d2 ♗c3! 21 ♕xg8+ ♘xg8 22 bxc3 ♕a5 with a clear advantage for Black) ♗xc3 19 bxc3 ♕xc3 20 ♕h6 ♔d7 21 ♖ae1 ♖cg8 22 ♕e3 (22 g3 ♖g6 23 ♕c1 ♖hg8 is unclear) ♕xe3 23 ♖xe3 ♘g6 24 f3 ♘h4 25 ♗a4+ ♔d8 with a sharp but balanced ending, Malishauskas–Krasenkov, Vilnius 1988.

(2) **17 ♘e2!** ♗xb2 (17 ... ♕c5 is well met by the exchange sacrifice 18 b3!) 18 ♖b1 ♗e5 was played in Short–van der Wiel, SWIFT Brussels 1987. Here Short played 19 ♕c1 and although White was still slightly better Black managed to escape from his difficulties. However White could

have tried other moves, for example 19 ♖b7 ♖c8 20 ♗b3 ♖c7 21 ♖b8+ ♖c8 22 ♖xc8+ ♘xc8 23 ♘g3 ♘e7 24 ♕h5 appears good for White, as does the simple 19 ♘g3, and if 19 ... ♖c8 then 20 ♕e2.

13 ♕h5   f4

Not 13 ... 0-0? 14 exf5 ♗xd5 15 f6 e4 16 fxg7 ♖e8 17 ♕xd5, nor 13 ... h6?! 14 f4! opening the position while Black's king is still in the centre.

14 c4   bxc4

After 14 ... b4 (14 ... ♗xd5 15 exd5 ♘e7 16 ♖ad1 b4 17 ♘b1 ♘g6 18 g3 with advantage to White, Vogt–Georgadze, Halle 1978) 15 ♘c2 ♖b8 White has a variety of promising ideas, since with d5 secured he can play on the queenside with b3 and a3, or on the kingside with g3. Finally ♘e1–f3–h4–f5 can be awkward. The speculative 14 ... 0-0 15 cxb5 ♘d4 16 ♘c2 ♘xb5 (16 ... ♘xc2 17 ♗xc2 axb5 18 ♗b3 is a safe positional plus for White) is dubious after 17 a4 (17 ♘cb4 ♘d4 18 ♖c1 is also promising) ♘a7 18 a5 ♘c6 19 b4 f5 20 ♘b6 ♖a7 21 exf5 ♗f7 22 ♕h3 ♕f6 23 ♗e4 ♘e7 24 ♖ad1 and White keeps control of d5.

15 ♗xc4   0-0

16 ♖ac1 *(61)* ♘e7

The position after 16 ♖ac1 is the key to the whole line and is critical for the assessment of Sveshnikov's variation. Black has a wide range of options:

(1) 16 ... ♘d4?! 17 ♘c2! ♘xc2

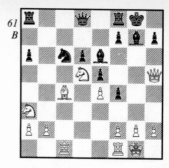

61
B

(17 ... f3 18 ♘xd4 fxg2 19 ♘f5! gxf1(♕)+ 20 ♔xf1 ♗xf5 21 exf5 h6 22 ♖c3! ♕g5 23 ♕xg5 hxg5 24 ♘e7+ ♔h7 25 ♖h3+ ♗h6 26 f6 e4 27 ♗d5 wins for White) 18 ♖xc2 ♔h8 19 ♖fc1 ♖a7 20 b4 ♖g8 21 a4 with an excellent position for White, Mokry–Vodichka, Decin 1979.

(2) 16 ... ♖a7!? and now:

(2a) 17 ♘xf4!? exf4 (17 ... ♗xc4? 18 ♖xc4 ♘a5 19 ♖a4 exf4 20 ♖xa5 ♗xb2 21 ♘c4 is good for White) 18 ♗xe6 ♘e7! (not 18 ... fxe6 19 ♖xc6) 19 ♗c4! (after 19 ♗d5 or 19 ♗f5 Black can take the bishop and then play 20 ... ♗xb2, when the sacrifice 21 ♖b1 ♗xa3 22 ♖b3 ♗c5 23 ♖h3 doesn't work because Black can advance his f-pawn and defend the second rank) ♘g6 (not now 19 ... ♗xb2? 20 ♖b1 ♗g7 21 ♖b3 intending ♖h3) 20 ♖c2 ♖e7 21 ♗d5 ♖e5 22 ♕d1 ♕h4 23 ♘c4 ♖h5 24 h3 ♖g5 25 ♔h1 ♗e5 and Black has enough for the pawn, Dvoris–Basagic, Sibenik 1988.

(2b) 17 ♖fd1 ♕b8!? (17 ... ♔h8? 18 ♘xf4 exf4 19 ♗xe6

really does work because f7 hangs after ... ♘e7) 18 b3 (18 ♘xf4 exf4 19 ♗xe6 ♘e7 is still unclear) ♘d4 19 ♘c2 ♘b5 and now 20 ♘cb4! appears good for White.

(3) **16 ... ♔h8** 17 ♖fd1 ♘d4 18 ♘c2 is slightly better for White.

(4) **16 ... ♖b8** (the main line) 17 b3 *(62)* and now:

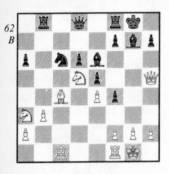

(4a) **17 ... ♔h8** 18 ♘xf4!? exf4 19 ♗xe6 ♘d4 20 ♗f5! ♘xf5 21 ♕xf5 ♗b2 22 ♘c4 ♗xc1 23 ♖xc1 is a very promising exchange sacrifice, while **17 ... ♗xd5** 18 ♗xd5 ♘b4 19 ♖fd1 ♘xa2 20 ♖c6, with ♘c4 to come, leaves Black very badly placed.

(4b) **17 ... ♕a5** (a recent idea) 18 ♘b1!? (18 ♘c2 ♕xa2 should lead to a draw after 19 ♕h4 h6! 20 ♘f6+ ♗xf6 21 ♕xf6 ♗xc4 22 ♕xh6 ♗xf1 23 ♕g5+) ♔h8 (not 18 ... ♕xa2? 19 ♘bc3 ♕a5 20 ♖a1 ♕c5 21 ♖xa6) 19 ♘bc3 f5 20 ♘e7 ♘xe7 21 ♗xe6 ♖f6! (not 21 ... fxe4? 22 ♘xe4 d5 23 ♖c5 ♕b4 24 ♘g5 h6 25 ♖c7) 22 exf5 e4! 23 ♕e2! (not 23 ♘xe4? ♖xe6 24 ♘g5 ♕xf5 and Black wins) d5, Estevez–Timoshchenko, Mana-

gua 1988, and now 24 ♕d2! f3 (24 ... ♘xf5 25 ♕xd5 ♕xd5 26 ♗xd5 e3 27 ♘e4 is very good for White) reaches the critical position. Black has some compensation for the pawn after 25 ♘xe4 ♕xd2 26 ♘xd2 fxg2 27 ♔xg2 ♘xf5, but 25 g4! appears quite unpleasant for Black (25 ... ♗h6 26 ♕d4).

(4c) **17 ... ♕d7** 18 ♖fd1 ♔h8 (not **18 ... ♗g4?** 19 ♕g5, while **18 ... ♘d4** 19 ♘c2 ♘xc2 20 ♖xc2 ♔h8 21 ♖d3 ♗g4 22 ♕h4 f5 23 f3 fxe4 24 fxe4 is a little better for White) 19 ♕h4 and now:

(4c1) **19 ... f5!?** 20 ♘xf4 exf4 21 ♗xe6 ♕xe6 22 ♖xc6 fxe4 23 ♖cxd6 ♕e8 reaching a very sharp position. It is perhaps surprising that nobody has repeated 19 ... f5!?, because in the only game played, Stanciu–Brkovic, Pernik 1983, the continuation **24 ♘c4** e3 25 fxe3 (not 25 ♖e1 ♗c3) fxe3 26 ♖e1 ♕f7! 27 ♘xe3 ♖be8 28 ♘c4! ♕e4! 29 ♕g3 was satisfactory for Black since he could now have forced a draw by 29 ... ♗d4+ 30 ♖xd4 ♖xd4 31 ♕e5+ ♕g7 32 ♕xg7+ ♔xg7. It seems to me that it was not necessary to play ♘c4 at once, and White should first try to defuse the advance of the e-pawn. Therefore **24 ♕g4** is logical, and after 24 ... e3 simply 25 ♕f3 (25 ♕e2!?), with ♘c4 coming next move, and Black has to prove that he has enough for the pawn. In any case no other players have been convinced by Black's sacrifice.

(4c2) **19 ... ♗xd5** 20 ♗xd5! (stronger than the old continuation 20 ♖xd5) ♘b4 (after **20 ... ♘d4** 21 ♖c4! both **21 ... f3** 22 ♘c2 ♘e2+ 23 ♔f1 ♘f4 24 gxf3 and **21 ... f5** 22 ♘c2 fxe4 23 ♘xd4 exd4 24 ♗xe4, Svesh-nikov–Vyzmanavin, Moscow II 1987, are good for White) and now:

(4c21) **21 ♖d2** f5 22 ♘c4 (22 ♕h3 should be met by **22 ... ♘xd5** 23 ♖xd5 ♕b7 24 ♕d3 fxe4 25 ♕xe4 f3 rather than **22 ... ♕e7** 23 exf5 e4 24 ♘c4 ♖f6 25 ♖e1 e3 26 fxe3 ♖h6 27 ♕g4 ♗c3 28 ♕xf4 ♖f6 29 ♖ed1 ♗xd2 30 ♖xd2 with advantage for White, Klovans–Vyzmanavin, USSR 1987) ♘xd5?! (22 ... ♖b5 23 ♖cd1 ♘xd5 is better) 23 ♖xd5 fxe4 24 ♖xd6 ♕f5 25 h3! h5 26 ♕e7 e3 27 fxe3 fxe3 28 ♖d7! and White stands well, Renet–Korchnoi, Lugano 1988.

(4c22) **21 ♖c3!?** ♘xa2 (after 21 ... f5 22 ♖h3 ♗f6 23 ♗e6! both **23 ... ♕e7** 24 ♕h5 fxe4 25 ♘c4 d5 26 ♘d6 and **23 ... ♗xh4** 24 ♗xd7 are good for White) 22 ♖h3 h6 23 ♘c4 ♖bd8 24 g4! and White has dangerous attacking chances since if Black exchanges on g3 the route is open for White's knight to move to f5.

17 ♖fd1

There is an interesting alternative in 17 ♘c7!? ♗xc4 (17 ... ♕xc7 18 ♗xe6 ♕b7 19 ♗b3! is good for White since **19 ... ♕xe4** loses to 20 ♗c2) 18 ♖xc4 ♖c8 19

♖fc1; perhaps **19 ... ♕d7** is the best reply.

17 ... ♖c8
18 ♘xe7+   ♕xe7 *(63)*

Up to this point the game has followed Matanovic–Sax, Buenos Aires 1978, which continued 19 ♕e2 ♔h8 20 ♗xa6 f5! with dangerous counterplay. Black went on to win and later it was suggested that 20 ♖c2 followed by doubling rooks on the c-file would have been good for White. Short prefers to double rooks on the d-file with his queen still actively posted on h5.

63
W

19 ♖c3!

Black has no immediate threats, so White can afford to take time out to prepare b3 followed by ♖cd3. Black must aim for ... f5, since this provides the only possible counterplay to off-set the backward d-pawn. The immediate 19 ... f5 fails to 20 exf5.

19 ...   ♔h8

Short's innovation caused Sax to use a lot of time over this and his next few moves, so that before long White was an hour ahead on the clock. 19 ... ♖c6? 20 ♗xe6 ♖xc3 21 ♗f5 wins.

20 b3 f5

20 ... d5 21 exd5 ♗xd5 22 ♖xd5 ♕xa3 fails after 23 ♗d3 e4 (23 ... h6 24 ♕f5 and 23 ... f5 24 ♗xf5 are even worse) 24 ♗xe4 h6 25 ♖xc8 ♖xc8 26 h3. Black could have tried 20 ... ♗d7, but then White can keep the advantage by 21 ♘b1! (intending ♖cd3 and ♘c3) f5 22 ♖cd3 fxe4 23 ♖xd6 followed by ♘c3.

21 ♖h3 h6
22 ♗xe6 ♕xe6
23 ♖hd3 ♖cd8

Although this looks passive it is the best way to defend the d-pawn, for example 23 ... ♖c6 24 ♕f3 or 23 ... fxe4 24 ♖xd6 ♕e7 25 ♘c4 with a clear plus for White in both cases. There is little point leaving a rook on the c-file when it will soon be blocked by ♘c4.

24 ♕e2!

It is easy to win a pawn, but if this involves allowing Black to advance his central pawns Black's powerful bishop may well provide enough compensation. One such line is 24 ♘c4 (24 ♕f3? ♕g6! 25 exf5 ♕xf5 followed by ... e4 is also bad) fxe4 25 ♖xd6 ♖xd6 26 ♖xd6 ♕e7 27 ♖xa6 e3 28 fxe3 fxe3 and the threats to White's king practically force him to play 29 ♖xh6+ (29 ♘xe3 ♕c5 30 ♕e2 e4 threatening ... ♗d4 is awkward) ♗xh6 30 ♕xh6+ ♔g8 31 ♕xe3, but 31 ... ♕f6 32 h3 ♕f1+ 33 ♔h2 ♕f4+ is a likely

draw because the knight and queenside pawns cannot assume a stable defensive configuration. White correctly prefers to keep the bind and cash in later.

24 ... fxe4

24 ... ♕g6 25 f3 d5 (25 ... fxe4 26 ♕xe4 is good for White) 26 ♖xd5 ♖xd5 27 exd5 e4 28 ♘c4 e3 may seem unclear, but White's passed pawn is just as far advanced as Black's and he has an extra pawn.

25 ♕xe4 f3
26 ♘c4! *(64)*

Much better than 26 ♖xf3 d5 27 ♕h4 (27 ♖xf8+ ♗xf8 attacks a3) ♖fe8 followed by the advance of the central pawns, with good compensation for the pawn.

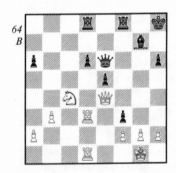

26 ... ♖f4

26 ... fxg2 27 ♖xd6 ♖xd6 28 ♖xd6 ♕f7 29 ♖d2 and 30 ♘e3 is also very good for White.

27 ♕d5 ♕g4

Black cannot avoid a miserable ending. Although he now succeeds in playing ... d5 his bishop remains blocked by the e5 pawn.

28 ♖xf3 ♖xf3

29	♕xf3	♛xf3
30	gxf3	d5
31	♔f1	♝f6

Despite White's doubled pawn the position should be a win since Black's d-pawn is easily blockaded by White's king and the bishop will be impeded by the central pawns. Moreover White has a powerful queenside pawn majority.

32	♘b6	d4
33	♔e2	

33 ♖c1! was more accurate, activating the rook before Black can play ... ♝g5. Then 34 ♖c8 is a threat, and after 33 ... ♔g7 34 ♖c7+ ♔g6 35 ♖d7 White gets his rook behind Black's passed pawn and follows up with ♔e2–d3. However the move played should also be sufficient to win.

33	...	♝g5
34	♘c4	♝f4
35	h3	♖g8

Black will have to play this sooner or later, for otherwise White plays ♔d3 and ♖g1, seizing the open file for his own use.

| 36 | b4 | ♖g2 |

The rook must move up the g-file to allow the Black king to cross, and at g2 it delays White's ♔d3.

37	a4	♔g7
38	b5	axb5
39	axb5	♔f6
40	b6	♔e6
41	b7	♖g8
42	♖b1	♖b8 *(65)*

The win still requires some work. White first secures the ad-

65
W

vanced pawn and moves his king up. Black is paralysed and can only adopt a waiting strategy.

43	♖b5	♔d7
44	♘a5	♔c7

White's only worry is that Black might try to liquidate to a rook and pawn ending by ... ♝g5–d8xa5. This might prove awkward to win as White would be left with only f- and h-pawns. The immediate 44 ... ♝g5 45 ♖xe5 ♝d8 fails to 46 ♖d5+ ♔e6 47 ♖xd8.

45	♔d3	♔d6
46	h4	

Definitely ruling out ... ♝g5.

46	...	♔c7
47	♖b2	♝h2
48	♔e4	

White's plan is to play ♖c2+ at a moment when Black must reply ... ♔d7 to prevent ♖c8. Then White will seize the g-file by ♖c1–g1. Finally the penetration of the rook combined with the advance of the White king to c4 and b5 will decide the game. The immediate 48 ♖c2+ fails to 48 ... ♔b6! 49 ♖c8 ♔xa5, so White must blockade the e-pawn before starting his plan.

48 ...   ♗f4

Black can only delay the end. This move covers c1 to prevent ♖c1–g1.

49   ♖c2+   ♚d7

Or 49 ... ♚b6 50 ♖c8 ♖xb7 51 ♘xb7 ♚xb7 52 ♖f8 (threat ♖xf4) ♗h2 53 ♖f6 and wins.

50   ♚d3!

Black is in zugzwang. The rook cannot move because of ♘c6, the king cannot move because of ♖c8 and ... h5 doesn't help.

50   ...   ♗h2
51   ♖c1   ♗f4

The same again! Black has to free g1.

52   ♖g1   ♚d6
53   ♚c4   Resigns

The finish might be **53 ... ♖f8** 54 ♘b3 (if White gets the chance to play ♘b3–c5 the winning process is simplified) ♖b8 55 ♘c5 ♖h8 56 ♖g6+ ♚c7 57 ♚b5 d3 58 ♖c6+ ♚b8 59 ♚b6 mating, or **53 ... ♚c7** 54 ♖g6 ♖h8 55 ♚c5 d3 56 ♖g7+ ♚b8 57 ♚b6 with a similar conclusion.

5 Dragon Variation

The Dragon is one of the most controversial lines in the Sicilian. At various times over the years it has appeared to be in its death throes, only to be suddenly revived by the discovery of new ideas for Black. Practitioners regard the variation as their private property, and defend it with an almost religious fervour against the many White players who wish to commit the heresy of mating Black down the h-file. The amount of opening analysis spawned by the Dragon is notorious, but much of this theory is concerned with the many White alternatives, so although I am recommending one of the main lines for White the quantity of analysis is not excessive. The material is divided amongst three games. I call the continuation 1 e4 c5 2 ♘f3 d6 3 d4 cxd4 4 ♘xd4 ♘f6 5 ♘c3 g6 6 ♗e3 ♗g7 7 f3 0-0 8 ♕d2 ♘c6 9 ♗c4 ♗d7 10 0-0-0 ♖c8 11 ♗b3 ♘e5 12 h4 h5 13 ♗g5 ♖c5 the 'main line'. Game 18 deals with all deviations from the main line before Black's 12th move, while game 19 covers Black's 12th and 13th move alternatives. The 'main line' itself is deferred until game 20.

The Dragon is characterized by the initial moves 1 e4 c5 2 ♘f3 d6 3 d4 cxd4 4 ♘xd4 ♘f6 5 ♘c3 g6, intending to develop Black's bishop actively at g7. If White plays quietly and castles kingside the bishop will still be useful in supporting Black's minority attack on the queenside, while if White aims to attack the enemy king and plays 0-0-0 the Dragon bishop comes into its own. Hosts of White players have seen their queensides disintegrate under the laser-like power of the g7 bishop, supported perhaps by ... ♕a5 and ... ♖c8 to step up the pressure on c3. The true Dragon player will analyse six exchange sacrifices on c3 before breakfast, and White players need to be constantly on the alert for combinations based on blowing open the long diagonal.

The critical lines are those in which White tries to deliver mate by advancing his h-pawn, when Black has two possible defences. He may ignore the advance and concentrate on developing his own attack, or he may block White by playing ... h5. This latter approach allows a possible sacrificial breakthrough by g4, but this has to be very well-timed or it just loses material. General principles aren't much help in the Dragon, since success or failure is determined by tactical considerations.

Game 18
Kroncke–Schroder
Correspondence, 1987

1	e4	c5
2	♘f3	d6
3	d4	cxd4
4	♘xd4	♘f6
5	♘c3	g6
6	♗e3	

If White intends castling queenside this move is the most usual. 6 ♗e2 only fits in with 0-0, since the bishop is usually better placed at f1 or c4 in the more aggressive lines resulting from castling on opposite wings.

6	...	♗g7

The Dragon differs from many other Sicilian systems in that Black often omits the typical move . . . a6. Time is of particular importance in the Dragon and Black simply cannot afford the tempo spent on preparing . . . b5, which can often be played without . . . a6 in case White castles queenside. The idea of playing . . . a6 and . . . b5 before castling has been tried, but after 6 . . . a6 (6 . . . ♘g4? loses material after 7 ♗b5+) 7 f3 ♘bd7 8 ♕d2 b5 9 a4! bxa4 (9 . . . b4 10 ♘d5 is also very good for White) 10 ♖xa4 ♗g7 11 ♗e2 0-0 12 0-0 ♘c5 13 ♖a3 ♗b7 14 ♖fa1 ♕c8 15 ♘b3 White had strong queenside pressure in Kavalek–Bilek, Sousse IZ 1967.

7	f3	(66)

This is more or less forced as 7 ♗c4 and 7 ♕d2 can both be met by 7 . . . ♘g4.

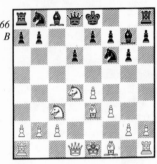

66
B

7	...	0-0

Or:

(1) **7 . . . a6** (7 . . . ♘bd7 exerts no pressure on d4 so simply 8 ♕d2 followed by 0-0-0, ♗c4 and ♗h6 gives White a strong attack) 8 ♕d2 ♘bd7 (8 . . . b5 9 a4! is similar to Kavalek–Bilek above) 9 ♗h6 (9 0-0-0 is also good) ♗xh6 (9 . . . 0-0 is suicidal since White's h4–h5 attack is much stronger than usual) 10 ♕xh6 b5 11 0-0-0 ♗b7 12 ♔b1, Bastrikov–Hasin, USSR 1961, and Black's king is stuck in the centre.

(2) **7 . . . ♘c6** (this can transpose to the main line if Black castles quickly, so we only explore lines in which Black plays . . . ♗d7 and . . . ♖c8 before . . . 0-0) 8 ♕d2 ♗d7 9 0-0-0 ♖c8 10 g4 and now:

(2a) **10 . . . ♘e5** 11 h4 h5 12 g5 ♘h7 13 f4 ♘g4 and now P. Littlewood–Mestel, London 1978, continued **14 ♗g1** 0-0 15 ♔b1 e5

16 ♘f3 ♗e6 17 fxe5 ♘xe5 18 ♘xe5 ♗xe5 19 ♘b5 ♖e8 and Black had no problems. However White can improve by playing f5 at some point, for example 15 f5 or, more provocatively, **14 f5!?** since although White's dark-squared bishop disappears after 14 ... ♘xe3 15 ♕xe3 0-0, it isn't easy to see a constructive plan for Black after 16 ♗h3.

(2b) **10 ... 0-0** 11 h4 and now:

(2b1) **11 ... b5** 12 ♘cxb5 ♘e5 13 h5 ♘xf3 (once Black has started sacrificing he must continue) 14 ♘xf3 ♗xg4 15 ♕g2 (15 ♗e2 ♘xe4 16 ♕e1! would be a safe answer to Black's aggression) ♕a5 16 a3 ♖xc2+! 17 ♔xc2 ♕a4+ 18 ♔d2 ♕b3 19 ♘c3 ♕xb2+ 20 ♔d3 ♕xa3 with horrendous complications, Mestel–Christiansen, Hastings 1978–9. This remarkable game concluded 21 ♗c1 (21 ♖c1 was probably better) ♕b4 22 ♗d2 ♖c8 23 hxg6 hxg6 (23 ... h5!? reserving h6 for the bishop was possible) 24 ♖h4 ♖xc3+ 25 ♗xc3 ♕xe4+ 26 ♔d2 ♘d5? (26 ... ♗xf3 27 ♖xe4 ♘xe4+ 28 ♔e3 ♗xg2 29 ♗xg7 ♔xg7 30 ♗xg2 ♘c5 was best and the strange ending resulting looks to be better for White) 27 ♗xg7 ♕e3+ 28 ♔c2 ♗xf3 29 ♗b2! e5 30 ♕d2 ♕c5+ 31 ♔b1 ♘e3 32 ♖c1 ♕b6 33 ♕h2 ♘f5 34 ♖c8+ ♔g7 35 ♖b4 Resigns.

(2b2) **11 ... ♕a5** 12 ♔b1 (12 h5 allows 12 ... ♘b4 with ... ♖xc3 to follow) ♖fd8? (12 ... ♘xd4 13 ♗xd4 ♖fd8 was better according to Hübner, who assesses the resulting position as slightly better for White) 13 ♘b3 ♕c7 14 h5 ♗e6 15 hxg6 fxg6, Hübner–Hort, match 1979 and now 16 ♘d5! would have given White a clear plus according to Hübner.

(2b3) **11 ... h5** 12 ♗e2 (it is by no means certain that this is White's best. Ligterink–Sosonko, Dutch Ch. 1978 went 12 gxh5 ♘xh5 13 ♖g1 ♔h7 14 ♗e2 ♘xd4 15 ♗xd4 ♗h6 16 ♗e3 ♗g7 17 ♗d4 ♗h6 Draw, but 14 ♔b1 avoiding the draw may be good for White) ♘e5 13 gxh5 ♘xh5 14 ♖dg1 (14 ♖hg1 is an alternative, but whether better or worse is not easy to decide) ♘c4 15 ♗xc4 (a defect of 12 ♗e2 is that this capture will involve a loss of a tempo) ♖xc4 16 ♖g5 (threatening 17 ♖xh5 gxh5 18 ♖g1) ♖c5 17 ♘d5 e6 18 ♖xh5 exd5 19 ♖xd5 ♖xd5 20 exd5 and White was a little better in Speelman–Liu Wenzhe, China 1981.

8 ♕d2 ♘c6

Or 8 ... d5 (other moves meet with common-sense replies, e.g. **8 ... ♗e6** 9 ♘xe6 fxe6 10 e5 or **8 ... a6** 9 0-0-0 b5 10 h4) 9 e5 ♘e8 (9 ... ♘fd7 10 f4 ♘b6 11 ♗e2 ♘c6, Popovic–Sax, Vrsac 1981, and now 12 0-0-0 ♗d7 13 ♘b3 looks unpleasant for Black since 13 ... e6 14 h4 gives White a very dangerous attack) 10 f4 f6 11 0-0-0 fxe5 (11 ... ♘c6 12 ♘f3) 12 fxe5 ♘c6 (12 ... ♗xe5 13 ♘f3 either regains the pawn with advantage or, after 13 ... ♗xc3 14 ♕xc3 e6

15 h4, gives White an enormous attack) 13 ♘f3 ♗g4 (13 ... e6 14 ♗h6 leaves Black with a very bad bishop) 14 ♘xd5 ♖xf3 15 gxf3 ♗xf3 16 ♗g2 ♗xd1 17 ♖xd1 ♗xe5 18 ♗c5 e6 19 ♘e7+ ♔g7 20 ♘xc6 ♕xd2+ 21 ♖xd2 bxc6 22 ♖d7+ with a good ending for White.

9   ♗c4 *(67)*

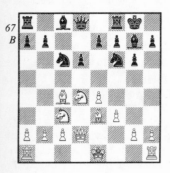

9 ...   ♗d7

This is by far the most common in practice, but a number of other moves have been tried:

(1) **9 ... a6** (too slow) 10 ♗b3 ♘e5 (10 ... ♘a5 11 h4 b5 12 h5 ♘xb3 13 axb3 ♗d7 14 ♗h6 ♗xh6 15 ♕xh6 e6 16 0-0-0 b4 17 ♘a2 ♕a5 18 ♔b1 is good for White) 11 h4 b5 12 h5 ♘xh5 13 ♗h6 e6 14 ♗xg7 ♔xg7 15 g4 ♘f6 16 0-0-0 with a dangerous attack, Yurtaev–Shur, USSR 1976.

(2) **9 ... a5** (this allows White to block the queenside) 10 ♗b3 ♗d7 11 a4 ♘xd4 12 ♗xd4 ♗e6 13 0-0-0 ♕d7 14 ♔b1 ♖fc8 15 ♖he1 ♖a6 16 ♕e2 ♖ac6 17 ♘d5 ♕e8 18 ♕b5 and White is clearly

better, Hardicsay–Honfi, Budapest 1977.

(3) **9 ... ♘xd4** (bringing White's bishop to d4 reduces the power of the Dragon bishop on g7) 10 ♗xd4 ♗e6 11 ♗b3 ♕a5 12 0-0-0 ♖fc8 (12 ... ♗xb3 13 cxb3 ♖fd8 14 ♔b1 ♖d7 15 g4 ♖ad8 16 ♕e2 ♗h8 17 h4 and 12 ... b5 13 ♔b1 b4 14 ♘d5 ♗xd5 15 exd5 ♕b5 16 ♕d3 ♕b7 17 ♖he1 a5 18 ♗a4 give White some advantage) 13 ♔b1 ♖c6 (13 ... b5 14 ♖he1 ♗xb3 15 cxb3 b4 16 ♗xf6 bxc3 17 ♗xc3 ♗xc3 18 bxc3 ♖xc3 19 ♖e3 ♖ac8 20 ♖xc3 ♕xc3 21 ♕xc3 ♖xc3 22 ♖c1 is a fairly typical line in this variation; White's outside passed pawn gives him a big advantage) 14 h4 ♗xb3 15 cxb3 b5 and now both 16 a3 and 16 h5 are good for White.

(4) **9 ... ♕a5** may be met by 10 ♗b3, and after 10 ... ♗d7 11 0-0-0 we reach the main line of this game. Note that the tempting 10 ♘b3 ♕b4 11 ♗e2 may not be good, e.g. 11 ... ♘a5 12 a3!? ♘xb3 13 cxb3 ♕xb3 14 ♖c1 ♗e6 15 ♗d1 ♕c4 16 ♘d5 ♗xd5 17 ♖xc4 ♗xc4 18 ♗xa7! ♘xe4! with a satisfactory position for Black.

(5) **9 ... ♘d7** (the most important 9th move alternative) 10 h4 *(68)* and now:

(5a) **10 ... h5** (a new idea of Larsen's) 11 ♗b3 (the flexible 11 0-0-0 may be more accurate with this move order) ♘c5 (11 ... ♘b6 12 0-0-0 ♘a5 13 ♕d3 ♗d7 14 g4 hxg4 15 h5 ♖c8 16 hxg6 ♘xb3+ 17 axb3 fxg6 18 e5! dxe5 19 ♕xg6

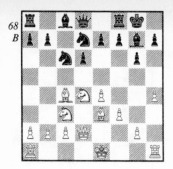

68
B

exd4 20 ♖h7 ♖f7 21 ♖dh1 wins)
12 0-0-0 ♘xb3+ 13 axb3 ♕a5 14
♔b1 ♗d7 15 g4 hxg4 16 h5
gxh5?? (a blunder; Sherzer
suggests 16 ... ♘xd4 17 ♗xd4
♗xd4 18 ♕xd4 g5, but the finesse
17 ♘d5! ♕d8 18 ♗xd4 appears
good for White) 17 ♘xc6 bxc6 18
♘d5 ♕d8 19 ♗h6 f6 20 ♖xh5
cxd5 21 ♗xg7 ♔f7 22 ♗xf8 ♕xf8
23 ♕xd5+ Resigns, Sherzer–Larsen, New York Open 1988.

(5b) **10 ... ♘b6** 11 ♗b3 ♘a5
(or 11 ... ♘e5 12 ♕e2) 12 ♕d3
♗d7 13 h5 ♖c8 14 hxg6 hxg6 15
0-0-0 ♘bc4 and White has two
promising lines:

(5b1) **16 ♗h6** e5 (16 ... ♗xh6?
17 ♖xh6 e5 18 ♖dh1 ♕g5+ 19
♔b1 exd4 20 ♘d5 f5 21 ♕xd4
♘xb3 22 axb3 ♘d2+ 23 ♕xd2
♕xd2 24 ♖h8+ ♔f7 25 ♖1h7+
♔e8 26 ♖e7+ mates) 17 ♗xg7
♔xg7 18 ♘de2 ♕g5+ 19 ♔b1 b5
(19 ... ♕xg2? 20 ♗xc4 ♘xc4 21
b3 is very good for White) 20 g3
b4? (20 ... ♖h8 21 ♖xh8 ♖xh8
22 a4! a6 23 ♗xc4 ♘xc4 24 b3
♘a3+ 25 ♔b2 b4 26 ♘d5 is
Black's best chance, but White

still has some advantage) 21 ♘d5
♗b5 22 f4! ♕d8 23 ♕f3 ♗c6 24
f5 f6 25 fxg6 ♗xd5 26 ♖h7+
♔g8 27 ♕h5 Resigns, Fleck–
Kozul, Cesme 1983.

(5b2) **16 ♗g5** ♘xb3+ 17 cxb3
♕a5 18 ♗xe7 ♘e5 19 ♕c2! and
Black has a depressing choice:

(5b21) **19 ... ♖xc3** 20 bxc3
♖c8 21 ♔b2 ♕b6 22 ♗g5 ♘c4+
23 ♔a1 ♘a3 24 ♕b2 ♘b5 25
♘xb5 ♖xb5 26 ♗e3! with a clear
plus for White, Wedberg–
Sosonko, Haninge 1988.

(5b22) **19 ... b5?** 20 ♔b1 ♖fe8
21 ♘d5! ♖xc2 22 ♘f6+ ♗xf6 23
♗xf6 wins.

(5b23) **19 ... ♘c6** 20 ♘xc6
♖xc6 21 ♔b1 ♖fc8 22 ♖d5! ♕b6
23 ♕d2 ♖xc3 24 bxc3 ♖xc3 25
♖xd6 ♖xb3+ 26 axb3 ♕xb3+
27 ♔c1 ♕a3+ 28 ♔d1 ♕a1+ 29
♕c1 ♕a4+ 30 ♔e2 ♗b5+ 31
♔f2 ♗d4+ 32 ♔g3 ♗e5+ 33 f4
and wins.

(5b24) **19 ... ♖fe8** 20 ♗xd6 b5
21 b4 ♕a6 22 ♘b3 ♗e6 23 ♘c5
♖xc5 24 ♗xc5 ♖xa2? 25 ♖d6
Resigns, Kruppa–Savchenko,
USSR 1984.

10 0-0-0 *(69)*
There are arguments in favour
of the alternative move order with
10 h4, but we shall adopt the most
usual sequence in which White
castles first.

10 ... ♕a5
When the Dragon was revived
in the 1960s, this was the most
popular line for Black. It frees the
f8 rook to come over to c8 so that
both Black rooks may participate

69
B

in the attack. It is unpopular at the moment both because of very bad practical results for Black and because of the depressing theoretical situation detailed below. It becomes clear that the time Black spends moving his queen to a5 only serves to present White with an important tempo by ♘b3 in the main line. 10 ... ♖c8 11 ♗b3 ♘e5 is covered in games 19 and 20, and we deal with the remaining lines now:

(1) **10 ... ♕c7** 11 ♗b3 ♖fc8 (11 ... ♘e5 12 ♗h6) 12 h4 ♘e5 13 h5 ♘c4 14 ♗xc4 ♕xc4 15 ♗h6 ♗h8 16 ♗g5 b5 17 hxg6 fxg6 18 ♗xf6 ♗xf6 19 ♘d5 ♗xd4 (19 ... ♕xa2 20 ♕h6! gives White a crushing attack) 20 ♘xe7+ ♔f7 (20 ... ♔f8 21 ♘xc8 ♖xc8 22 c3 is very good for White) 21 ♖xh7+ ♗g7 22 c3 ♖h8 (White plays ♕f4+ after most moves) 23 ♕f4+ ♗f5 24 ♘xf5 ♖xh7 25 ♘xd6+ ♔g8 26 ♘xc4 ♗h6 27 ♕xh6 ♖xh6 28 ♘e3 and with three solid pawns for the exchange White has good winning chances in the ending.

(2) **10 ... ♕b8** 11 h4 and now:

(2a) **11 ... b5** (11 ... a5? 12 ♗h6) 12 ♗d5! ♖c8 13 ♔b1 (13 ♗xc6 ♗xc6 14 h5 b4 15 ♘ce2 ♘xh5 16 ♖xh5 gxh5 17 ♘f5 ♖c7 18 ♗h6 was also very good for White in Wahls–Ristic, Dortmund II 1989) b4 14 ♘ce2 ♘xd5 15 ♘xc6 ♖xc6 (15 ... ♘c3+ loses to 16 ♘xc3 bxc3 17 ♘xb8 ♖axb8 18 ♕d5 ♖xb2+ 19 ♔a1 ♗e6 20 ♕a5) 16 exd5 ♖a6 17 ♗d4 with an excellent position for White, Mikhalchishin–Sirov, USSR 1988.

(2b) **11 ... ♖c8** 12 ♗b3 a5 (12 ... b5 13 h5) and White has two tempting lines:

(2b1) **13 a4** ♘xd4 14 ♗xd4 b5 15 ♘d5 e5 16 ♗xe5 bxa4 (after 16 ... dxe5 17 ♘xf6+ ♗xf6 18 ♕xd7 ♖a7 19 ♕d6 the only question is whether the extra pawn is enough to win) 17 ♗xf6! axb3 (17 ... ♕xb3 18 ♘e7+ ♔f8 19 ♘xc8 ♖xc8 20 ♗xg7+ ♔xg7 21 ♕d3 wins) 18 c3! ♖c4 (there is nothing better as White already has a decisive attack) 19 ♗xg7 ♔xg7 20 h5 ♖a4 21 ♔b1 ♕b5 22 ♕g5! Resigns, D'Adamo–Teipelke, corr. 1986.

(2b2) **13 h5** a4 (13 ... ♘xd4 14 ♗xd4 a4 15 ♗d5 e5 16 hxg6! is crushing) 14 ♗d5 ♘xh5 (or 14 ... e6 15 hxg6! exd5 16 ♗h6! fxg6 17 ♗xg7 ♔xg7 18 ♕h6+ ♔f7 19 ♘xd5 with a very strong attack) 15 g4 ♘f6 16 ♘f5 ♗xf5 17 gxf5 ♘b4 18 fxg6! ♘fxd5 19 ♗d4! (a very nice move) ♗xd4 (the lines **19 ... fxg6** 20 exd5, **19 ... ♘f6** 20 gxh7+ ♔h8 21 ♖dg1 and **19 ...**

e5 20 gxh7+ ♚h8 21 ♖dg1 f6 22 exd5! exd4 23 ♖xg7 ♚xg7 24 ♕h6+ ♚f7 25 ♖g1 all win for White) 20 ♕xd4 e5 21 gxf7+ ♚f8 (21 ... ♚xf7 22 ♖xh7+ ♚g8 23 ♕g1+ ♚xh7 24 ♕g2 wins) 22 ♕g1 ♘f6 23 ♖h6! ♘xa2+ 24 ♘xa2 ♕c7 25 ♘b4 ♕xf7 26 ♖xd6 ♘e8 27 ♖d3 and although material is equal, Black's king is horribly exposed, Agdestein–Karlsson, Gausdal 1987.

| 11 | ♗b3 | ♖fc8 |
| 12 | ♚b1 | ♘e5 |

12 ... ♖ab8 (a bit slow, so White can afford to spend time preparing h4 with g4, which cuts out the reply ... h5) 13 g4 b5 14 h4 b4 15 ♘d5 ♘xd5 16 exd5 ♘xd4 17 ♗xd4 ♗xd4 18 ♕xd4 ♕c5 19 ♕d2 a5 20 h5 a4 21 hxg6 axb3 22 gxf7+ ♚f8 23 ♕h6+ ♚xf7 24 ♕h5+ ♚f6 25 g5+ Resigns, Schmidt–Bobotsov, Varna 1964.

| 13 | h4 | ♘c4 |

After 13 ... b5 14 ♘cxb5 ♕xd2 15 ♗xd2 it is hard to believe that Black can have enough for the pawn. Kuzmin–Garcia Martinez, Hastings 1973/4 continued 15 ... ♘c4 16 ♘c3 ♘xe4 17 ♘xe4 ♗xd4 18 ♗g5 ♗e5 19 ♗xe7 ♘xb2 20 ♖xd6! ♗e8 21 ♖d5 with a clear plus for White.

| 14 | ♗xc4 | ♖xc4 |
| 15 | ♘b3 *(70)* | ♕c7 |

This appears to be the best square:

(1) **15 ... ♕e5** (a recent idea, but there is an obvious danger of the queen being trapped) 16 ♗d4

♕e6 17 g4 (17 h5 a5 18 h6 ♗h8 19 ♘d5 a4 20 ♗xf6 ♗xf6 21 ♘xf6+ ♕xf6 22 ♘d4 ♖ac8 23 ♖he1 a3 was unclear in Hebden–Jonsson, London 1988) ♖ac8 18 ♖he1 ♗c6 19 ♘d5 ♗a4 20 c3 b5 21 ♕h2 and White has the advantage, Koch–Ristic, Dortmund II 1989.

(2) **15 ... ♕a6** (dubious) 16 e5 ♘e8 (16 ... dxe5 17 ♘c5 ♕d6 18 ♕e2!) 17 h5 (17 ♘d5 is also strong) ♖ac8 (17 ... ♗xe5 18 hxg6 followed by ♗d4 is good for White) 18 hxg6 fxg6 (or 18 ... hxg6 19 ♗h6 ♗xe5 20 ♘d5 with a strong attack) 19 ♗d4 with a distinct plus for White.

(3) **15 ... ♕d8** (also poor) 16 ♗h6 ♗h8 (perhaps 16 ... ♕f8 is relatively best, but after 17 ♗xg7 ♕xg7 18 g4 Black has no real counterplay) 17 h5 ♖ac8 18 hxg6 fxg6 19 e5 ♘e8 20 exd6 e6 21 ♗g5 and Black is in a mess, Ciocaltea–Drimer, Romania 1968.

| 16 | ♗d4 |

One should also take note of a promising alternative for White here, namely 16 g4 and now 16 ...

♗e6 17 h5 a5 (17 ... ♖c8 18 ♘b5
♕d8 19 ♘5d4 ♗d7 20 hxg6 fxg6
21 e5 ♘e8 22 ♕h2 was very good
for White in Bangiev–Ovhinikov,
USSR 1976) 18 hxg6 fxg6 19 ♗d4
a4 20 ♗xf6 exf6 (20 ... ♗xf6 21
♘d5 ♗xd5 22 ♕xd5+ ♔g7 23
♖xh7+ wins) 21 ♘d5 ♕d8 22
♘d4 ♗f7 23 ♕h2 h6 24 ♘e3 left
Black with a miserable position in
Gonzales–Schroder, corr. 1987.

16   ...   ♗e6

Or 16 ... ♗c6 17 h5 a5 18 hxg6
hxg6 19 a4 e6 (Black wants to
take on a4 without allowing ♗xf6
followed by ♘d5, but this is too
slow) 20 ♖h4 ♗xa4 21 ♖dh1
♖xd4 22 ♘xd4 ♗e8 23 ♘db5
with a large advantage for White,
Wang Zili–Velimirovic, Thessaloniki Ol. 1988.

17	**h5**	**a5**
18	**hxg6**	**hxg6**
19	**a4**	**♖b4**

After 19 ... ♖c8 20 g4 ♖xd4
21 ♘xd4 ♕b6 Black had some
counterplay in Hartston–Hollis,
London 1967, but 20 ♖h4! looks
very unpleasant for Black.

20   ♖h4 (71) b5

Or 20 ... ♖c8 (20 ... ♗xb3 21
cxb3 e5 22 ♗e3 ♖xb3 23 ♖c1
♕d7 24 ♗h6 ♗h8 25 ♗g5 ♗g7
26 ♖ch1 ♖xc3 27 ♕xc3 was excellent for White, Hartston–Kol-
bek, Dresden 1969) 21 ♖dh1
♗xb3 22 cxb3 e5 23 ♗e3 ♖xb3
24 ♘b5 ♕d8 25 ♗h6 ♗f8 26
♗xf8 ♔xf8 27 ♖h8+ ♘g8 28
♖xg8+ Resigns, Savic–Simic,
corr. 1979.

21   ♘xb5   ♕b7

The theoretical main line continues 21 ... ♕c4 22 ♘c3 ♖ab8
and although this is good for
White, it turns out that 22 ♖dh1!
is even better. Black cannot reply
22 ... ♖xa4 because of 23 ♘xd6
exd6 24 ♕g5 (the main threat is
25 ♖h8+ ♗xh8 26 ♖xh8+, but
both 25 ♗xf6 and 25 ♕xf6 are
lesser threats) ♘h5 25 ♗xg7
♔xg7 (25 ... ♖c8 26 ♗c3) 26
♖xh5 with a crushing attack.
Therefore Black has nothing
better than 22 ... ♖c8, but then
White has a pleasant choice. He
may play 23 ♘c3, effectively gaining a tempo over an already promising line, since Black needs to
double rooks on the b-file to
create any threats. Alternatively
he may continue 23 g4 followed
by ♕h2 with an enormous attack.

22   ♖dh1

The position of the queen on b7
is no better; White's attack on the
h-file is just too strong.

22   ...   ♖xa4

23   ♘c3

Not 23 ♘xd6 exd6 24 ♕g5
because of 24 ... ♖xd4.

23 ... ♗xb3

Or 23 ... ♖b4 24 g4 ♗xb3 25 ♕h2 ♗xc2+ (25 ... ♗a2+ 26 ♘xa2) 26 ♔a1 ♘h5 27 ♗xg7 ♔xg7 (27 ... ♖xb2 28 ♖xh5!) 28 ♖xh5! gxh5 29 ♕xh5 f6 30 ♕h7+ ♔f8 31 ♕g6 mating.

24 cxb3 ♖b4

After 24 ... ♖xd4 25 ♕xd4 ♕xb3 26 ♘d5 e5 27 ♕c3 White has a clear material and positional advantage.

25 ♘d5 e5
26 ♖h8+! Resigns

Because of 26 ... ♗xh8 27 ♖xh8+ ♔xh8 28 ♕h6+ ♘h7 29 ♘f6 mating.

Game 19
Nunn–Mestel
London (GLC) 1986

1	e4	c5
2	♘f3	d6
3	d4	cxd4
4	♘xd4	♘f6
5	♘c3	g6
6	♗e3	♗g7
7	f3	0–0
8	♕d2	♘c6
9	♗c4	♗d7
10	0–0–0	♖c8
11	♗b3	♘e5
12	h4 *(72)*	h5

Or:

(1) **12 ... ♕a5** 13 ♔b1 ♘c4 14 ♗xc4 ♖xc4 (the only difference compared to game 18 is that Black's rook is on f8 instead of a8, but this difference is crucial) 15 h5! (15 ♘b3, as in game 18, is still promising, but this may be even better) ♖xc3 (when the rook is on

a8 this move is good) 16 h6! (White saves his h-pawn because 16 ... ♖c5 17 hxg7 hits the rook, so Black must play 17 ... ♖fc8 transposing to the game) ♖fc8 (16 ... ♗h8 17 ♕xc3 is very good for White) 17 hxg7 ♖3c5 18 c3 (it seems to me that 18 b4 ♕b6 19 ♘b3 ♖xc2 20 ♗xb6 ♖xd2 21 ♘xd2 axb6 22 ♖c1 is very good for White) ♕a4 19 ♗g5 ♖xg5 20 ♕xg5 with advantage to White, Shabalov–Yurtaev, Moscow GMA 1989.

(2) **12 ... a5** 13 h5 (13 a4 is also good) a4 (13 ... ♘xh5 14 g4 ♖xc3 15 bxc3 ♘f6 16 ♗h6 a4 17 ♗xg7 ♔xg7 18 ♗xa4! ♗xa4 19 ♘f5+ Resigns, Draskovic–Lazic, corr. 1974) 14 ♘xa4 ♗xa4 15 ♗xa4 ♘c4 16 ♕d3 (Black suffers from the lack of a white-squared bishop) ♕a5 17 ♗b3 d5 18 hxg6 hxg6 19 g4! dxe4 20 fxe4 ♘xg4 21 ♗g1 ♕g5+ 22 ♔b1 ♘ge5 23 ♕h3 ♖fd8 24 ♗f2 ♘d2+ 25 ♖xd2 ♕xd2 26 ♗e3 ♕a5 27 ♘e6 fxe6 28 ♕xe6+ Resigns, Fatalibekova–Akhsharumova, Moscow 1975.

(3) **12 ... ♘c4** (the most important 12th move alternative) 13 ♗xc4 ♖xc4 14 h5 and now:

(3a) **14 ... b5?** 15 hxg6 fxg6 16 e5 dxe5 17 ♘e6 is bad and **14 ... ♕a5** 15 ♔b1 (15 ♘b3 is also good) transposes to line 1 above.

(3b) **14 ... ♕c7** 15 hxg6 fxg6 16 ♘de2 ♖c8 17 ♔b1 ♗e6 18 ♘f4 ♕d7 19 ♘xe6 ♕xe6 20 ♖c1 ♘d7 21 ♕d5 ♕xd5 22 ♘xd5 ♖e8 23 b3 ♖c6 24 c4 and White's superior pawn structure gives him a permanent advantage in the ending.

(3c) **14 ... ♘xh5** (the critical move) 15 g4 ♘f6 16 ♘b3!? *(73)* (rarely played, but promising) and now:

73
B

(3c1) **16 ... a5** 17 ♗h6 ♗xh6 18 ♖xh6 (with the threat of ♖dh1 followed by ♖xh7 and ♕h6) ♔g7 (intending ... ♖h8) 19 e5! dxe5 (19 ... ♘xg4 20 fxg4 ♗xg4 21 ♖dh1 is very good for White) 20 g5 ♘g8 21 ♕h2 ♖e8 22 ♖xh7+ ♔f8 23 ♕xe5 f6 24 gxf6 and White wins.

(3c2) **16 ... ♖xc3** 17 bxc3 ♕c7 18 e5 ♘e8 19 ♕h2 h5 20 gxh5

♗xe5 21 f4! ♕xc3 (21 ... ♗xc3 22 hxg6) 22 ♗d4 ♗xd4 23 ♖xd4 with a large advantage for White.

(3c3) **16 ... ♖e8** 17 e5 ♘xg4 18 fxg4 ♗xg4 19 ♖dg1 and now:

(3c31) **19 ... h5** 20 e6! ♗xe6 (20 ... f5 21 ♘d5 ♕c8 22 ♘d4 and now 22 ... ♔h7? 23 ♖xg4! fxg4 24 ♕d3 won for White in Ye Jiangchuan–Velimirovic, Asia–Yugoslavia 1984) 21 ♗d4 (Gufeld's suggestion of 21 ♖xh5! is a good alternative, the point being that 21 ... gxh5 loses to 22 ♗h6 ♖g4 23 ♖xg4 followed by ♕g5) ♗g4 22 ♖xg4 hxg4 23 ♗xg7 ♔xg7 24 ♕h6+ ♔f6 25 ♘d5+ ♔e6 26 ♖e1+ ♔d7 (26 ... ♔xd5 27 ♕h1+ is attractive) 27 ♕g7 ♖f8 (27 ... ♔c8 28 ♕xf7 ♔b8, Caturian–Poletaev, corr. 1983, and now 29 ♘f6 ♖h8 30 ♕xc4 exf6 31 ♕xg4 gives White a winning position) 28 ♘d2 ♖c5 29 ♖xe7+ ♕xe7 30 ♘xe7 ♔xe7 31 ♘e4 ♖f5 32 ♘xd6 with advantage to White because of Black's exposed king.

(3c32) **19 ... dxe5** and now there are two possible moves. My suggestion was **20 ♕xd8 ♖xd8** 21 ♘d2 (or 21 ♘a5!?, aiming to keep the knight in a more active position) ♖xc3 (21 ... ♖b4 22 a3) 22 bxc3, when it seems to me that Black's four pawns are too far back to provide enough compensation for the rook. However, in the 1988 correspondence game Kauranen–Nesis White preferred to play for the attack by **20 ♕g2!?**, threatening 21 ♘d2 and 21 ♕xb7.

This policy was a success after 20 ... ♕c8?! (this must be bad; Black should prevent ♗h6 and secure the g4 bishop by 20 ... h5, even if this means sacrificing the queenside pawns) 21 ♗h6 ♗h8 22 ♘d2 ♖xc3 23 bxc3 ♗d7 24 ♕g3 (White has an extra rook and an attack) ♗c6 25 ♖h2 ♕f5 26 ♕h4 ♕f6 27 ♗g5 ♕g7 (very thematic for the Dragon; pity about the pawn on e5) 28 ♗xe7 h5 (28 ... e4 29 ♗f6) 29 ♖h3 a5 30 ♗c5 b5 31 ♘e4 b4 32 ♘d6 ♖b8 33 ♘f5 Resigns.

(3c4) **16 ...** ♕c7 and now there are two promising lines:

(3c41) **17 e5** dxe5 (17 ... ♘xg4 18 fxg4 ♗xg4 19 exd6 exd6 20 ♘d5 wins) 18 g5 ♗f5 19 gxf6 exf6 20 ♗h6 g5 21 ♗xg7 ♔xg7 is recommended by Sapi and Schneider, but 22 ♕e3! followed by ♘d2 and ♘de4 appears good for White. Combined with a later ♖d2 and ♘d5 Black will be hard pressed to defend his seriously weak pawn at f6. If Black exchanges on e4 he will be mated down the h-file.

(3c42) **17 g5** (normally a bad move, but this position is a special case against White gains a lot of time) ♘h5 18 ♘d5 ♕d8 19 ♗d4 ♗xd4 (19 ... e5 20 ♗xa7) 20 ♘xd4 ♗c6 21 b3 ♗xd5 (21 ... ♖c5 22 b4 ♖c4 23 ♘e3 is also good for White!) 22 bxc4 ♗xc4 23 ♘f5 f6 24 ♖xh5! gxh5 25 ♖g1 e6 26 gxf6+ ♔h8 27 ♘e7 1–0, Thesing–Ballmann, Zug 1989.

13 ♗g5 *(74)*

74
B

13 ... ♘c4

13 ... ♖c5 is covered in game 20. Other 13th moves:

(1) **13 ... a6** (ignoring the threat) 14 g4 hxg4 15 h5 ♘xh5 16 ♘d5 ♖e8 17 ♖xh5 gxh5 18 ♕h2 (this gives White a crushing attack just as in game 20 below) gxf3 19 ♕xh5 ♗g4 20 ♕h4 ♖c7 21 ♖h1 ♘g6 22 ♕h7+ ♔f8 23 ♗h6 Resigns, Hechler–Masur, corr. 1980.

(2) **13 ... ♘h7** 14 ♗h6 ♗xh6 15 ♕xh6 ♖xc3 16 bxc3 and now:

(2a) **16 ... ♕a5** 17 ♔b1 (17 ♘e2 ♗b5 18 ♖he1 ♘f6 19 ♖d4 ♖c8 20 ♖b4! e6 21 ♘d4 ♗d7 22 ♕e3 b5 23 ♔b2 ♖c5 24 ♘e2 ♘c6 25 ♕f4 ♘e8 26 a3 was also good for White in Tal–Mista, Dubna 1973) ♕xc3 (17 ... ♖c8 18 f4 ♘c4 19 f5 gives White the advantage) 18 ♘e2 ♕c5 19 g4 ♘xf3 (19 ... hxg4 20 f4 ♕e3 21 h5 wins) 20 ♖d5! ♕f2 21 gxh5 g5 (21 ... ♕xe2 22 hxg6 ♘f6 23 g7 wins) 22 hxg5 ♕e3 23 ♖hd1! and White won easily, Geller–Kuzmin, USSR Ch. 1978.

(2b) **16 ... ♕c7** 17 ♔b1! ♘c4 (17 ... ♕xc3 leads to line 1) 18 g4

hxg4 (18 ... ♘f6 19 ♘f5!) 19 f4
(19 h5? g5) ♖c8 20 ♖d3 ♕a5 21
h5 g5 and now 22 e5!? was good
for White in Lobron–Miles, Biel
1986 after 22 ... dxe5 23 ♗xc4
♖xc4 24 ♘b3 ♕c7 25 fxg5 ♗f5
26 g6, but according to Lobron it
was simpler to play 22 ♗xc4!
♖xc4 23 ♘b3 ♕d8 24 fxg5 ♕f8
25 e5! ♕xh6 (25 ... ♗f5 26 exd6
♗xd3 27 ♕xf8+ ♘xf8 28 dxe7
wins) 26 gxh6 ♗f5 27 exd6 exd6
28 ♖xd6 when White's material
advantage and threats against the
Black king give him a winning
position.

14   ♕e2

After 14 ♕d3 Black can reply
14 ... ♘e5, since 15 ♕e2 would
be an invitation for Black to sacrifice at c3.

14   ...   ♘a5
15   ♔b1

For the moment Black has no
threats because ... ♖xc3 isn't
dangerous when the knight prevents the queen moving to a5, so
White takes the opportunity to
make a useful consolidating
move.

15   ...   a6

This move represents the point
of the manoeuvre ... ♘c4–a5.
Black threatens to trap the knight
on d4 by ... e5 and if White were
now forced to spend a tempo
moving the queen Black would
play ... b5 with good counterplay. Everything depends on
whether White can successfully ignore the threat of ... e5.

16   g4 *(75)*

16   ...   e5

Or 16 ... ♘xb3 17 axb3 hxg4
(for 17 ... e5, see the note to
Black's 18th move) 18 h5! gxf3 (18
... ♘xh5 19 fxg4 ♘g3 20 ♕h2
♘xh1 21 ♖xh1 leads to mate) 19
♘xf3 ♗g4 (19 ... ♘xh5 20 ♖dg1
threatening ♖xh5 is very strong)
20 ♖dg1 (20 h6 ♗h8 21 e5 is also
good, but not 21 h7+ ♘xh7
when Black can block the h-file by
... ♗h5) gxh5 (20 ... ♗xh5 21
♗xf6 exf6 22 ♖xh5 gxh5 23 ♕g2
wins) 21 ♗xf6 exf6 and now 22
♖xg4 hxg4 23 ♘d4 is one dangerous attacking possibility.

17   gxh5!

Geller–Miles, Linares 1983,
continued 17 ♘f5 gxf5 18 gxf5
♘xb3 19 axb3 ♗c6 20 ♖hg1 ♔h7
21 ♖g2 ♖g8 and White went on
to win, but Mestel was evidently
not convinced about White's
compensation, and in this I agree
with him.

17   ...   exd4
18   ♘d5! *(76)*

Geller's notes to his game gave
18 h6 ♗h8 (**18 ... dxc3** 19 hxg7
♔xg7 20 ♖xd6 wins) 19 h7+
♔xh7 20 h5 and wins, but **18 ...**

♗xh6! 19 ♗xh6 ♘xb3 20 axb3 dxc3 is a big improvement, when the position is totally unclear. Later I discovered that Timman had suggested 18 ♘d5! in 1983, but during the game I was unaware of this!

76
B

18 ...   ♘xb3

The only real defence to the threat of 19 h6 ♗h8 20 h7+ ♚xh7 21 h5 is to play ... gxh5. Unfortunately 18 ... gxh5 (trying to deflect White's rook by 18 ... d3 19 ♖xd3 gxh5 fails after 20 ♖g1 ♚h7 21 ♘xf6+ ♗xf6 22 ♖xd6 ♗xg5 23 ♖xg5 winning easily) loses to 19 ♖hg1 ♚h8 20 e5 dxe5 21 ♕xe5 ♘xd5 (or 21 ... ♖e8 22 ♗xf6 ♕xf6 23 ♕xf6 ♗xf6 24 ♘xf6 ♖e7 25 ♖xd4 with a won ending) 22 ♕xg7+ ♚xg7 23 ♗xd8+ ♚h7 24 ♗xa5 with a strong attack and a bonus pawn to come. Thus Black tries to exchange on b3 before taking on h5, but in this position White doesn't need to recapture. If Black wanted to exchange on b3 he should have done so at move 16, with the continuation 16 ...

♘xb3 17 axb3 e5 18 gxh5 exd4 19 ♘d5. I think White can still win even in this case, but it is much more complex: 19 ... gxh5 20 ♖dg1 ♚h7 (20 ... ♚h8 21 f4 ♗g4 22 ♖xg4 hxg4 23 h5! ♚h7 24 h6 ♗h8 25 ♕d3 ♚g8 26 h7+ wins) 21 f4 ♗g4 22 ♕d3! ♚g8 (22 ... ♚h8 23 ♖xg4 hxg4 24 h5 is worse) 23 ♖xg4 hxg4 24 h5 (this seems to be good even when White has a tempo less) ♘xd5 (24 ... ♖e8 25 h6 ♗h8 26 h7+ ♚f8 27 ♘xf6 wins) 25 ♗xd8 ♘b4 (25 ... ♘xf4 26 ♕f1) 26 ♕d2 d3 27 cxd3 ♖c2 28 ♕xb4 ♖xb2+ 29 ♚c1 ♖xd8 30 d4 and White should win.

19 h6!

Stronger than transposing to the above analysis by 19 axb3.

19 ...   ♗b5

Trying to generate counterplay, but there is no defence. The main line runs 19 ... ♗h8 (19 ... ♘xd5 20 hxg7) 20 h7+ ♚xh7 21 h5 ♚g8 (21 ... ♗g7 22 hxg6+ ♚g8 23 ♘xf6+ ♗xf6 24 ♕h2) 22 ♕h2! (not 22 hxg6 fxg6 23 ♕h2 ♚f7) gxh5 (22 ... ♘g4 23 fxg4 ♕xg5 24 hxg6 mates) 23 ♘xf6+ ♗xf6 24 ♕xh5 ♖e8 25 ♖dg1 ♚f8 26 ♕h6+ ♗g7 27 ♕xg7+ ♚xg7 28 ♗e7+ and mate next move.

20 ♕h2   d3
21 cxb3

Not 21 c3? d2! with dangerous counterthreats.

21 ...   ♘xd5

After 21 ... ♖c2 22 hxg7 ♖xh2 23 gxf8(♕)+ ♚xf8 24 ♖xh2

Black loses the knight on f6.

22 hxg7

Not 22 ♗xd8? ♗e5.

22 ... ♖c2

Black cannot avoid a fatal loss of material.

23 ♗xd8 ♖xd8
24 ♖d2 Resigns

24 ... ♘e3 is met by 25 ♕f2.

Game 20
Mestel–Kudrin
Hastings 1986/7

1	e4	c5
2	♘f3	d6
3	d4	cxd4
4	♘xd4	♘f6
5	♘c3	g6
6	♗e3	♗g7
7	f3	0-0
8	♕d2	♘c6
9	♗c4	♗d7
10	0-0-0	♖c8
11	♗b3	♘e5
12	h4	h5
13	♗g5	♖c5
14	♔b1	

This is not only a useful move, it leaves Black with little choice but to play ... b5, when curiously enough White's kingside breakthrough becomes stronger because in one variation Black does not have the move ... ♕b6 attacking b2.

14 ... b5
15 g4 *(77)*

15 ... a5 *(78)*

Declining the sacrifice, but acceptance is a major alternative for Black: 15 ... hxg4 16 h5 and now:

77
B

(1) **16 ... ♖xc3** with a further branch:

(1a) **17 ♕xc3 ♘xh5 18 fxg4 ♗xg4 19 ♖dg1 ♕d7** is unclear, while **17 ♗xf6 ♖xb3 18 ♗xg7 ♖xb2+** wins for Black.

(1b) **17 bxc3** and Black has one bad move and one good move:

(1b1) **17 ... ♘xh5** and now the simple **18 ♗h6!** (threat 19 ♖xh5 gxh5 20 ♕g5) e6 19 ♖dg1 gives White a strong attack for no material investment. In Ulybin–Tiviakov, USSR 1987 White chose a more complex line by **18 ♖xh5 gxh5 19 ♕h2 ♘c4** (otherwise White plays ♕xh5 and ♖h1) **20 ♕xh5 f6 21 ♘xb5! ♗xb5** (White also has the advantage after 21 ... fxg5 22 ♗xc4+ e6 23 ♘xd6) **22 ♗h6 ♕d7** (22 ... ♕c8 23 ♖g1 f5 24 ♗xg7 ♔xg7 25 exf5 gives White more than enough for the piece according to Ulybin) **23 ♗xg7 ♔xg7 24 ♖g1** with a crushing attack.

(1b2) **17 ... ♘xf3! 18 ♘xf3 ♘xe4 19 ♕h2 ♘xc3+ 20 ♔c1 ♕a5 21 hxg6** (21 ♖d4 g3! is unclear) **♘xa2+ 22 ♗xa2 ♕a3+ 23 ♔d2 ♕c3+ 24 ♔c1** (24 ♔e2

♕xf3+ 25 ♔e1? ♕e4+ and 26 ... ♕xg6 gives Black 5 pawns and attacking chances for a rook) ♕a3+ Draw, Lanka–Smirin, USSR 1989.

(1c) **17 h6!** (although never tried in practice I think this is a good move) and now:

(1c1) **17 ... ♖xb3** 18 hxg7 ♖xb2+ 19 ♔a1! (threat 20 ♗xf6 exf6 21 ♖h8+) ♔xg7 (19 ... ♘h5 20 ♗f6!) 20 ♗xf6+ ♔xf6 21 ♕f4+ ♔g7 22 ♕h6+ ♔f6 23 fxg4! and White has a massive attack.

(1c2) **17 ... ♘xf3** 18 ♘xf3 ♖xf3 19 hxg7 ♔xg7 20 ♗h6+ (20 e5!? is also possible, with the idea that after 20 ... dxe5 21 ♗h6+ ♔g8 22 ♗g7 ♖h3 23 ♖xh3 gxh3 24 ♕h6 ♘h7 25 ♗xe5 Black is mated) ♔g8 21 ♗g7! ♖h3 (21 ... ♘h5 22 ♕h6) 22 ♖xh3 gxh3 23 ♕h6 ♘h7 24 ♗c3 e5 25 ♕xg6+ ♔h8 26 ♕xd6 with advantage to White.

(2) **16 ... ♘xh5** 17 ♘d5 ♖e8 (17 ... ♖xd5 18 ♗xd5 is bad since 18 ... gxf3 lets White break through by 19 ♘f5!) 18 ♖xh5 gxh5 19 ♕h2 ♖xd5 (or 19 ... ♖c4 20 ♗xc4 bxc4 21 ♕xh5 f6 22 f4! and after 22 ... fxg5 23 fxe5 dxe5 24 ♖h1 exd4 25 ♕h7+ ♔f7 26 ♖f1+ ♔e6 27 ♕xg7 White's attack is too strong, so Karpov–Sznapik, Dubai Ol. 1986 finished 22 ... ♘f7 23 ♗h4! ♕b8 24 ♖h1 c3 25 b3 ♕b7 26 f5 ♘e5 27 ♘e6 Resigns) 20 ♗xd5 ♕b6 (now it becomes clear that interpolating ♔b1 and ... b5 favours White

since b2 is not attacked) 21 ♕xh5 e6 22 ♗b3 and White has a winning attack, for example:

(2a) **22 ... a5 (22 ... ♘g6** 23 ♗e3 ♕c7 24 ♖h1 and **22 ... ♘xf3** 23 ♘f5 ♘xg5 24 ♘xg7 ♔xg7 25 ♕xg5+ ♔f8 26 e5! dxe5 27 ♖h1 both win for White) 23 f4 ♘c4 (23 ... ♘g6 24 f5) 24 ♗h6 ♕xd4 (24 ... ♔f8 25 ♗xg7+ ♔xg7 26 ♕g5+ ♔f8 27 ♕f6 or 24 ... ♕d8 25 ♗xc4 bxc4 26 e5! f5 27 ♗g5 ♕c7 28 ♗f6) 25 ♖xd4 ♗xd4 26 ♗xc4 bxc4 27 e5 Resigns, Short–Mandl, Bundesliga 1986.

(2b) **22 ... ♕c5** 23 ♗h6 ♗f6 24 f4 ♘g6 25 ♘f5 ♗c6 26 ♕xg4 d5 27 ♘g3 ♕e3 28 e5 ♗xe5 29 fxe5 ♕xh6 30 ♘h5 ♖c8 31 c3 ♕e3 32 ♗c2 ♔f8 33 ♖xg6 fxg6 34 ♖f1+ ♔e7 35 ♕b4+ ♔d8 36 ♕d6+ Resigns, Chandler–Mestel, British Ch. Play-Off 1986.

16 ♗xf6

The alternative 16 gxh5 has not been played much but it could also be good, e.g. 16 gxh5 a4 (16 ... ♘xh5 17 ♘d5 ♖e8 18 a3 was good for White in Sznapik–Sehner, Slupsk 1987) and now:

78
W

(1) **17 ♗d5** b4 18 ♘ce2 e6? (18 ... ♘xd5 19 exd5 ♖xd5 20 h6 is better but still good for White according to Sznapik) 19 h6! ♗h8 20 h7+! ♚xh7 21 h5 exd5 22 hxg6+ ♚g8 23 ♖xh8+ ♚xh8 24 ♗xf6+ Resigns, Sznapik–Komeljenovic, Biel Open 1987.

(2) **17 h6** ♗h8 18 ♗d5 (after 18 h7+ not **18 ... ♚xh7?** 19 h5 ♘xh5 20 ♖xh5+ gxh5 21 ♕h2 and wins but **18 ... ♘xh7!** with unclear complications) ♚h7! (White's attack has been blocked) 19 a3 ♕b6 20 ♗a2 b4 21 axb4 ♕xb4 22 ♗xf6 ♘xf3! with a very dangerous attack for Black, Ulybin–Savchenko, Simferopol 1988.

(3) **17 ♗xf7+!?** ♚xf7! (not 17 ... ♖xf7? 18 hxg6 ♘xg6 19 h5 ♘f8 20 ♖dg1 ♚h7 21 e5! with a decisive attack, Ivanovic–Feick, Berlin Open 1988) 18 hxg6+ (18 f4 b4!) ♘xg6 19 h5 ♘e5 20 h6 ♘c4 (20 ... ♗h8?! 21 f4 ♘c4 22 ♕e2! gives White more chances) 21 ♕g2 ♗h8 22 h7 ♕a5, Ivanovic–Kosanovic, Stara Pazova 1988, and now 23 ♗xf6! ♗xf6 (23 ... ♕b4 24 ♘b3 axb3 25 cxb3 ♗xf6 26 ♘d5! is good for White) is unclear after 24 ♘d5!? or even 24 h8(♕) ♗xh8 25 ♘d5.

16	...	♗xf6
17	gxh5	a4
18	♗d5	

Better than 18 hxg6 axb3 19 ♘xb3 ♖xc3 20 gxf7+ ♚xf7 21 ♕xc3 (with ♖+3♙ v ♗+♘ White might appear to have good winning chances, but in fact Black can just hold the balance) ♘c4 22

♘d4 ♕b6 23 ♕d3 ♕xd4 24 ♕xd4 ♗xd4 25 ♖xd4 ♚g6 and Black drew this ending in Chandler–Petursson, Hastings 1986/7.

18	...	e6
19	hxg6	exd5
20	h5	♖xc3

In Wiech–Nizynski, Poland 1987, Black was successful with 20 ... ♗g5 21 ♕g2 ♖xc3 22 bxc3 ♘c4 23 ♖dg1 ♕a5 24 ♕xg5 ♕xc3 25 gxf7+ ♚xf7 26 ♕xd5+ ♚e8 27 ♕a8+ ♚f7 28 ♕d5+ ♚e8 and White had nothing better than perpetual check. However 21 f4 ♘c4 (21 ... ♖xc3 22 bxc3 transposes to the main line, but this could be an important finesse of move order for Black if the suggestion of 21 ♕h6 in the next note turns out to be strong) 22 ♕h2 ♗h6 23 ♘xd5 appears much more dangerous.

21 bxc3

Not 21 ♕xc3? since the tempo saved by keeping the queen active is more important than the damage done to White's pawn structure. However 21 ♕h6 fxg6 22 hxg6 ♕e7 23 bxc3 is an interesting alternative since White transfers his queen to a better position with gain of time.

21	...	♗g5
22	f4	♗h6 *(79)*

Not 22 ... ♘c4 23 ♕g2 ♗xf4 24 gxf7+ ♚h8 25 h6 ♖xf7 26 ♖dg1 ♗g5 27 ♕xg5 ♖f1+ 28 ♖xf1 ♕xg5 29 ♖f8+ ♚h7 30 ♖f7+ ♚h8 when White plays 31 h7! ♕d8 (31 ... ♗h3 32 ♖f8+

♔xh7 33 ♖xh3+ wins the queen) 32 ♖g1 ♘e5 (relatively the best) 33 ♖g8+ ♕xg8 34 hxg8(♕)+ ♔xg8 35 ♖f6 with excellent winning chances.

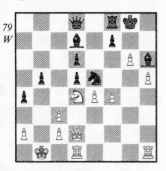

79
W

23 ♖dg1

A very committal move. White plays for mate, but if he cannot break through the move is probably a mistake. Instead White should prefer 23 exd5, not only improving his material situation but also securing c6 and e6 as potential knight outposts. In this case I believe White has some advantage, although of course the position is still very complicated.

23 ... ♕e7?

Any error will have fatal consequences in such a double-edged position. Here Black misses a good chance with 23 ... dxe4! 24 gxf7+ (24 ♕g2 f5! 25 fxe5 dxe5 is unclear) ♔h8 25 ♕g2 (25 ♖g6 ♘xg6 26 hxg6 ♔g7 27 ♕h2 ♖h8 28 f5 ♕f6 and Black survives) ♘xf7 26 ♕xe4 ♕e8! (26 ... ♖e8 27 ♕g6 is good for White) 27 ♕d5 ♕e3! and Black develops counterplay. In this case Black should be at least equal.

24 ♕g2 ♗xf4

Forced as 24 ... ♘g4 (if the knight goes anywhere else Black is mated by gxf7+) 25 f5 ♘f6 26 gxf7+ ♔h8 27 ♕g6 wins outright.

25 g7 ♖b8
26 h6 ♘g6
27 ♘f5 ♗xf5
28 exf5 ♕e5
29 fxg6

and Black lost on time while playing 29 ... f5. White wins by 30 ♖e1 ♗e3 31 ♖xe3 followed by ♕xd5+ and mate.

6 Kan Variation

This line, which starts 1 e4 c5 2 ♘f3 e6 3 d4 cxd4 4 ♘xd4 a6, is notable for the flexibility afforded to Black, since by delaying his piece development he keeps the maximum possible range of options open. Because there are many reasonable choices at each move it is pointless to give precise lines against all possible move orders, so in this chapter there will be a greater emphasis on general principles. The continuation recommended in this chapter, 5 ♗d3, is the most common line in practice. At the moment Black's most popular reply is to set up a 'hedgehog' position by 5 ... ♘f6 6 0-0 d6 (or 6 ... ♕c7 7 ♕e2 d6). After 7 c4 Black may choose to develop his bishop on e7 immediately, but he sometimes brings the queenside out first in order to keep open the option of ... g6 and ... ♗g7. The 'hedgehog' name is derived from the way Black curls up on the first two ranks, moves like ... ♘bd7, ... b6, ... ♗b7, ... ♖e8, ... ♕c7, ... ♗f8, ... ♖ac8 and ... ♕b8 being typical. Black's slow development invites White to attack, but experience has shown that the unwary attacker can easily impale himself on Black's spines, and such at-tacks have to be well-organized if they are to stand much chance of success. Moreover White has to watch out for Black's ... b5 and ... d5 breaks. Game 22 deals with the lines arising after 5 ... ♘f6, including the 'hedgehog'. All Black's other 5th moves, such as 5 ... ♗c5, 5 ... ♘c6, 5 ... ♘e7 and 5 ... g6, are in game 21.

Game 21
Kengis–Nevednici
USSR 1979

1	e4	c5
2	♘f3	e6
3	d4	cxd4
4	♘xd4	a6
5	♗d3	*(80)*

5	...	♗c5

Black's alternatives are arranged in descending order of importance:

(1) **5 ... ♘c6** (it is surprising

hat this solid line is not played more frequently; although the symmetrical position gives Black few winning chances, it is hard for White to prove any advantage) 6 ♘xc6 and now:

(1a) **6 ... dxc6** 7 ♘d2 e5 8 ♕h5 ♗d6 9 ♘c4 ♗c7 (9 ... ♘f6 10 ♘xd6+ ♕xd6 11 ♕e2 ♗e6 12 0-0 gives White the chance to make his black-squared bishop a potent force, as in Jansa–Cebalo, Smederevska Palanka 1978 after 12 ... ♘d7 13 ♖d1 ♕e7 14 b3 0-0 15 a4 a5 16 ♗a3 ♘c5 17 ♗c4!) 10 ♗g5 ♘f6 11 ♕e2 h6 12 ♗h4 ♕e7 13 0-0-0 (13 0-0?! allowed Black to stir up trouble by 13 ... g5 14 ♗g3 h5 15 f3 h4 in Ligterink–Miles, Lone Pine 1979) ♗e6 14 f4 ♗xc4 (14 ... ♗g4 15 ♗xf6 ♗xe2 16 ♗xe7 ♗xd1 17 ♗d6 ♗xd6 18 ♘xd6+ ♔d7 19 ♘xf7 wins material for White) 15 ♗xc4 b5 16 ♗b3 0-0 17 ♗xf6 ♕xf6 18 ♖d7 and White's pressure against f7 gives him some advantage, Tseshkovsky–Miles, Bled-Portoroz 1979.

(1b) **6 ... bxc6** (out of favour ever since the famous Fischer–Petrosian game mentioned below) 7 0-0 d5 (**7 ... e5** 8 f4 ♗c5+ 9 ♔h1 ♗e7 10 ♕h5 ♘g6 11 f5 ♘f4 12 ♗xf4 exf4 13 f6 ♗d4 14 fxg7 ♗xg7 15 ♖xf4 ♕e7 16 ♘c3 is very good for White, Ravinsky–Vorotnikov, USSR 1963, while **7 ... g6?!** 8 e5 ♗g7 9 f4 d6, van der Wiel–Anand, Thessaloniki Ol. 1984, should have been met by 10 exd6 ♕xd6 11 ♘d2 ♕d4+ 12

♔h1 ♘f6 13 ♘c4 ♘d5 14 ♘d6+ ♔e7 15 c3 with a fine position for White) 8 c4 ♘f6 9 cxd5 cxd5 10 exd5 ♘xd5 (**10 ... exd5** 11 ♘c3 ♗e7 12 ♕a4+ ♕d7 13 ♖e1! ♕xa4 14 ♘xa4 ♗e6 15 ♗e3 0-0 16 ♗c5 is Fischer–Petrosian, match, 1971, which was won by Fischer, while **10 ... ♕xd5** 11 ♘c3 ♕d7 12 ♗g5 ♗e7 13 ♕e2 ♗b7 14 ♖ac1 0-0 15 ♖fd1, although keeping Black's pawns intact, gave White a dangerous initiative in Mikhalchishin–Gorchakov, USSR 1972) 11 ♗e4 ♖a7 (**11 ... ♖b8** 12 ♕f3 f5 13 ♗xd5 ♕xd5 14 ♕xd5 exd5 15 ♖d1 ♗e6 16 ♘c3 ♖d8 17 ♗g5 ♖d7 18 ♘e2 gives White the better ending and **11 ... ♗e7** 12 ♘c3 ♗b7 13 ♕a4+ ♕d7 14 ♕xd7+ ♔xd7 15 ♖d1 is also promising after **15 ... ♖ad8** 16 ♘xd5 ♗xd5 17 ♗xd5 exd5 18 ♖xd5+ ♔e6 19 ♖xd8 ♖xd8 20 ♗e3, Matanovic–Roos, Le Havre 1966, or **15 ... ♗f6** 16 ♘xd5 ♗xd5 17 ♗xd5 exd5 18 ♖xd5+ ♔e6 19 ♖d2 ♖hd8 20 ♖e2+, Averbakh–Taimanov, USSR Ch. 1960) 12 ♕d4 ♖d7 13 ♘c3 ♘xc3 (13 ... ♗b7 14 ♘xd5 ♗xd5 15 ♗xd5 ♖xd5 16 ♕a4+ wins the a-pawn) 14 ♕xc3 and Black's uncastled king gives him plenty of problems, Belyavsky–Kurajica, Sarajevo 1982.

(2) **5 ... g6** 6 c4 ♗g7 (this is an attempt to reach a kind of hedgehog position, but with the bishop more actively deployed at g7) 7 ♘b3 and now:

(2a) **7 ... ♘e7** 8 ♘c3 d5 (8 ...

0-0 9 0-0 ♘bc6 10 ♗e2 b6 11 ♗f4
f5 12 exf5 ♖xf5 13 ♕d2 with
advantage to White, Ljubojevic–
Panno, Buenos Aires 1980) 9 cxd5
exd5 10 ♗g5! h6 11 ♗xe7
♗xc3+ 12 bxc3 ♕xe7 13 0-0
dxe4 14 ♗xe4 0-0 15 ♖e1 ♕c7 16
♕f3 ♘d7 17 ♘d4 ♔g7 18 ♖ab1
and White has a big lead in development, Donchev–Prie, Tou-
lon 1988.

(2b) **7 ... d6** 8 ♘c3 ♘f6 9 ♗f4
(9 0-0 followed by ♗f4 transposes
to lines given in game 22, but
White can do better here because
Black has no time for ... ♘c6 and
... ♘e8) 0-0 10 ♗e2 e5 (10 ...
♘e8 11 c5 is particularly unpleasant when Black's queen is
undefended) 11 ♗e3 ♗e6 12 0-0
♘c6 13 f3 ♖c8 14 ♖c1, Ljubojevic–Rajkovic, Yugoslavia 1980,
with a good position for White.
The plan of directly attacking the
d-pawn by ♗f4 and ♗e2 is a
logical way to exploit Black's ...
♗g7, and in this case it gives
White the advantage.

(3) **5 ... ♘e7** (Black aims to
play ... ♘c6, but only when he
can recapture with a piece) 6 ♘c3
(6 0-0 ♘ec6 7 c3 is also possible,
when 7 ... ♗e7 8 ♗e3 0-0 9 f4 d6
10 ♘f3 ♘d7 11 ♘bd2 gave White
a small but enduring plus in Georgiev–Peev, Bulgaria Ch. 1980–1)
♘ec6 7 ♘b3 ♗e7 8 ♕h5! d6 9
♗e3 ♘d7 10 f4 b5 11 0-0-0 b4?!
12 ♘a4! e5 13 f5 0-0 14 g4! with
an automatic attack for White,
Mikhalchishin–Dorfman, Lvov
1983.

(4) **5 ... ♕b6** 6 c3! d6 (6 ...
♘c6 7 0-0 ♘xd4 8 cxd4 ♕xd4 9
♘c3 is dangerous for Black) 7 0-0
♘f6 8 a4 ♗e7 9 ♘d2 ♕c7 10 a5
0-0 11 ♘c4 ♘bd7 12 ♕e2 ♖e8 13
♗g5! ♗f8?! (13 ... h6 14 ♗h4 b5
is just slightly better for White) 14
♗h4 with a good game for White,
Lazic–Martinovic, Yugoslavia
1987.

(5) **5 ... ♕c7** 6 0-0 ♘c6?!
(Black can transpose to game 22
by 6 ... ♘f6) 7 ♘xc6 ♕xc6 (or
else Black has an inferior version
of variation 1 above) 8 c4 (8 ♘d2
is probably also good) g6 9 ♘c3
♗g7 10 ♖e1 ♘e7 11 ♗g5 d6 12
♕d2 with a very good position for
White.

(6) **5 ... b5** 6 0-0 ♗b7 7 ♕e2
♘e7 8 a4 b4 9 ♘d2 ♘bc6 10
♘4b3 ♘g6 11 f4 with advantage
to White, Matanovic–Taimanov,
Yugoslavia 1965. One of the main
advantages of 5 ♗d3 as opposed
to 5 ♘c3 is that an early ... b5 by
Black is hardly ever a worry, since
White may undermine Black's
queenside pawns by a4 without
fearing a loss of time after ... b4.

    6 ♘b3 ♗a7

It makes little difference
whether Black plays 6 ... ♗a7 or
6 ... ♗b6, since he must exchange
on e3 within a few moves in any
case.

    7 ♕e2 ♘c6
    8 ♗e3 ♗xe3
    9 ♕xe3 *(81)*
    9 ... d6
Or:
(1) **9 ... e5** 10 ♘c3 ♘ge7 11

81
B

0-0-0 d6 12 ♗c4 b5 13 ♗d5 ♘xd5
14 ♘xd5 ♗e6 15 f4 0-0 with a
roughly equal position, Wahls–
Farago, Altensteig 1987, but 12
♖d2 followed by ♖hd1 and ♗e2
creates a more dynamic impres-
sion.

(2) **9 ... ♘f6** (this move order is
sometimes played, but it may be
inaccurate) 10 e5!? (after 10 ♘c3
Black should play 10 ... d6; trying his luck with 10 ... 0-0 is bad
after 11 e5 ♘g4 12 ♗xh7+!) ♘g4
11 ♕g3 h5 (11 ... ♘cxe5? 12 ♗e2
h5 13 h3 h4 14 ♕c3 wins for
White) 12 h3 ♘gxe5 13 ♕xg7 and
White has some advantage.

(3) **9 ... ♘ge7** 10 ♘c3 0-0 11 0-
0-0 ♕c7 (or 11 ... b6 12 f4 ♗b7
13 ♘he1 ♕c7 14 ♔b1 d6 15 ♕h3
♘b4 16 a3 ♘xd3+ 17 ♖xd3 ♘c6
18 ♕h4! with dangerous threats,
Vilela–Lebredo, Cuba 1983) 12 f4
d6 13 ♕h3 ♘b4 14 ♖hf1! e5 15 f5
d5 16 exd5 ♘exd5 17 ♘xd5 ♘xd5
18 ♕h4 ♘f6 19 g4 e4 20 g5 exd3
21 ♖xd3 ♕e5 22 gxf6 ♕xf6 23
♕xf6 gxf6 24 ♖d6 with a very
good ending for White, Korlov–
Batakov, corr. 1984.

10   ♘c3   ♘f6
11   0-0-0

White has an interesting alternative in 11 g4!?, when **11 ... b5**
12 0-0-0 0-0 13 g5 ♘e8 14 f4 left
White with a favourable version
of the main line in Anand–Ninov,
Baguio City 1987. Anand finished
off efficiently: 14 ... b4 15 ♘e2 a5
16 ♘bd4 ♘xd4 17 ♘xd4 ♕b6?!
18 e5! ♗b7 19 ♖hf1! dxe5 20 fxe5
♖d8? 21 ♗xh7+! ♔xh7 22 g6+
♔g8 23 ♕h3 ♘f6 24 exf6 fxg6 25
fxg7 Resigns. The critical response to 11 g4 is probably **11 ...
♘xg4** 12 ♕g3 ♘f6 13 ♕xg7 ♖g8
14 ♕h6 ♗d7 intending ... ♕e7
and ... 0-0-0, and it is not clear
how much advantage White can
claim.

11   ...   0-0

There are quite a few alternatives:

(1) **11 ... e5** 12 ♖d2 (12 ♗e2 0-
0 13 f4 exf4 14 ♕xf4 ♘e8 15 ♘d4
♗e6 16 ♘f5 was a little better for
White in Psakhis–Vyzmanavin,
Moscow Ch. 1981) ♗e6 13 ♖hd1
♕c7 14 ♗e2 ♖d8 15 g4! 0-0 (15
... h6?! 16 f4 exf4 17 ♕xf4 ♘e5
18 ♘d4 0-0 19 g5 d5 20 ♔b1 was
good for White, Varjomaa–Tor-
nefjell, corr. 1979) 16 ♕g3 ♗xb3
17 cxb3! ♘d4 18 ♔b1 b5 19 ♗d3
♕c6 20 f3 ♖fe8 21 ♕g2 b4 22 g5!
and the outpost on c4 for White's
bishop aided an already dangerous kingside attack in Lekander–
Schoneberg, corr. 1980.

(2) **11 ... b5** 12 ♖d2 (12 g4!?
looks good) 0-0 13 ♖hd1 ♕c7 14
f4 b4 15 ♘e2 e5 16 fxe5 dxe5 17

🗒f1 ♘d7 18 ♘g3 ♘b6 19 ♘f5 with strong pressure for White, Byrne–Larsen, Biel IZ 1976.

(3) **11 ... ♕c7** may transpose into the main line after 12 f4 0-0, but it allows White the alternative of 12 g4!, which looks unpleasant for Black.

    12   f4   **♕c7** *(82)*

    13   g4

There seems to be no general agreement as to whether White needs to prepare this with 🗒hg1. The alternative attacking ideas are:

(1) **13 ♕h3** ♘b4 14 g4 b5 15 g5 ♘xd3+ (15... ♘e8 16 ♕h4 f6 17 a3 fxg5 18 fxg5 ♘xd3+ 19 🗒xd3 🗒b8 was unclear in Vogt–Velikov, E. Germany–Bulgaria 1987) 16 🗒xd3 ♘e8 17 f5 b4 led to a sharp finish in Bronstein–Suetin, Moscow Ch. 1982 after 18 ♕h4 bxc3 19 🗒h3 cxb2+ 20 ♔b1 f6 21 ♕xh7+ ♔f7 22 🗒g1 🗒g8 23 🗒h6 exf5 24 🗒xf6+ ♘xf6 25 gxf6 ♔xf6 26 ♕xg8 ♗b7 27 ♕h7 ♗xe4 28 ♕g6+ ♔e5 29 ♕g3+ Draw.

(2) **13 🗒hg1** (this is probably good enough for a slight advantage) b5 14 g4 b4 15 g5 ♘e8 16 ♘e2 (16 ♘b1 a5 17 🗒g4!? a4 18 ♘3d2 ♗a6 19 ♗xa6 🗒xa6 20 🗒h4 g6 21 ♕h3 f5 22 gxf6 🗒xf6 23 ♘c4 may be slightly better for White, Wedberg–Spraggett, New York Open 1987) ♕a7 (16... a5 17 ♘bd4 ♘xd4 18 ♕xd4 ♗a6 19 ♔b1 was a little better for White in Arnason–Suetin, Sochi 1980) 17 ♕h3! g6 18 f5 exf5 19 exf5 ♘e7 20 ♘g3! ♕e3+?! (20... a5 is better, but still favours White) 21 ♔b1 ♗xf5 22 ♗xf5 ♘xf5 23 🗒de1 ♕f4 24 🗒gf1 ♕h4 25 ♕xh4 ♘xh4 26 🗒e4 with an excellent ending for White, Arnason–Kirov, Plovdiv 1986.

    13 ...   **b5**

Accepting the offer must be a critical test of White's willingness to play g4 without the preparatory 🗒hg1. In Short–Velikov, European Club Ch. 1987 the continuation was 13 ... ♘xg4 14 ♕g3 ♘f6 15 🗒hg1 ♘e8 16 ♔b1 (16 f5!? is natural) ♘e7?! (16... b5 and 16... f6 have been suggested as possible improvements) 17 ♘d4 ♕c5 18 ♘f3 f6 19 e5! with a very strong attack, Short–Velikov, European Club Ch. 1987. Velikov must have found an improvement because he repeated this line in a later game Ivanovic–Velikov, Saint John Open 1988. Unfortunately Ivanovic varied by 16 ♕h4, so we don't know what Velikov's intention was. Despite this hint, I believe White has good compensation for the pawn and it would require a brave Black player to take this line on.

14 g5 ♘d7
15 f5!?

15 ♕h3 ♘b4 16 a3 ♘xd3+ 17 ♕xd3 d5 gave Black counterplay in Georgadze–Bohlig, Halle 1978, although White won this game too.

15 ... b4
16 ♘e2 a5

It is almost impossible to assess positions in which the players are attacking on opposite wings. Unless one of the players is well in front it is likely that a single tempo will decide the race and obscure tactical points will often have a crucial influence on the play.

17 ♕h3

Attacking e6 directly, and creating a concealed threat to h7.

17 ... exf5
18 exf5 ♘de5

The pin along the c8–h3 diagonal is awkward for White since he cannot move his kingside pawns, nor can he unpin by ♕h4 since ... ♘xd3+ and ... ♗xf5 repulses the attack. Bringing the knight to d5 is the only way to make progress.

19 ♘f4 a4
20 ♘d5 ♕d8 *(83)*

Now that b3 and g5 are under attack, White is committed to the sacrificial path.

21 ♖hg1! ♘xd3+?

Black decides to eliminate one of the attacking pieces, but in

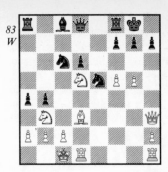

doing so brings the d1 rook into the attack. The best defence was 21 ... axb3! 22 ♘f6+ gxf6 23 ♕h6! (23 gxf6+ ♘g6 leads nowhere as the f5 pawn is pinned while 24 ♕h6 ♕xf6 25 fxg6 fxg6 26 ♗xg6 ♕f4+ 27 ♕xf4 ♖xf4 28 ♗e8+ ♔f8 29 ♗xc6 bxa2 30 ♔d2 ♖d4+ wins for Black) ♘g6! (23 ... ♔h8 24 gxf6 ♖g8 25 ♖g7 ♘xd3+ 26 ♖xd3 ♗xf5 27 ♖h3! leads to mate at h7) 24 fxg6 fxg6 25 ♗xg6 ♖a7! 26 gxf6 hxg6 (26 ... ♕xf6 27 ♗xh7+ ♔h8 28 ♖g8+! ♖xg8 29 ♗g6+ mates, or 27 ... ♔f7 28 ♖df1) 27 ♖xg6+ (27 ♕xg6+ ♔h8 leads to nothing as the d1 rook cannot reach the h-file, ♖d5 being met by ... ♘e5) ♔f7 reaching a remarkable position in which it appears that White must mate, but it isn't certain that he can do so. In the first edition I commented that I couldn't see a mate after 28 ♖g7+ ♔e6 (28 ... ♔e8 29 ♕e3+ ♘e5 30 ♕xa7 ♕xf6 31 axb3 is very good for White, with material equality but weak Black pawns and an exposed Black king) 29 ♕h3+ ♔xf6 30 ♕h6+

♔e5 (30 ... ♔f5 31 ♖g2! does mate), for example 31 ♖g3 ♗f5 32 c4 ♗e4! I still don't see a mate, and nobody wrote to me suggesting one, but if we return to the position after 27 ... ♔f7 White can gain a massive advantage by 28 ♖e1 ♘e5 29 ♖g7+ ♔e6 (29 ... ♔e8 30 ♖xa7 ♕xf6 31 ♕h5+ ♔d8 32 axb3 is similar) 30 ♖xa7 bxa2 (30 ... ♕xf6 31 ♕h3+ and ♕xb3+) 31 ♕h3+ ♔d5 32 ♕b3+ ♔c6 33 ♕xa2, with a slight material plus for White together with a raging attack.

22   ♖xd3   ♘e5

Now White wins by force.

23   ♘f6+   gxf6
24   ♕h6!

Once again 24 gxf6+ ♘g6 repulses the attack, but now 24 ... ♘g6 loses to 25 ♖h3 ♖e8 26 fxg6 fxg6 27 ♕xh7+ ♔f8 28 ♕h8+ and ♖h7 mate. 24 ... ♔h8 25 ♖h3 ♗xf5 26 g6! ♗xg6 27 ♖xg6 is also mate, so Black must take the rook.

24...   ♘xd3+ *(84)*

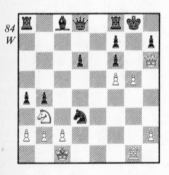

84
W

Black is hoping for 25 cxd3 ♔h8 when **26 gxf6 ♖g8 27 ♖g7 ♗xf5** defends, as does **26 g6 fxg6 27 fxg6 ♕c7+** and **28 ... ♕g7.**

25   ♔b1!   fxg5

25 ... ♔h8 26 g6 fxg6 27 fxg6 threatens both 28 ♕xh7 mate and 28 g7+, while 25 ... ♕b6 26 ♖g3 only makes matters worse.

26   f6   ♕xf6
27   ♕xf6   g4

The only way to avoid mate. Although rook, bishop and two pawns amount to enough material to balance a queen, Black still suffers from his bad king position.

28   ♕g5+   ♔h8
29   ♕f6+   ♔g8
30   ♘d4   ♘e5
31   h3

Intending 32 hxg4 followed by ♘f5.

31   ...   h5
32   ♕g5+   ♘g6
33   ♕xh5   gxh3
34   ♕d5

Attacking a8 and g6. White finishes the game with the same energy he has displayed throughout.

34   ...   ♗e6
35   ♘xe6   h2
36   ♖xg6+   Resigns

36 ... fxg6 37 ♘xf8+ and ♕xa8 wins all the black pieces.

Game 22
Nunn–Gheorghiu
Hamburg 1984

1	e4	c5
2	♘f3	e6
3	d4	cxd4

4	♘xd4	a6
5	♗d3	♘f6
6	0-0 *(85)*	

6 ... d6

The surprising move **6 ... e5** (6 ... d5 7 e5 is very bad for Black since the natural 7 ... ♘fd7 loses to 8 ♘xe6!) was played in Fedorowicz–Dorfman, New York 1989, and now 7 ♗g5! exd4 (7 ... h6 8 ♗xf6 ♕xf6 9 ♘e2 d6 10 ♘bc3 ♗e6 11 f4 is good for White) 8 e5 ♗e7 (**8 ... ♕a5** 9 ♕d2! and **8 ... h6** 9 exf6 hxg5 10 ♖e1+ are very bad for Black) 9 exf6 ♗xf6 10 ♗xf6 ♕xf6 11 ♖e1+ ♔f8 12 ♗e4 is a little better for White since Black will still have an isolated pawn after White regains the front d-pawn.

Black has a major alternative in **6 ... ♕c7** 7 ♕e2 (7 c4 ♘c6 8 ♘xc6 dxc6 is now considered satisfactory for Black because White has spent a move on c4, which in this position only serves to weaken d4) d6 (7 ... ♘c6 is bad because of 8 ♘xc6 and 9 e5, while 7 ... ♗c5!? 8 ♘b3 is a speciality of Eingorn; the two examples **8**

... ♗e7 9 c4 d6 10 ♘c3 0-0 11 ♗d2 b6 12 ♘d4 ♗b7 13 ♔h1 ♘c6 14 ♘xc6 ♗xc6 15 ♖ae1 ♕b7 16 a4 ♘d7 17 b4 ♕c8 18 f4, Govedarica–Eingorn, Novi Sad 1988 and **8 ... ♗a7** 9 ♔h1 d6 10 c4 ♘c6 11 ♗g5 ♗d7 12 ♘c3 ♘d4 13 ♘xd4 ♗xd4 14 ♖ac1 ♕c5 15 ♗d2, Smyslov–Eingorn, USSR Ch. 1988 were both very slightly better for White, but the idea is an interesting one and I expect to see more of it; perhaps 8 ♗e3 is the best reply) 8 c4 g6 (this is the move which gives 6 ... ♕c7 its distinctive flavour; if Black develops his bishop at e7 we reach positions similar to those in the main line below, but after ... g6 White's prospects of a direct kingside attack are reduced; on the other hand d6 is weakened) 9 ♘c3 (it is also worth considering b3 and ♗b2) ♗g7 10 ♖d1 (White's idea is to attack d6 by ♗c2, ♘f3 and ♗f4) 0-0 *(86)* and now:

(1) **11 ♗c2 ♘bd7** (**11 ... b6** 12 ♘f3 ♘fd7 13 ♗e3 ♘c6 14 ♖ac1 ♗b7 15 ♗b1 is good for White,

Ivanovic–Cvitan, Vrsac 1987, while **11 ... ♘c6** 12 ♘xc6 bxc6 13 ♗f4 e5 14 ♗e3 ♗e6 15 ♗b3 ♖fd8, Cabrilo–Gheorghiu, New York Open 1988, gives White a slight plus after 16 h3 or 16 ♖d3) 12 ♘f3 ♗g4 (not 12 ... b6 13 ♗f4! ♘e5 14 ♘xe5 dxe5 15 ♗e3 ♗b7 16 ♘a4 b5 17 cxb5 axb5 18 ♘c5 ♗c6, Ljubojevic–Hulak, Wijk aan Zee 1987, and now 19 b4! followed by ♗b3 is good for White) 13 ♗f4 (not 13 ♗g5 ♘de5 14 ♘d2 b5! and Black seized the initiative in Klinger–Jukic, Berne Open 1988) and now 13 ... ♘de5 14 ♘d2 b5?! 15 h3 ♘f6?! 16 cxb5 axb5 17 ♗b3 b4 18 ♘b5 ♕b8 19 ♘xd6 was good for White in Cabrilo–Kovacevic, Vrnjacka Banja 1988. However Black's play was poor in this example; had he played 13 ... ♘ge5 White would have a slightly inferior version of line 2a below in which his bishop is on c2 instead of the better square b1.

(2) **11 ♘f3** (this may be more accurate since White often prefers to retreat his bishop to b1) and now:

(2a) **11 ... ♘bd7** 12 ♗f4 ♗g4 13 ♖ac1 b6 14 ♗b1 ♘ge5 15 b3 ♘xf3+ 16 ♕xf3 ♘e5 17 ♕e2 and now:

(2a1) **17 ... ♗b7** 18 ♕d2 (18 ♗e3 ♖fd8 19 ♕d2 ♖ab8?! 20 h3 ♗a8 21 f4 ♘c6 22 ♕f2, Armas–Gheorghiu, Romania Ch. 1987, was slightly better for White, but Black can try 19 ... ♗f8 or 19 ... ♘g4) ♖fd8 19 ♗g5! ♖d7 (Black

would like to play 19 ... f6 20 ♗e3 g5, but this allows 21 ♘a4) 20 h3, intending f4, with advantage to White, Armas–Ionescu, Romania Ch. 1988.

(2a2) **17 ... ♖b8** (this seems to be more accurate; Black first of all secures the weak b6 pawn) 18 h3 ♗b7 19 ♕d2 ♖fd8 20 ♗g5 (the immediate 20 ♗e3! transposes to Armas–Gheorghiu above, which was slightly better for White) f6 21 ♗e3 g5 22 ♗d3 (now 22 ♘a4 is met by 22 ... ♗c6) ♗c6 23 ♘b5 ♕f7 with equality, Wolff–Hulak, Toronto 1989.

(2b) **11 ... ♘c6** (in many lines it makes no difference whether Black plays ... ♘bd7 or ... ♘c6 because he will continue with ... ♘f6–g4–e5xf3+ followed by ... ♘e5 in any case, but here we examine one independent line) 12 ♗f4 ♘d7 13 ♖ac1 ♘de5 14 b3 ♕e7 (14 ... ♘xf3+ will transpose to line 2a) 15 ♗b1 (White aims to expel the e5 knight by moving his ♘f3 and ♗f4 away) ♖d8 (15 ... ♗d7 16 ♘e1 ♖fd8 17 ♕d2 ♗e8 18 ♗g5 f6 19 ♗h6 ♗xh6 20 ♕xh6 also gave White an edge in Timoshchenko–Eingorn, Tallinn 1989) 16 ♗e3 ♗d7 17 ♘d2! ♗e8 18 f4 ♘d7 ♘f3 ♖ab8 and White retains a slight advantage, Kuzmin–Eingorn, Moscow 1989.

7 c4 *(87)* **♗e7**

Other 7th moves:

(1) **7 ... g6** 8 ♘c3 ♗g7 9 ♘b3! 0-0 10 ♗e2 ♘c6 11 ♗f4 ♘e8 (Black has little choice as 11 ...

87
B

♘e5 12 c5 is very awkward) and
after 12 ♕d2 b6 13 ♖fd1 ♘e5 14
♖ac1 ♕c7 Black equalized in
Nunn–Gheorghiu, Vienna 1986.
However 12 c5! is unpleasant for
Black, for example **12 ... dxc5** 13
♕xd8 ♘xd8 14 ♘a4! or **12 ... e5**
13 ♗e3 ♗e6 14 ♘d5.

(2) **7 ...** ♗**d7** 8 ♘c3 ♘c6 9
♘xc6 ♗xc6 10 ♕e2 ♗e7 11 b3
0-0 12 ♗b2 ♖e8 (**12 ...** ♘**d7** 13 f4
is slightly better for White, while
after **12 ...** ♕**b8** 13 a4 ♖e8 14
♖ae1 ♘d7 15 f4 ♗h4! 16 ♖d1
♗f6 17 b4!? the position was
unclear in Nunn–Bischoff, Dortmund 1987; 14 f4! was more accurate, not committing the a1
rook for the moment) 13 f4 d5!?
14 cxd5 exd5 15 e5 ♘e4 16 ♘xe4!
dxe4 17 ♗xe4 ♗b5 and now **18**
♕**g4?!** ♗d2! 19 ♗xh7+!? was
unclear in Arnason–Toshkov,
Jurmala 1987. White can draw by
18 ♕**c2** ♗xf1 19 ♗xh7+ ♔h8 20
♔xf1 ♖c8 21 ♕d3! g6 22 ♗xg6
hxg6 23 ♕xg6 ♕d2, but **18** ♕**f3!?**
is the most promising, not only
playing for a possible attack by

♕h3, but also lining up against
the b7 pawn.

(3) **7 ... b6**. Normally this
transposes to lines considered below.

8   ♘c3

White has two main attacking
plans, which are distinguished by
the development of his queen's
bishop. Firstly he may build up a
slow kingside attack by b3, ♗b2,
♘c3, ♕e2, f4, ♖ae1 and so on,
with the ultimate aim of a
breakthrough by f5. The other
plan is to prepare for e5 by ♘c3,
♕e2, f4, ♗d2 and ♖ae1. The
important point is that with the
bishop on b2 the e5 plan is much
less effective, because White ends
up with a pawn on e5 and this
would block the bishop on b2.

8   ...   0-0
9   ♕e2

Moves such as ♕e2, ♔h1 and
f4 are logical because they do not
commit White to one plan or the
other. My view is that the e5 plan
is most effective against ... ♘bd7
by Black, because then the
queen's knight blocks the retreat
of the one on f6. Therefore it is
often useful to delay committing
the c1 bishop until Black has
moved his b8 knight. Against ...
♘c6 White will take on c6, then
play b3 and ♗b2, and against ...
♘bd7 White will play ♗d2 and
♖ae1.

9   ...   b6

Black also delays for as long as
possible.

10   f4

Despite the above (rather subjective) comments it is quite reasonable to play b3 straight away, the advantage being that White can sometimes manage without ♔h1. After 10 b3 ♗b7 11 ♗b2 *(88)* there are two lines:

88
B

(1) **11 ... ♘c6** (as the earlier explanation makes clear, this move plays into White's hands since we reach positions similar to the main line below, but with White having saved about half a tempo by missing out ♔h1) 12 ♘xc6 ♗xc6 and Black has been highly unsuccessful from this position:

(1a) **13 ♖ad1 ♕b8?!** 14 a3 (what on earth is this for?) ♖d8? (it doesn't matter about the tempo spent on a3 in view of the way Black plays) 15 f4 ♘d7 16 ♘d5! ♗f8 17 ♖f3! ♖e8 18 ♖h3! g6 19 ♕g4 ♕d8 20 ♖f1 ♗g7 21 ♗xg7 ♔xg7 22 f5! with a massive attack, Ivanovic–Ermenkov, Plovdiv 1983.

(1b) **13 f4 ♘d7** 14 ♖ad1 b5? 15 cxb5! axb5 16 ♗xb5 ♕b6+ 17 ♖f2! ♗xb5 18 ♕xb5 ♕xb5 19

♘xb5 ♖xa2 20 ♗xg7 ♖fa8 21 ♖xa2 ♖xa2 22 ♗d4 e5, Hellers–Adamski, Eeklo 1985, and now 23 ♗c3 gives White a won ending.

(1c) **13 ♖ae1 ♖e8** 14 f4 g6 15 e5! dxe5 16 fxe5 ♗c5+ 17 ♔h1 ♘g4 18 ♗e4! ♘xe5 19 ♗xc6 ♘xc6 20 ♕f3 again with a tremendous attack for White, Ermenkov–Gheorghiu, Prague 1985.

(2) **11 ... ♘bd7** 12 ♖ad1 (12 f4 is also playable) ♖e8 (12 ... ♕c7 13 ♗b1 ♖fe8 14 f4 ♖ac8 15 ♘f3 ♗f8 16 ♔h1 ♗c6 was less accurate and after 17 e5! ♗xf3 18 ♖xf3 dxe5 19 fxe5 ♘g4 20 ♖xf7! White had a very dangerous attack in Plachetka–Ravikumar, Copenhagen 1980) 13 ♗b1 ♕b8 14 f4 ♗f8 15 ♔h1 ♖a7 16 ♘f3 ♗a8 with a double-edged position, Akesson–Mestel, Copenhagen 1980, although I still favour White.

10	...	**♗b7**
11	**♔h1** *(89)*	

89
B

11	...	**♘c6**

Or:

(1) **11 ... ♘bd7** 12 ♗d2 ♕c7 13 ♖ac1 (13 ♖ae1 ♖fe8 14 ♖f3 g6

15 Rg3! Kh8 16 Rh3 e5 17 Nf3 exf4 18 Bxf4 Bf8 19 Qf2 Nc5 20 Bc2 was also good for White in Ivanovic–Peev, Balasiha 1977) g6 14 b4 Rac8 15 a3 Qb8 (the advantage of playing f4 is that the weakening of c4 created by White playing b4 cannot be exploited by ... Ne5) 16 Nf3 Rfe8 17 Rce1 Bf8 18 Ng5 h6 (18 ... e5 19 f5 gave White a strong attack at no material cost in Commons–Najdorf, Lone Pine 1976) 19 Nxf7! Kxf7 20 e5 Ng8 21 Qg4 Ne7 22 Bxg6+! Nxg6 23 f5 Ndxe5 24 fxe6+! (24 fxg6+ Kg8 is unclear) Ke7 (24 ... Kg7 25 Rxe5 dxe5 26 Rf7+ mates) 25 Qxg6! (the climax of a magnificent combination) Kd8 26 Rxe5 dxe5 27 Bxh6 Rxc4 (27 ... Bxh6 28 Rd1+ mates) 28 Qxe8+ (White gives up his queen after all) Kxe8 29 Rxf8+ Ke7 30 Rxb8 Bc6 31 Nd1 b5 32 Kg1 Kxe6 33 Rb6 Resigns, Commons–Peev, Plovdiv 1976.

(2) 11 ... Re8 (dubious as it allows White to play for e5 without delay) 12 Nf3 g6 (12 ... Nbd7 13 e5 dxe5 14 fxe5 Ng4 15 Bf4 Bxf3 16 Rxf3 and 12 ... Nc6 13 e5 dxe5 14 fxe5 Ng4 15 Bf4 are good for White) 13 e5! Nh5, Sax–Bellon, Dubai Ol. 1986 and now Sax recommends 14 Be4 Nc6 15 g4 Ng7 16 f5!, when the lines 16 ... exf5 17 gxf5 dxe5 18 fxg6 hxg6 19 Nxe5, 16 ... gxf5 17 gxf5 Nxf5 (17 ... exf5 18 Bd5) 18 Bxf5 exf5 19 Nd5 and 16 ... dxe5 17 fxg6 f5 (17 ... hxg6 18 Nxe5) 18 gxf5 exf5 19 Bd5+ Kh8 20 Nxe5 are all good for White.

12 Nxc6   Bxc6
13 b3   Nd7

Or 13 ... Qc7 14 Bb2 Rad8 and now:

(1) 15 Rad1 g6 16 Bb1 Nh5 17 Rd3 (17 g4 Ng7 18 f5! exf5 19 gxf5 was probably better) e5! 18 fxe5 dxe5 19 Rxd8 Rxd8 20 Nd5 with just an edge for White, Matulovic–Tringov, Vrnjacka Banja 1986.

(2) 15 Rae1 (intending Nd5) Bb7 16 Bb1 Nd7? (16 ... g6 is probably better, when 17 Qd3 is only a slight plus for White) and now 17 Qh5 Rfe8 18 Re3 Nf6 19 Qh3 g6 20 f5! gave White a decisive attack in Nunn–Gheorghiu, Biel 1983, which is annotated in detail in *Secrets of Grandmaster Play* by Peter Griffiths and the present author. For some reason Gheorghiu repeated the whole line in the game Mokry–Gheorghiu, Prague 1985. That game continued 17 Qg4 Bf6 18 Re3 g6 19 Rh3 Kh8?? 20 Nd5! winning, as 20 ... exd5 is met by 21 Qh4. Of course 19 ... Rfe8 is better, but 20 Qg3 intending f5 gives White a dangerous attack in any case.

14 Bb2   g6

14 ... Bf6 leaves d6 weak and after 15 Rad1 Qc7 16 Bb1 Rfd8?! (16 ... Rad8 was a better chance) 17 Rd3 g6 18 Rfd1 Nc5 19 Nd5! exd5 20 Bxf6 Nxd3 21 exd5! Nxf4 22 Qf3 Nh5 23 Bxd8 Rxd8 24 dxc6 White had a clear

advantage in Marjanovic–Rajkovic, Yugoslavia Ch. 1983.

15 ♖ad1

The purpose of this (rather than ♖ae1) is to prevent the development of Black's e7 bishop to the long diagonal. After 15 ... ♗f6, for example, 16 ♗b1 ♕c7 17 ♕d2 attacks d6.

15 ... ♖e8
16 ♗b1 *(90)*

90
B

16 ... ♕c7

The alternatives are:

(1) **16 ... ♖a7** 17 a4 (the direct 17 ♕d3 was also tempting) ♗f8 18 ♗c2 ♕a8 19 ♕f2 ♘c5? (19 ... ♖c7 was better) 20 ♘d5! exd5 21 cxd5 ♗xa4 22 bxa4 ♗g7 23 ♗xg7 ♔xg7 24 e5! and White stands well, Popovic–Kotronias, Pucarevo 1987.

(2) **16 ... ♕b8** 17 f5 (17 a4!? is possible, but I like 17 ♕d3 b5 18 cxb5 axb5 19 ♘e2! b4 20 ♘d4 ♗b7 21 ♕h3 with dangerous threats on the kingside) b5 18 fxe6 fxe6 19 cxb5 axb5 20 ♘d5!? ♗xd5 (20 ... exd5 21 exd5 ♗f6 22 ♕d2 ♗xb2 23 dxc6 is good for White)

21 exd5 e5 22 ♕g4 ♘f6 23 ♕e6+ ♔g7 was unclear in Prasad–Gheorghiu, Biel Open 1985.

(3) **16 ... ♗f8** 17 e5! dxe5 18 ♗e4! gives White a dangerous attack. The game Vogt–Gheorghiu, E. Germany–Romania 1984 continued 18 ... ♕c7 (18 ... ♗xe4 19 ♘xe4 ♗g7 20 ♗xe5 ♗xe5 21 fxe5 ♔g7 22 ♕f2 wins after **22 ... ♕e7** 23 ♕f6+! ♔g8 24 ♕xe7 ♖xe7 25 ♖xd7 or 22 ... ♖e7 23 ♘g5 ♕g8 24 ♘xf7 ♖f8 25 ♖xd7!) 19 ♕f3 ♗xe4 20 ♘xe4 f5 (20 ... ♗g7 21 fxe5 ♘xe5 22 ♘f6+ ♔h8 23 ♗xe5 wins material) 21 ♖xd7 fxe4 22 ♕d1 ♕c6 23 ♗xe5 ♖ac8 24 ♕d4 ♗e7 (**24 ... ♖e7** 25 ♖d6 drops the b-pawn, while **24 ... b5** 25 ♕a7! and **24 ... ♗c5** 25 ♖g7+ ♔f8 26 ♗d6+ lead to mate) 25 f5! (the immediate 25 ♗h8 ♗f8 26 ♖g7+ ♔xh8 27 ♖xg6+ is met by ... e5, but if Black now plays 25 ... exf5 this line wins) ♖cd8 (25 ... gxf5 26 ♗h8 ♗f8 27 ♖xf5! exf5 28 ♖g7+ mates) 26 ♖xe7! (26 fxg6! ♖xd7 27 gxh7+ ♔xh7 28 ♖f7+ ♔h6 29 ♕e3+ ♗g5 30 ♕h3+ also wins) exf5 (26 ... ♖xd4 27 ♖g7+ is mate next move) 27 ♖xe8+ ♕xe8 28 ♕xb6 Resigns.

17 ♕d3

A flexible move attacking d6 and preparing ♕d4 or ♕h3 according to circumstance.

17 ... ♗f8

This move cost Black forty minutes, presumably checking that the line 18 ♕d4 e5 (18 ... ♗g7 19 ♕xg7+ wins) 19 ♘d5 ♗xd5 20

♕xd5 exf4 21 ♖xf4 ♘e5 22 ♖df1 ♖a7 presented no dangers.

18   ♘b5!?

A shock for Black. After 18 ... axb5 19 ♕c3 e5 20 cxb5 ♖ac8 21 bxc6 ♕xc6 22 ♕f3 Black cannot exchange at f4 since he has no satisfactory way to cover f7, so White gets to play 23 f5, when Black's white squares look very sickly.

18   ...   ♗xb5
19   cxb5   axb5

19 ... a5 20 ♖c1 ♘c5 21 ♕c3 is much worse as Black has to play the weakening ... e5.

20   ♕xb5   ♕b7

The upshot of White's mini-combination is that he has the two bishops and a queenside pawn majority. Now 21 a4! would have been logical, relieving the b1 bishop of its defensive duty and pinning down the b6 pawn. If Black remains passive the b1 bishop can eventually move to b5. During the game I didn't like 21 a4! ♘c5 22 ♕c4 ♖ac8, but 23 f5 e5 24 ♖f3 gives Black no way to exploit the position of White's queen (24 ... ♘e6 25 fxe6!), and consolidation by 25 ♕e2 will be good for White.

21   ♕e2?!   b5!

Black takes the chance to prevent a4. Now ... b4 would permanently cripple White's queenside pawns, so ...

22   b4

Black cannot transfer his knight to c4 because b5 is weak, for example 22 ... ♕a6 (threat ... ♘b6) 23 ♗d3 ♕xa2 24 ♗xb5

♕a7 (24 ... ♖ed8 25 ♗xd7 and ♖a1) 25 ♗c6 followed by ♗d4 and b5, with an excellent position for White.

22   ...   ♖a6 *(91)*

Another useful defensive move, covering d6 in preparation for ... ♗g7. Here I thought for a long time trying to find a way to keep the advantage.

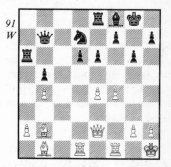

91
W

23   ♖f3!   ♗g7
24   ♗xg7   ♔xg7
25   ♖fd3   ♕c7
26   ♖h3

The point of White's manoeuvre is that he gains a tempo by attacking b5 to transfer his rook to the h-file, reviving some threats against Black's king.

26   ...   ♖b6

Not 26 ... ♕c4? 27 ♕b2+ and 28 ♖c3 trapping the queen.

27   ♕d2

The threat is 28 e5 d5 29 f5 and the queen gets to h6.

27   ...   ♘f6

Once again Black finds a good defence, relieving the pin down the d-file.

28   f5   exf5

28 ... e5 29 ♕h6+ ♔g8 30 g4! is very unpleasant.

29 exf5 d5!

All these difficult moves were very time-consuming, so that Black had only a couple of minutes left to reach move 40. At first sight White can win by 30 fxg6 fxg6 31 ♕h6+ ♔g8 32 ♗xg6 hxg6 33 ♕h8+ (33 ♕xg6+ ♕g7 34 ♕f5 ♖ce6 defends) ♔f7 34 ♖h7+ ♔e6 35 ♖e1+ (35 ♕xf6+ ♔xf6 36 ♖xc7 ♖be6 gives Black enough for the pawn in view of his active rooks and king), but then comes 35 ... ♔f5! 36 ♖f1+ ♔g5! 37 h4+ ♔g4 and White's queen is trapped.

30 fxg6?!

The immediate 30 ♖f1! was much better, when the defence Black plays in the game would have been prevented.

30 ... fxg6

31 ♖f1

Now truly threatening 32 ♕h6+ ♔g8 33 ♗xg6.

31 ... ♘g4!

Suddenly Black exploits White's weak back rank. If 32 ♕xd5? then 32 ... ♘f2+ wins.

32 ♕d4+ ♖f6 (92)

White cannot take the rook or the knight, nor can he play ♖hf3. The move played supports the back rank and attacks the knight.

33 ♗d3 h5

Forced, but good. The draw would now be in sight if it were not for Black's time-trouble.

34 ♖xf6 ♘xf6

92
W

35 ♖f3 ♖e1+

36 ♗f1 ♕e7?!

36 ... ♕e5 37 ♕xe5 ♖xe5 38 ♗xb5 gives White good winning chances as the d-pawn cannot pass over the d3 square. However 36 ... ♕d6! was more accurate, for example 37 ♔g1 (37 h3 ♖e4 38 ♕c3 ♖xb4 39 ♖xf6 ♕xf6) ♖e4 38 ♕c5 (38 ♕c3 d4 39 ♕d3 ♘g4! 40 g3 ♖e1 threatening ... ♘e5 is unpleasant) ♕xc5 39 bxc5 ♖e1 and a draw is inevitable (40 ♖c3 d4).

37 ♔g1 ♖e4

Black can also choose to wait, since progress isn't easy for White, but in time-trouble it is very natural to break the pin.

38 ♕c3 d4

Not 38 ... ♖xb4 39 ♖xf6 d4 because of 40 ♖e6!

39 ♕d3

With two moves still to make Black suddenly finds himself in trouble over the b5 pawn. 39 ... ♕xb4 loses to 40 ♖xf6, so the best chance is 39 ... ♘d5 40 ♕xb5 ♘xb4. Then 41 ♗c4 ♖e1+ 42 ♔f2 ♔h6 isn't dangerous, so White's winning prospects are very slight.

39 ... ♘g4?

40 h3

and Black's flag dropped before he could make his 40th move. After 40 ... ♘e3 41 ♕xb5 ♘xf1 42 ♖xf1 ♖e2 43 ♕d3 ♕e3+ 44 ♕xe3 dxe3, suggested by Black after the game, White can win by 45 a4! (but not 45 b5 ♖xa2 46 ♖b1 ♖d2! 47 ♔f1 ♖f2+ 48 ♔e1 ♖xg2 49 ♖b4 ♖d2 50 b6 ♖d8 51 b7 ♖b8 when Black has drawing chances) ♖b2 46 b5 ♖a2 47 b6 ♖xa4 48 ♖b1 ♖d4 49 ♔f1! (49 b7 e2) ♖d8 50 b7 ♖b8 51 ♔e2 etc. Obviously Black has other ways to play, but the two connected passed pawns give White good winning chances in any case.

7   Maroczy Bind

This most commonly arises if Black plays an early ... g6, for example 1 e4 c5 2 ♘f3 ♘c6 3 d4 cxd4 4 ♘xd4 g6, aiming to reach a Dragon position without having played ... d6. This restricts White's options quite severely, since he has to be careful not to allow Black to play ... d5 in one go, saving a crucial tempo. An effective way out of this dilemma is to continue 5 c4, setting up the formation of pawns on c4 and e4 known as the Maroczy bind. The asset of this formation is the automatic restraint of ... b5 and ... d5, Black's basic freeing thrusts. Black does sometimes succeed in organizing ... b5, but this is normally only good when White has made a mistake. White's main asset is his space advantage, leading to the corollary that he should avoid exchanges which would relieve the cramp in Black's position. If Black does succeed in liquidating to an ending, White's c4 pawn and black-squared weaknesses can become a liability. Play often becomes a matter of slow manoeuvring as White tries to increase his space advantage and force weaknesses in the Black position while his opponent remains crouched on his back two

ranks waiting for the first sign of over-extension to launch a counterattack. The Maroczy Bind can also occur if Black adopts an unusual move order, for example 1 e4 c5 2 ♘f3 ♘c6 3 d4 cxd4 4 ♘xd4 d6 and now 5 c4 will probably transpose to this chapter after 5 ... ♘f6 6 ♘c3 g6. Although the Maroczy Bind is slightly passive for Black, players such as Larsen, Petursson and Velimirovic have shown that by patiently waiting for a lapse of concentration from White this line can offer winning chances for Black. The theoretical opinion is that White should maintain a slight advantage, but White players should not believe that this is a line in which they cannot lose.

Game 23
Karpov–Kavalek
Nice Olympiad 1974

1	e4	c5
2	♘f3	♘c6
3	d4	cxd4
4	♘xd4	g6
5	c4	

Here Black has two possibilities. He may play 5 ... ♗g7 in order to force White's ♗e3, but in doing this he forfeits the chance to take on d4 at a moment when

White must recapture with the queen. The alternative is 5 ... ♘f6, which will often transpose to 5 ... ♗g7 if Black does not take up the chance to play ... ♘xd4. The 5 ... ♗g7 systems are examined in game 24, while in this game we look at 5 ... ♘f6.

5 ...   ♘f6
6   ♘c3 *(93)*

6 ...   d6

If Black adopts the move order 6 ... ♘xd4 7 ♕xd4 d6 (possibly to avoid 7 ♘c2 as in the next note) then White has an interesting alternative based on playing ♗d3 rather than ♗e2, providing the e4 pawn with useful extra protection, for example 6 ... ♘xd4 7 ♕xd4 d6 8 ♗g5 ♗g7 9 ♕d2 0-0 (9 ... ♗e6 10 ♖c1 ♖c8 11 b3 ♕a5 12 f3 h6 13 ♗e3 0-0 14 ♗d3 ♔h7 15 0-0 a6 16 h3 ♘d7 17 f4 f5 18 exf5 ♗xf5 19 ♗e2! was good for White in Polugayevsky–Belyavsky, USSR Ch. 1975) 10 ♗d3 (10 f3 is also interesting, for example after 10 ... ♗e6 11 ♖c1 ♕a5 12 b3 a6? 13 ♘d5! ♕xd2+ 14 ♔xd2 ♗xd5 15 cxd5 ♖fc8 16 ♖xc8! ♖xc8 17 g3 ♔f8 18 ♗h3 ♖c7 19 ♖c1 ♖xc1 20 ♔xc1 White was winning in Byrne–Garcia Padron, Torremolinos 1977—12 ... ♖fc8 was better when 13 ♗e2 a6 14 ♘a4 transposes to Karpov–Kavalek) ♗e6 (10 ... a5 11 0-0 a4 12 ♖ac1 ♗e6 13 ♕c2 gave White his usual space advantage in Portisch–Reshevsky, Petropolis 1973) 11 ♖c1 ♕a5 12 0-0 ♖fc8 13 b3 a6 14 ♖fe1 ♔f8! (14 ... b5? 15 ♘d5! ♕xd2 16 ♗xd2 ♗xd5 17 exd5 bxc4 18 ♗xc4 ♔f8 19 b4 with a clear plus for White, Geller–L. Garcia, Bogota 1978) 15 ♖c2 (15 f4 is Jansa's double-edged suggestion) b5 16 cxb5 axb5 17 ♖ec1 b4 18 ♘b5 ♖xc2 19 ♖xc2 with just an edge for White, Polugayevsky–Jansa, Sochi 1974.

7   ♗e2   ♘xd4

This is Black's last chance to force White to recapture on d4 with his queen. If he plays 7 ... ♗g7 White should transpose to game 24 by 8 ♗e3. At one time 8 ♘c2 was thought the best reply to 7 ... ♗g7, but after 8 ... ♘d7 9 ♗d2 a5! (not 9 ... ♘c5?! 10 b4 ♘e6 11 ♖c1 0-0 12 0-0 f5 13 exf5 gxf5 14 f4 ♘ed4 15 ♘xd4 ♘xd4 16 ♗e3 with a positional advantage for White, Nunn-Rind, Manchester 1980) 10 0-0 0-0 11 ♖c1 ♘c5 Black has a much better version of the Maroczy Bind than in other lines. In Nunn–Petursson, Wijk aan Zee 1990 I made matters worse by 12 b3? ♘b4! and Black had a clear advantage.

8 ♕xd4 ♗g7
9 ♗g5 *(94)* ♗e6

Or:

(1) **9 ... ♗d7** 10 ♕d2 h6 (after 10 ... ♗c6 White should continue with 11 f3) 11 ♗f4 a6 12 0-0 ♗c6 13 f3 0-0 14 a4 ♘d7 15 a5! ♘c5 16

94
B

♖a3 with a small advantage for White, Pomar–Cordovil, Malaga 1972.

(2) **9 ... h6** 10 ♗e3 0-0 11 ♕d2 ♔h7 (11 ... ♕a5 12 0-0 forces ... ♔h7 in any case) 12 0-0 ♗e6 13 f4 (13 ♗d4 ♖c8 14 b3 a6 15 ♕e3 ♘d7 16 ♗xg7 ♔xg7 17 f4 ♕b6 18 ♕xb6 ♘xb6 19 f5 ♗d7 20 ♖ad1 only gave White a slight edge in Timman–Ribli, Amsterdam 1973) ♖c8 (after 13 ... ♕a5 14 f5 forces 14 ... ♗d7 since 14 ... gxf5 15 exf5 ♗xf5 allows 16 ♖xf5, so White avoids wasting a tempo on b3) 14 b3 ♕a5 (14 ... a6 15 ♖ad1 ♕a5 16 ♗d4 is good for White after both **16 ... b5** 17 f5 ♗d7 18 ♗xf6! exf6 19 ♘d5 ♕xd2 20 ♖xd2, Nunn–van der Sterren, Groningen 1974–5 and **16 ...** ♗d7 17 ♗xf6 exf6 18 ♘d5 ♕c5+ 19 ♔h1 a5 20 f5, Nunn–I. Ivanov,

London 1987, so it makes sense for Black to try to force White's rook to the less active square c1) 15 a3 (15 ♖ac1 is also possible, although 15 ... a6 16 f5 ♗d7 17 h3 ♗c6 18 ♗d3 ♘d7 was unclear in Gulko–Petrosian, Biel IZ 1976) a6 16 f5 ♗d7 17 b4 ♕e5 (Larsen–Fischer, match 1971) and now, according to various analyses of this famous match, 18 ♖ad1 would have been good for White.

10 ♖c1 *(95)*

10 0-0 is possible, and after 10 ... 0-0 11 ♕d2 a6 (11 ... ♖c8 12 b3 b5?! is doubtful because of 13 e5! when **13 ... dxe5** 14 ♕xd8 ♖fxd8 15 ♘xb5 gives White the better ending and **13 ... b4** 14 exf6 exf6 15 ♗e3 bxc3 16 ♕xc3 f5 17 ♗d4 ♗xd4 18 ♕xd4 gives White the better middlegame, Bukic–Romanishin, Moscow 1977) 12 f3 (not 12 ♖c1 allowing 12 ... b5! with equality) ♕a5 13 ♖fd1 ♖fc8 14 ♘d5 ♕xd2 15 ♖xd2 ♖xd5 (15 ... ♘xd5? 16 exd5 ♗d7 17 ♗xe7! ♗h6 and now not **18 ♖c2** ♗f5 and 19 ... ♖e8, but **18 ♖ad1!** ♗xd2 19 ♖xd2 ♖e8 20 ♗xd6 with a clear plus for White, Britton–Donaldson, Rhodes 1980) 16 cxd5 ♔f8 White can claim a very slight plus. In general these endings with an open c-file are very drawish unless Black has weakened his queenside by playing ... b5 (which both allows a4 and gives White an entry point at c6), or White can quickly seize the c-file by playing his bishop to the h3–c8 diagonal.

Neither situation exists here, so White's advantage is insignificant and in practice Black would have few problems reaching the draw.

10 ... ♛a5

If Black omits this move, we again face move order questions. After 10 ... 0-0 11 ♛d2 ♜c8 12

95
B

b3 a6 the obvious **13 f3** allows 13 ... b5!? 14 cxb5 axb5 15 ♞xb5 ♜xc1+ 16 ♛xc1 ♛a5+ 17 ♛d2 ♜a8 18 ♛xa5 ♜xa5 19 a3! ♝xb3 20 ♚f2 ♝a4 21 ♜b1, Tukmakov–Vaganian, USSR 1984, and now 21 ... ♝xb5 22 ♜xb5 ♜xa3 is a simple draw. Therefore White should prefer **13 0-0**, when **13 ... ♛a5** 14 f3 transposes to the next note, while **13 ... b5** 14 cxb5 axb5 15 ♝xb5 ♛a5 (15 ... ♜xc3 16 ♛xc3 ♞xe4 17 ♛e3) 16 ♝d3 also seems good for White, e.g. 16 ... ♜xc3 17 ♛xc3 ♛xc3 18 ♜xc3 ♞xe4 19 ♜xe4 ♝xc3 20 ♝xe7.

11 ♛d2 0-0

After 11 ... ♜c8 12 f3! Black is in a rather awkward situation since he has the wrong rook on c8 if he wants to castle. The point is that with the f-rook on c8 White is

never threatening ♞d5, because after the sequence ... ♛xd2 ♞xe7+ ♚f8 White just loses his knight. With the a-rook on c8, however, Black will sooner or later have to waste time meeting this threat. So **12 ... 0-0** 13 b3 a6 14 0-0, for example, is better for White than the positions in the note to 10 ♜c1. It is also too dangerous to take the c-pawn, for example **12 ... ♝xc4** 13 ♞d5! ♛xa2 14 0-0 ♞xd5 15 ♜xc4! ♜xc4 16 ♛xd5 ♜a4 17 ♝b5+ ♚f8 18 ♜c1! and in Geller–Stean, Teesside 1975 Black resigned because of 18 ... ♝d4+ 19 ♛xd4! ♜xd4 20 ♝h6+ mating. In fact White had an even more convincing win by 14 ♞b4, since 14 ... ♛b3 15 ♝d1 traps the queen.

If Black doesn't castle he soon runs out of things to do, e.g. 12 ... a6 13 b3 b5 14 ♞d5! (as mentioned earlier, ... b5 makes this a much better proposition) ♛xd2+ 15 ♚xd2 ♝xd5 16 cxd5 ♚d7 17 a4 h6 18 ♝e3 ♜xc1 19 ♜xc1 ♜b8 20 ♜c6 with a very good ending for White, Nunn–Reuben, London 1978.

12 f3 ♜fc8
13 b3

By securely defending c4 and e4 White has prevented any tricks based on an immediate ... b5 so Black has nothing better than to prepare this thrust with ... a6.

13 ... a6
14 ♞a4

White chooses a favourable

moment to exchange queens. Black's last move weakened b6 and he must waste a tempo preventing White's knight fork.

14 ... ♛xd2+

After 14 ... ♛d8 White may either play 15 c5 (as suggested by Karpov) based on the idea 15 ... dxc5 16 ♛xd8+ ♖xd8 17 ♞b6 when 17 ... ♖ab8 allows 18 ♗f4, or continue more quietly by 15 ♗e3 ♖ab8?! (15 ... ♞d7) 16 ♗a7 ♖a8 17 ♗b6 ♛f8 18 ♗e3 ♖ab8 19 ♞b6 ♖c7 20 0-0 ♞d7 21 ♞d5 with an excellent position, Nunn–Blum, London 1979.

15 ♚xd2 *(96)*

96
B

15 ... ♖c6

After Black lost with this move in Karpov–Kavalek attention turned to 15 ... ♞d7, but this doesn't seem to be any better, for example 16 g4 ♚f8 17 h4 ♖c6 18 ♖c2 ♞c5 19 ♞c3 a5 20 ♞d5 ♖e8 21 ♗e3 ♗c8 22 h5 e6 23 ♞c3 f5 24 hxg6 hxg6 25 exf5 exf5 26 gxf5 ♗xf5 27 ♖cc1, Averbakh–Popov, Polanica Zdroj 1976, or 16 h4 (this is perhaps even stronger) ♚f8 17 h5 h6 (17 ... ♖ab8 18

hxg6 hxg6 19 ♞c3 is also good for White) 18 ♗e3 g5 19 g3 ♖cb8 20 ♞c3 b5 21 ♞d5!, Psakhis–Pigusov, USSR 1980 when in both cases White had a good ending. It is curious that the exchange of queens is just what White needs to start a kingside attack by h4–h5. The explanation is that Black's counterplay by ... b5 would be very dangerous with queens on the board, since it would lead to an attack against the centralized white king. With queens off this counterplay is relatively harmless.

16 ♞c3 ♖ac8

Karpov suggested 16 ... ♖e8 as a possible improvement, so as to trap White's bishop in case of 17 ♞d5 ♞d7 18 ♞xe7+?! ♖xe7 19 ♗xe7 f6 20 ♗d8 b6. 16 ... ♖cc8 was played in Sakharov–Pereira, corr. 1976, which finished in a draw after 17 ♞a4 ♖c6! I don't suppose Karpov would have agreed a draw if Kavalek had 'found' 16 ... ♖cc8!

17 ♞d5 ♚f8
18 ♗e3 ♞d7

Defending such an ending is an unpleasant task at the best of times, doubly so against Karpov. White has the choice of expanding on the queenside by a timely b4, or of gaining space on the other flank by g4 and h4, as in the note to Black's 15th move. Until White shows his hand Black can only wait.

19 h4 ♗xd5

Black resolves to do away with the dangerous knight. 19 ... h5 was well met by 20 ♘f4 and Karpov's suggestion of 19 ... f5 would require strong nerves in view of Black's king position.

| 20 | exd5 | ♖6c7 |
| 21 | h5 | ♔g8?! *(97)* |

This move is probably a mistake. 21 ... ♖e8 followed by ... e6 would have opened the position up for White's two bishops, but by activating his rooks on the central files Black would have developed counterplay against White's king.

| 22 | f4! |

Most players would have rejected this as it allows Black's knight to settle at e4 (supported by ... f5). Karpov, however, is actually aiming to provoke ... f5, which gives him the lever g4 by which he can prise open Black's kingside.

22	...	♘c5
23	♗g4	♘e4+
24	♔d3	f5
25	♗f3	b5

It looks as though Black's counterplay has got off the ground at last but White defuses it adroitly.

26	g4	bxc4+
27	♖xc4	♖xc4
28	bxc4	♘c5+

Black had little choice as he could not allow the white rook to occupy the b-file, nor could he play ... ♖b8 without losing a pawn at e4.

| 29 | ♗xc5! |

If there are rooks on the board opposite coloured bishops tend to lose their drawish influence. Here Black runs into trouble because his king is badly placed and he will have two or even three pawns stuck on white squares, where they cannot be defended by his bishop.

| 29 | ... | ♖xc5 |

Black plays for a counterattack by ... ♖a5. 29 ... dxc5 30 h6 ♗d4 31 ♖b1 is also unpleasant, the a6 pawn being particularly weak.

| 30 | h6 | ♗f8 |

It looks horrible to bury the bishop but Black lacked a reasonable alternative, for example 30 ... fxg4 (30 ... ♗f6 31 ♖b1 threatens 32 gxf5 gxf5 33 ♖b8+ ♔f7 34 ♗h5 mate) 31 ♗xg4 ♗f8 (31 ... ♗f6 32 ♗e6+ ♔f8 33 ♖b1) 32 ♗e6+ ♔h8 33 f5 ♖a5 34 ♖b1 ♖a3+ 35 ♔e2 ♖xa2+ 36 ♔f1 ♗xh6 37 f6 and the pawn slips through (37 ... exf6 38 ♖b8+ wins a piece).

| 31 | ♔c3 |

Karpov also analyses 31 g5 ♖a5 22 ♖b1 as good for White,

but the variations are by no means simple and in practice it is not surprising that he chose to prevent 31 ... ♖a5 by simple means (32 ♔b3, and the rook has to go back).

| 31 | ... | fxg4 |
| 32 | ♗xg4 *(98)* | |

98
B

| 32 | ... | ♔f7?! |

Black resolves to extract his king, even at the cost of the h7 pawn. Despite its dangerous appearance, he would probably have done better to try 32 ... ♖c7 33 ♗e6+ ♔h8 34 f5 ♖b7! (preventing 35 ♖b1 ♗xh6 36 f6 exf6 37 ♖b8+), when White finds it hard to make progress because of Black's attack on the h6 pawn.

| 33 | ♗e6+ | ♔f6 |
| 34 | ♗g8 | ♖c7 |

34 ... ♗xh6 35 ♖xh6 ♔g7 leads to a lost rook and pawn ending after 36 ♖xh7+ and 37 ♖xe7.

| 35 | ♗xh7 | e6 |

35 ... ♔f7 is refuted by 36 f5 g5 37 f6! exf6 38 ♗f5 ♔g8 39 h7+ ♔h8 40 ♖b1 and 41 ♖b8.

| 36 | ♗g8 | exd5 |
| 37 | h7 | |

Not 37 ♗xd5? ♖h7.

| 37 | ... | ♗g7? |

Loses by force. 37 ... ♖xc4+ 38 ♔d3 ♗g7 39 ♗xd5 (39 h8(♕) ♗xh8 40 ♖xh8 ♖c8 and 41 ... ♔g7) ♖c8 leads to the same position as the game but with White having a pawn less. Black would still be worse, but he would have chances of a draw.

38	♗xd5	♗h8
39	♔d3	♔f5
40	♔e3	♖e7+
41	♔f3	a5
42	a4	♖c7
43	♗e4+	♔f6
44	♖h6	♖g7

44 ... ♔g7 45 ♖xg6+ ♔xh7 46 ♖g1+ ♔h6 47 ♖h1+ and 48 ♖h7+ wins the rook.

| 45 | ♔g4 | **Resigns** |

Black is totally paralysed.

Game 24
Vaganian–Ivkov
Moscow 1985

1	e4	c5
2	♘f3	♘c6
3	d4	cxd4
4	♘xd4	g6
5	c4	♗g7
6	♗e3 *(99)*	
6	...	♘f6

Black can also play ... ♘h6 followed by ... f5, either with or without ... d6, but this idea does not equalize:

(1) **6 ... d6** 7 ♘c3 ♘h6 8 ♗e2 0-0 9 0-0 f5 10 exf5 gxf5 (10 ... ♘xd4 11 ♗xd4 ♗xd4 12 ♕xd4

99
B

♘xf5 13 ♕d2 ♗d7 was good for White after both 14 ♗f3, Tal–Kupreichik, Sochi 1970 and 14 ♗g4, Vilela–Estevez, Cienfuegos 1980) 11 f4 ♕b6 (11 ... ♗d7 12 ♕d2 ♘g4 13 ♗xg4 fxg4 14 ♘d5 is a little better for White, Szabo–Larsen, Vinkovci 1970) 12 ♘xf5 ♕xb2 13 ♘xh6+ ♗xh6 14 ♖c1 ♗g7 15 ♖c2 (15 ♘d5 sacrificing the a-pawn was possible) ♕a3 16 ♕d2 with an edge for White, Spassov–Nicevski, Sofia 1976.

(2) **6 ... ♘h6** 7 ♘c3 0-0 8 ♗e2 f5 9 exf5 ♗xd4 10 ♗xh6 ♖xf5 11 0-0 d6 (11 ... ♕b6 is met by 12 ♘d5!) 12 ♗f3 (12 ♕d2 ♕a5 13 ♔h1 ♗f7 14 f4 was also promising in Shamkovich–Vasyukov, USSR 1965) ♗g7 13 ♗e3 ♗d7 14 ♖e1 b6 15 ♗e4 ♖f7 16 ♗g5! ♗f6 17 ♗xf6 ♖xf6 18 ♕d2 ♕f8 19 ♖ad1 ♖d8 20 ♘d5 with a clear plus for White, Kudrin–I. Ivanov, New York 1983.

In this note we have seen a pawn structure with white pawns on c4 and f4 against black d-, e- and f-pawns. This structure arises frequently in the Maroczy Bind

and it is almost always good for White. Black's problem is that any central pawn advance leaves him with either a backward pawn or hanging pawns, while if the pawns stay where they are White can just build up pressure down the d- and e-files. Similar comments apply in the case where Black plays ... f5 and recaptures on f5 with a piece. The hanging pawns are a more important factor than the temporary piece activity Black obtains.

7 ♘c3 0-0

Black has a major alternative in 7 ... ♘g4, which has recently become more popular. This new respectability has been based partly on an original idea for Black involving kingside pawn expansion, and partly on a realization that the older lines are not so bad for Black as had been thought. White has his typical space advantage, but Black's position is solid and Larsen in particular has achieved quite good results for Black.

After 7 ... ♘g4 8 ♕xg4 ♘xd4 (or 8 ... ♗xd4 9 ♗xd4 ♘xd4 10 0-0-0 e5 11 ♕g3 d6 12 f4 f6 13 f5! ♔f7 14 ♘b5 ♘xb5 15 cxb5 with an excellent position for White, Mestel–Karlsson, Las Palmas 1982) 9 ♕d1 *(100)* Black has three possibilities:

(1) **9 ... e5** 10 ♗d3 (this gives White a positional advantage with no risk, but there seems nothing wrong with the older tactical line 10 ♘b5 0-0 11 ♕d2!

100
B

101
B

♕h4 12 ♗d3 d5 13 cxd5 ♘xb5 14 ♗xb5 ♕xe4 15 0-0 ♖d8 16 ♖fd1 when 16 ... ♗e6 fails to 17 f3 ♕xd5 18 ♕e2 trapping Black's queen) 0-0 11 0-0 d6 12 ♕d2 ♗e6 (12 ... f5 13 exf5 gxf5 14 f4 ♘c6 15 ♖ad1 ♕e7 16 ♗e2 ♘d4 17 ♗xd4 exd4 18 ♘d5 gave White a clear plus, Andersson–Rogers, Malta 1980) 13 ♖ac1 a6 14 b3 ♖c8 15 f3 and now both **15 ... f5** 16 exf5 gxf5 17 f4 ♕f6 18 ♘e2 ♖cd8 19 ♘xd4 exd4 20 ♗f2, Ghitescu–Radovici, Romania Ch. 1977, and **15 ... ♕a5** 16 ♖fd1 f5 17 exf5 ♘xf5 18 ♗e4, Tal–Partos, Nice 1974, were very good for White.

(2) **9 ... ♘c6** 10 ♕d2 ♕a5 11 ♖c1 0-0 12 ♗e2 d6 13 0-0 ♗e6 14 b3 ♖ac8 15 f4 with a good position for White, Polugayevsky–Suetin, Kislovodsk 1972.

(3) **9 ... ♘e6** (the main line) 10 ♖c1 *(101)* and now:

(3a) **10 ... ♕a5** and now it is unclear whether the bishop should be developed at e2 or d3:

(3a1) **11 ♗d3** with a further branch:

(3a11) **11 ... ♗xc3+** 12 ♖xc3

♕xa2 13 ♕c1 ♕a5 14 c5 is extremely dangerous for Black.

(3a12) **11 ... d6** 12 0-0 (better than 12 ♕d2 ♗d7 13 0-0 ♘c6 14 ♖fe1 0-0 15 ♗h6 ♕e5! 16 ♗xg7 ♕xg7 17 ♖cd1 ♘c5 18 ♗f1 a5 with equality, Nogueiras–Korchnoi, Montpellier 1985) 0-0 13 ♗b1 ♗d7 14 f4 ♘c5 15 ♘d5 with advantage to White in Mednis–D. Byrne, US Ch. 1973.

(3a13) **11 ... b6** 12 0-0 ♗b7 13 f4!? (probably better than 13 ♕d2 g5 14 ♖fd1 d6 when 15 f3 ♗e5 16 ♔h1 ♗f4 17 ♗xf4 ♘xf4 18 ♗f1 ♘e6 19 a3 ♕e5 20 ♘d5 h5 21 b4 ♔f8 22 ♖e1 ♖c8 was equal in Popovic–Cebalo, Yugoslavia 1988, and 15 a3 h5 16 ♖c2 ♗d4 17 b4 ♕e5 18 ♘d5 ♗xe3 19 fxe3 ♖c8 20 ♖f1 ♘g7 21 ♕f2 f6 was unclear in Ljubojevic–Korchnoi, Tilburg 1987) 0-0 14 ♗b1 d6 15 ♖f2 ♖ac8 16 ♘d5 ♗xd5 17 exd5 ♘c5 18 a3 and White is better, A. Rodriguez–Hernandez, Cuba Ch. 1988.

(3a2) **11 ♗e2** b6 12 0-0 ♗b7 13 f3 g5 (Larsen's plan increases the black-squared pressure and reserves e5 for the queen, but the obvious danger is that Black's king has to stay in the centre) 14 ♖f2! (a number of other games had continued with ♕d2, but the rook transfer to d2 appears the best way of meeting Black's double-edged plan) h5 15 ♗f1 ♕e5 16 ♖d2 d6 17 ♘d5 ♔f8 18 b4 ♗h6 19 ♕b3 g4 20 ♗xh6+ ♖xh6 21 ♕e3 ♕g7 22 f4 with a distinct advantage for White, Short–Larsen, Hastings 1987/8.

(3b) **10 ... b6** 11 ♗d3 (11 b4 is also good, for example 11 ... ♗b7 12 ♗d3 0-0 13 0-0 ♘d4 14 ♗b1 ♘c6 15 a3 d6 16 ♕d3 ♖c8 17 f4 and White has consolidated his space advantage, Suba–Taimanov, Bucharest 1979, or 13 ... ♖c8 14 f4 with attacking chances for White) ♗b7 12 0-0 ♕b8 (Black intends a variant of Larsen's plan to dominate the black squares on the kingside; normal development would lead to positions similar to Suba–Taimanov above) 13 ♕d2 ♕d6 14 ♘d5 g5 15 b4 h5 16 ♖fd1 ♗e5 17 h3 ♗f4 18 ♗f1! and Black's attack has become bogged down while White has all sorts of threats against Black's king and queen, Mochalov–Kapengut, USSR 1st League 1976.

(3c) **10 ... d6** 11 b4! (when Black's knight is on e6 White should in general aim to play b4 as quickly as possible, preventing Black cementing his knight on c5 by ... a5) 0-0 12 ♗e2 and now:

(3c1) **12 ... b6** 13 ♕d2 (13 0-0 may be better, for example 13 ...

♗b7 14 ♘d5 ♕d7 15 ♗g4! f5 16 ♗h3 ♘c7 17 ♘xc7 ♕xc7 18 exf5 gxf5 19 c5! with a fine game for White, Adorjan–Larsen, Hastings 1986/7) ♗b7 14 f3 (14 ♘d5 ♘c7! was played in Rogers–Hernandez, Calcutta 1988, and now 15 0-0 e6 16 ♘xc7 ♕xc7 17 f3 would have kept an edge for White) f5 15 exf5 gxf5 16 ♘d5 ♖f7 17 0-0 ♘f8 18 ♖fd1 with advantage to White, Smejkal–Radulov, Skara 1980.

(3c2) **12 ... a5** 13 a3 axb4 14 axb4 ♗d7 (14 ... ♖a3 15 ♘d5) 15 0-0 ♗c6 16 ♕d2 ♖a3 (16 ... ♗xc3 17 ♕xc3 ♗xe4 fails to 18 ♗h6 ♖e8 19 ♖ce1 followed by ♗g4 with a catastrophe at g7) 17 ♘d5 ♔h8 18 ♗b6 ♕d7 19 f4 with a fine position for White, Portisch–Pfleger, Manila 1974.

(3d) **10 ... 0-0** 11 b4 will quickly transpose into 3b or 3c.

8 ♗e2 *(102)* d6

Black may try to do without this move:

(1) **8 ... a5** 9 0-0 a4 10 c5!? (an attempt at outright refutation; 10 ♘db5 would be similar to 9 ... a5 below) d5 11 cxd6 ♕xd6 12 ♘db5

♕b4 (12 ... ♕xd1 13 ♖axd1 gives White some endgame advantage) 13 a3 ♕a5 14 f4 e5 15 fxe5 ♘xe5 16 ♖xf6! ♗xf6 17 ♘d5 ♗d8? (17 ... ♖a6! 18 ♖c1! ♗d7 19 ♖c5 ♕d8 is better, although White has an ominous initiative) 18 ♗d4! f6 19 ♗c3 ♕a6 20 ♘bc7 ♕a7+ 21 ♗d4 ♕b8 22 ♘xa8 with a clear plus for White, Nunn–Haik, Paris 1983.

(2) **8 ... b6** (an important alternative) 9 0-0 ♗b7 10 f3 (when Black develops his bishop at b7 the extra protection of the e-pawn afforded by f3 is usually a good idea) and now Black has an extensive range of possibilities:

(2a) **10 ... ♘h5** 11 ♘xc6! ♗xc6 (11 ... dxc6 12 c5 is good for White) 12 ♖c1 f5 13 exf5 gxf5 14 f4 ♘f6 15 ♗f3 ♖c8 16 b3 ♕e8 17 ♘d5 ♕f7 18 ♘xf6+ ♕xf6 19 ♖c2 ♗xf3?! 20 ♖xf3 d6 21 ♖d2 ♔h8 22 ♗d4 gave White his standard favourable position in Nunn–Ristoja, Malta 1980.

(2b) **10 ... d6** (this is inconsistent with the choice of ... b6) 11 ♕d2 ♕d7 12 a4!? e6 13 ♖fd1 ♖fd8 14 ♘xc6 ♕xc6 15 a5 bxa5 16 ♘b5 with unpleasant threats to d6, a7 and a5, Gheorghiu–Bellon, Las Palmas 1976.

(2c) **10 ... ♖c8** 11 ♕d2 ♘h5 (11 ... ♖e8 12 ♖ac1 ♕c7 13 b4! ♘h5 14 ♘xc6 ♗xc6 15 ♘d5 ♕b8 16 f4 ♘f6 17 ♗f3 d6 18 ♗d4 was very good for White in Nunn–Karlsson, Helsinki 1981) 12 ♖fd1 ♘e5 13 b3 f5 14 exf5 gxf5 15

♘d5! ♕e8?!, Kir. Georgiev–Kristensen, Saint John Open 1988, and now 16 f4! ♗xd5 (16 ... ♘g4 17 ♘xf5 ♘xe3 18 ♘xg7 ♖xg7 19 ♕xe3 wins) 17 cxd5 ♘g4 18 ♘xf5! ♗xa1 19 ♖xg4 ♘f6 (19 ... ♗f6 20 d6! e6 21 ♘e7+ ♗xe7 22 dxe7 ♖f6 23 ♕xd7 wins and 19 ... ♗c3 20 ♕d3 ♘g7 21 d6 are no better) 20 ♘h6+ ♔g7 21 ♖xa1 ♔xh6 22 f5+ ♔g7 23 ♗h6+ ♔h8 24 ♗xf8 ♘xg4 25 ♕d4+ ♘f6 26 ♗h6 wins for White.

(2d) **10 ... ♘xd4** 11 ♗xd4 d6 12 ♕d2 ♘d7 13 ♗xg7 (13 ♗e3 is promising) ♔xg7 14 f4 ♖c8 15 ♖ad1 ♘f6 16 e5 dxe5 17 fxe5 ♘g8 18 ♕e3! with some advantage for White, Cvetkovic–Cebalo, Yugoslavia 1985.

(2e) **10 ... ♘e8** 11 ♕d2 ♘c7 12 ♖ad1 ♘e6 13 ♘db5 d6 14 ♘d5 ♖b8 15 f4 ♘c5 16 ♗f3 a6 17 ♘d4 ♘xd4 18 ♗xd4 ♗xd4+ 19 ♕xd4 b5, Agapov–Kimelfeld, USSR 1985, and now 20 e5 would have kept some advantage for White.

(2f) **10 ... e6** 11 ♕d2 (11 ♘db5 is probably also good, e.g. 11 ... d5 12 cxd5 exd5 13 exd5 ♘e7 14 d6 ♘f5 15 ♗f2 ♘e8 16 d7 ♘f6 17 g4 ♘e7 18 ♗h4 with advantage, A. Rodriguez–Pinal, Sagua la Grande 1984) d5 12 ♘xc6 ♗xc6 13 cxd5 exd5 14 e5 ♘d7 15 f4 ♘c5 16 ♖ad1! f6 (16 ... ♘e4 17 ♘xe4 fxe4 18 ♕d6! ♗b7 19 ♗c4 is also unpleasant) 17 ♘xd5 fxe5 18 ♗c4 ♔h8 19 fxe5 ♖xf1+ (19 ... ♗xe5 20 ♗d4 ♕d6 21 ♗xe5+ ♕xe5 22 ♖fe1 ♘e4 23 ♖xe4! Resigns, Kuporosov–Jakovic, USSR 1984) 20 ♖xf1 ♕h4 21 ♖f4! ♕h5 22 ♘e7 ♗b7 23 b4 ♘e4 24 ♕d7 ♖b8 25 ♘c8! ♖xc8 26 ♕xb7 ♖d8 27 ♕xe4 ♗xe5 28 ♗e2 Resigns, Kuporosov–Malishauskas, USSR 1985.

9   0-0 *(103)*

103
B

9   ...   ♗d7

Or:

(1) **9 ... a5** (certainly not 9 ... ♘g4 losing a piece after 10 ♗xg4 ♗xg4 11 ♘xc6) 10 f3 ♘d7 11 ♘db5 ♘c5 12 ♕d2 a4 13 ♖fd1 ♕a5 14 ♖ac1 ♗e6 15 ♘d5 ♕xd2 16 ♖xd2 ♗xd5? (16 ... ♖fd8 is only slightly better for White) 17 cxd5 ♘b4 18 ♖xc5! dxc5 19 ♗xc5 ♘xa2 20 ♗xe7 and Black is in trouble, Andersson–Larsen, Linares 1983.

(2) **9 ... ♖e8** (another Larsen idea) and now:

(2a) **10 ♖b1** a6 11 ♕d2 ♗d7 12 ♖fd1 ♖c8 13 f3 ♘xd4 14 ♗xd4 ♗e6 15 ♘d5 ♘xd5 16 cxd5 ♗xd4+ 17 ♕xd4 ♗d7 18 ♖bc1 ♕a5 with equality, Speelman–Larsen, Hastings 1988/9.

(2b) **10 f3** ♘d7 11 ♕d2 ♘c5 (taking twice on d4 is also pos-

sible) 12 ♖fd1 ♕a5 13 ♖ab1 ♘xd4 14 ♗xd4 ♗xd4+ 15 ♕xd4 ♘e6 16 ♕f2 ♗d7 and White has no advantage, Andersson–Larsen, Naestved 1985.

(2c) **10 a3** ♗d7 11 f3 a6 12 b4 ♖c8 13 ♖c1 ♘xd4 14 ♗xd4 ♗h6! 15 ♖c2 ♗e6 and Black is at least equal, Short–Larsen, Naestved 1985.

(2d) **10 ♕d2** ♘g4, 10 ♖c1 ♘xd4 11 ♗xd4 ♗h6 and 10 f4 e5 are other points of Larsen's move, so what is the best answer? Probably White should play 10 ♘c2, avoiding the knight exchange and preparing solid development by ♖c1.

10   ♕d2

It is also possible to move the knight on d4, thereby frustrating Black's plan of ... ♘xd4 and ... ♗c6. In Korchnoi–Soos, Rome 1982, White continued 10 ♘b3 ♘a5 (10 ... a5 11 a4 ♘b4 12 f3 ♗c6 13 ♕d2 ♖c8 14 ♔h1 ♗d7 15 ♘d5 was also better for White, Tarjan–Strauss, USA 1982) 11 f3 ♘xb3 12 axb3 a6 13 b4 ♗e6 14 ♕d2 ♖c8 15 b3 ♘d7 16 ♖a2, while Schmidt–Kagen, Lucerne 1982, went 10 ♘c2 ♗e6 11 ♕d2 a5 12 f4 a4 13 ♖ab1 ♗g4 14 ♗d3 ♗c8 15 h3 ♘d7 16 ♗e2 and in both cases White had a good position. It could well be that these lines are as strong as the traditional continuations 10 ♖c1 and 10 ♕d2, but they do not seem to have been tested in recent years.

A separate question is whether White should play 10 ♖c1 or 10 d2. I have preferred the latter move for two reasons. Firstly, the rook on c1 is sometimes vulnerable to unwelcome attacks by ... ♘xd4 and ... ♗h6, and secondly White often starts a queenside advance by a3 and b4 later on. If Black plays ... a5 White needs a rook on b1 to force through b4, but playing the rook to c1 and then to b1 loses a tempo. The lines after ♖c1 and ♕d2 are quite similar, so the material from the first edition of the book is also worth reviewing, but here we shall only examine the lines which follow 10 ♕d2.

10 ...   ♘xd4

10 ... ♖c8 11 f3 a6 12 ♖ac1 ♘xd4 13 ♗xd4 ♗e6 14 b3 is passive and White has a very comfortable position, Smejkal–Diez del Corral, Skopje Ol. 1972.

11 ♗xd4   ♗c6
12 f3   a5

The move order is flexible, but White always answers ... ♘d7 by ♗e3 (to avoid freeing exchanges) and ... a5 by b3 (or else Black plays ... a4 followed by ... ♕a5, with an active position).

13 b3   ♘d7

Or 13 ... ♖e8 (13 ... ♘h5?! 14 ♗e3! f5 15 exf5 gxf5 16 f4 was good for White in Kavalek–Larsen, USA–Nordic match 1986) 14 ♖fd1 ♘d7 15 ♗e3 ♘c5 16 ♖ac1 (16 ♖ab1 appears more consistent) ♕b6 17 ♘b5 ♖ec8 18 ♕e1 (18 ♘d4 is better) ♗xb5! 19 cxb5 ♗h6 with equality, Arnason–Karlsson, Helsinki 1986.

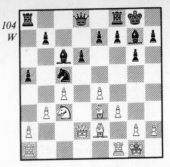

14 ♗e3   ♘c5 (104)
15 ♖ab1

In order to make progress White must expel the knight from c5, and so he needs to play a3 and b4. 15 ♖ab1 appears the most logical, and this intuitive assessment is supported by the fact that after the alternative 15 ♖ac1 (this position can also arise via 10 ♖c1) ♕b6 (15 ... f5 16 exf5 gxf5 17 ♘d5 ♖f7 18 ♖fd1 b6! 19 ♗g5 ♖a7 was unclear in Vaganian–Yudashin, USSR Ch. 1988) 16 ♘b5 ♖fc8 17 ♖fd1 ♕d8 18 ♘d4 (18 ♗f1 ♕f8 19 ♘c3 b6 20 ♘d5 ♖ab8 21 ♖b1 ♗e5 22 ♗h6 ♗g7 23 ♗g5 ♖b7 24 ♖e1 ♘e6 25 ♗e3 ♘c5! was level, Sax–Petursson, Reykjavik 1988), Nunn–Velimirovic, Dubai Ol. 1986, Black can play 18 ... ♗d7 19 ♖b1 ♘e6 20 ♘xe6 ♗xe6 with equality (instead of 18 ... ♕f8?! 19 ♖b1 ♗f6 20 a3 ♕g7 21 b4 axb4 22 axb4 ♘e6 23 ♘xe6 fxe6 24 b5 ♗e8 25 f4 with a clear plus for White in the game).

15 ...   ♕b6

Or 15 ... b6 (after 15 ... e6 16 ♗d1! intending ♘e2–d4, a3 and b4 Black's panic reaction 16 ... f5

17 exf5 ♖xf5 18 ♘e2 was good for White in Tringov–Haik, Vrnjacka Banja 1986) 16 ♗d1 (White's problem is that the immediate a3 may be met by ... a4; the idea of ♗d1 is to be able to take the Black knight when it arrives at b3, but White has other ways to nullify ... a4, for example with the slow preparatory plan of ♖fc1–c2, ♗f1 and ♕f2 to line up against the weak pawn on b6) ♕b8 17 a3 ♖c8 18 ♘d5 ♗xd5?! (probably bad, but White is slightly better in any case) 19 exd5 a4 20 b4 ♘b3 21 ♕e2 with an excellent position for White, Anand–Larsen, Cannes 1989.

16   ♖fc1

After 16 ♘b5 (not 16 a3? ♘xb3) ♖fc8 17 ♖fd1 ♕d8 18 ♘d4 ♕f8 19 a3 (19 ♗f1 may be better, but I doubt if White has more than a tiny edge) ♗d7! (not 19 ... ♗f6? 20 b4 axb4 21 axb4 ♘e6 22 ♘xe6 fxe6 23 f4 with the same advantage for White as in Nunn–Velimirovic above) 20 b4 axb4 21 axb4 ♘e6 22 ♖a1 ♖xa1 23 ♖xa1 ♖a8 24 ♖xa8 ♕xa8 25 ♘xe6 ♗xe6 Black is completely equal, Jansa–Petursson, Naestved 1988.

16   ...   ♖fc8
17   ♖c2

Again this is useful preparation for a3 and b4. Now Black cannot meet 18 a3 by 18 ... ♘xb3 because 19 ♘d1! wins material.

17   ...   ♕d8

There is no point to 17 ... ♕b4 because after 18 ♕c1 Black will be driven back by a3 with great loss of time.

18   ♗f1   ♗e5

White intends ♕f2, followed by a3 and b4, so Black has to organize some counterplay. With ... ♗e5 he hopes to become active with ... e6 and ... ♕h4, but the exposed bishop on e5 is a target which causes White to switch plans away from his queenside pawn advance to a more aggressive idea.

19   ♘d1!?

The knight transfer to h6, which gains time along the way when ♘g4 hits the bishop, is not a very thematic approach, but chess cannot always be played according to the recipe book.

19   ...   ♕e8 (105)

Preparing ... b5 is the most natural way to counter White's slow build-up towards a kingside attack. Moreover the queen defends the f7 pawn which might come under fire after ♘f2–g4–h6+.

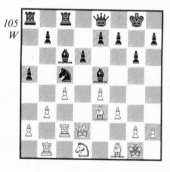

105 W

20   ♘f2   b5?!

It would have been better to

play 20 . . . ♗g7, so as to meet 21 ♘g4 by 21 . . . h5. Then White could hardly venture into the lion's den by 22 ♘h6+ ♔h7, so the knight would have to return to f2. After 20 . . . ♗g7 White should switch plans again by 21 ♘d3 b6 22 ♕f2, followed by a3 and b4.

21	♘g4	♗g7
22	cxb5	♗xb5
23	♘h6+	♔f8

Unfortunately Black has to go to f8 because 23 . . . ♔h8 loses a pawn after 24 ♘xf7+, while 23 . . . ♗xh6 24 ♗xh6 gives White a permanent advantage.

24	♗xb5	♕xb5
25	♕d5	♕e8
26	e5!	♖d8?!

In a difficult position Black fails to offer the most resistance. He should try to give up a pawn to reach an ending in which the off-side knight on h6 gives White problems. Therefore 26 . . . ♘e6 was the best (26 . . . ♖a6 27 exd6 is bad since 27 . . . ♖xd6 28 ♕xf7+! wins a clear pawn), with the idea 27 ♖xc8 ♖xc8 28 exd6 exd6 29 ♕xd6+ ♕e7 30 ♕xe7+ ♔xe7 with excellent counterplay. White should prefer 29 ♘g4!, when the weak pawns on d6 and a5 make Black's position unattractive, but his chances would certainly be much better than in the game.

27	exd6	exd6
28	♖e1	♖ac8?

The final collapse. 28 . . . ♘e6 was necessary to meet the threat of 29 ♖xc5, when 29 ♘g4 gives White a positional advantage but nothing decisive.

29	♖xc5!	♖xc5
30	♕xc5	Resigns

8   Taimanov Variation

The first moves of this system run 1 e4 c5 2 ♘f3 e6 3 d4 cxd4 4 ♘xd4 ♘c6 (or 2 ... ♘c6 and 4 ... e6). In a way this resembles the Kan Variation, since Black keeps the f8–b4 diagonal open for his bishop, but here White cannot play ♗d3, so there are fewer options for the first player. The variation I am recommending for White, 5 ♘b5, is the most obvious way to exploit the substitution of ... ♘c6 for a6. The main line leads to a kind of Maroczy Bind position in which White's knight is on a3 instead of d4. This provides more support for the c4 pawn, so White is not normally forced to play b3, but on the minus side the knight is distinctly offside on a3 and in many lines White tries to bring it back via b1 or c2. Black's best strategy is watchful waiting as in the Maroczy Bind. One difference between this line and the Maroczy Bind is that Black's bishop is on e7 instead of g7, so that White may be able to play for a direct kingside attack by advancing his g- and h-pawns. As usual, such a strategy carries many risks, but with the knights on a3 and c3 holding up Black's counterplay by ... b5 or ... d5 White may have enough time to break through.

Game 25
Chandler–Pritchett
British Ch. 1985

1	e4	c5
2	♘f3	e6
3	d4	cxd4
4	♘xd4	♘c6
5	♘b5	*(106)*

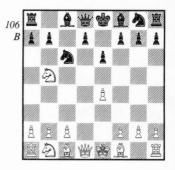

106
B

5	...	d6

Not 5 ... ♗c5 (5 ... ♘f6 6 ♘1c3 transposes to Chapter 9) 6 ♗f4 ♕f6 7 ♕c1 ♗f8 8 ♘1c3 when both **8 ... ♘ge7** 9 ♗e3! b6 10 ♕d2 ♗xe3 11 ♕xe3 d5 12 0-0-0 a6 13 exd5 exd5 14 ♘c7 d4 15 ♖xd4 ♘xd4 16 ♘xa8, Gufeld–Plaskett, Hastings 1986/7 and **8 ... a6** 9 ♗d6+ ♗xd6 10 ♘xd6 ♕d4 11 ♕f4 (11 ♕d1 is also good) ♘f6 12 ♖d1 ♕b4 13 ♕d2, Mokry–Plaskett, Trnava 1984, gave White a clear advantage.

6 c4 ♘f6

Black can also play 6 ... a6 7 ♘5c3 ♘f6, when White can transpose to the main line by playing 8 ♘a3, but in practice White has usually chosen to try exploiting Black's move order by developing his knight to d2 instead. After 6 ... a6 7 ♘5c3 ♘f6 8 ♗e2 ♗e7 9 0-0 0-0 10 ♗e3 Black has tried:

(1) **10 ... ♕c7?!** (usually wrong in this system, since after White plays ♖c1 Black will be in danger from tactics based on ♘b5 or ♘d5) 11 ♘a3 (reasonable now that Black is committed to a bad line) b6 12 ♕e1 ♗b7, Dieks–Marjanovic, Manila 1974, and now 13 ♖c1 followed by f3 and ♕f2 would be good for White.

(2) **10 ... ♗d7** 11 f4 ♕b8 12 ♘d2 b6 13 a3 ♘a7 14 ♗f3 ♗c6 15 ♘b3 ♘d7 16 ♘d4 ♗b7 17 f5 with a slight plus for White, Karpov–Taimanov, USSR Ch. 1976.

(3) **10 ... ♖e8** 11 a3 ♗f8 12 ♕b3 ♘d7 13 ♘d2 b6 14 ♘f3 ♗b7 15 ♖fd1 and again White is slightly better, Bronstein–Lombardy, Teesside 1975.

(4) **10 ... b6** 11 ♕b3 (the immediate 11 ♘d2 is also good, and after 11 ... ♖b8 12 ♖c1 ♗b7 13 ♕b3 ♘d7 14 ♖fd1 ♘ce5 15 f4! ♘g6 16 ♗f3! ♕c7 17 f5! ♘ge5 18 ♘d4 ♘c5 19 ♕c2 White was doing well in Gufeld–Hort, Dortmund 1983) ♖b8 12 ♖d1 ♕c7 13 a3!? ♗d7 14 ♘d2 ♖fc8 (14 ... ♘a5 is just slightly better for White) 15 ♖dc1! ♕d8 16 ♕d1

♖c7, Psakhis–Holm, Plovdiv 1983 and now 17 b4! intending ♘b3 is good for White according to Psakhis.

7 ♘1c3

Now 7 ♘5c3 makes no sense, for Black gains a tempo by missing out ... a6.

7 ... a6

After 7 ... ♗e7 8 ♗f4 e5 9 ♗g5 a6 10 ♗xf6 gxf6 11 ♘a3 ♘d4 12 ♘c2 ♘xc2+ 13 ♕xc2 White has an evident positional advantage, Chiburdanidze–Taborov, USSR 1979, so Black must push the knight away.

8 ♘a3 *(107)*

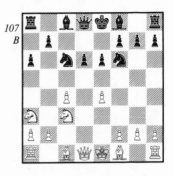

8 ... ♗e7

The speculative pawn sacrifice **8 ... d5** 9 cxd5 exd5 10 exd5 ♘b4 was played a few times, but is now considered bad after 11 ♗e2, for example:

(1) **11 ... ♗c5** 12 ♗e3! ♗xe3 13 ♕a4+ ♘d7 (13 ... b5 14 ♕xb4 ♗b6 15 0-0 ♗a5 16 ♗xb5+! axb5 17 ♖fe1+ ♔d7 18 ♕xb5+ ♔c7 19 d6+! ♕xd6 20 ♖ac1 wins for White, while 13 ...

♗d7 14 ♕xb4 ♕b6 15 ♕xb6 ♗xb6 16 ♘c4 ♗d4 17 ♖d1 leaves Black with nothing for the pawn) 14 ♕xb4 (14 fxe3 ♕h4+ 15 g3 ♕e7 16 ♖d1 is also good) ♗c5 15 ♕e4+ ♔f8 16 0-0 b5 17 ♘c2 and Black has no real compensation for the pawn, Karpov–van der Wiel, Brussels 1986.

(2) **11 ... ♗e7** 12 ♗f3 ♗f5 13 0-0 0-0 14 ♘c4 ♗c5 15 ♗e3 ♗d6 16 ♘xd6 ♕xd6 17 ♕d2 ♖fd8 18 ♖ad1 ♘d3 19 ♗e2 ♘xd5 20 ♗xd3 ♘xc3 21 ♗xf5 ♘xd1 22 ♖xd1 ♕xd2 23 ♖xd2 and White won the ending in Lawton–Gayson, British Ch. 1987.

Some Black players have experimented with delayed castling, but this increases the danger that White will gain time by missing out ♗e3, for example **8 ... b6** 9 ♗e2 ♗b7 10 f4 (10 0-0 is less accurate, because after 10 ... ♘b8! White has no good way to defend the e4 pawn, since the reply 11 f3 cuts out the plan based on f4 recommended in this game) ♘b8 11 ♗f3 ♘bd7 12 0-0 ♗e7 13 ♕e2 0-0 14 g4!? d5 15 exd5 exd5 16 g5 ♖e8 17 ♕g2 ♘e4, Geller–I. Sokolov, Panchevo 1987, and now 18 cxd5 is good for White according to Geller.

9 ♗e2 0-0
10 0-0 b6

By far the most popular move. The alternative is to play for ... b5 directly in order to save time, but the problem is that a premature ... b5 just leaves Black with a weak b-pawn, for example:

(1) **10 ... ♖b8** 11 ♗e3 ♕a5 12 ♘c2 ♗d7 13 f4 b5 14 cxb5 axb5 15 a3 ♖fc8 16 g4 ♕d8 17 g5 ♘e8 18 ♗xb5 ♘a5 19 a4, Mednis–Schmidt, Nice 1977, and Black does not have enough for the pawn.

(2) **10 ... ♗d7** 11 ♗e3 ♕b8 (**11 ... ♘e5** 12 f4 ♘g6 13 ♕e1 ♗c6 14 ♗f3 ♕e8 15 ♘c2 ♖c8 16 a4 a5 17 g3 ♘d7 18 h4 gave White attacking chances in Yudashin–Osnos, USSR 1986, while **11 ... ♖b8** 12 f4 ♕a5 13 ♘c2 b5 14 cxb5 axb5 15 a3 is also slightly better for White) 12 f3 ♘a7, Agapov–Taimanov, USSR 1987, and now 13 ♕d3!? ♗c6 14 ♖fd1 ♘d7 15 ♗f1 ♘e5 16 ♕e2 gives White an edge according to Agapov. If Black cannot force through ... b5 then his piece deployment looks very strange.

11 ♗e3 *(108)*

11 ... ♘e5

This is a major branch. Black has a number of possibilities, but since this line is governed largely by general principles rather than specific variations, we do not waste time considering numerous very similar lines. Instead we only seriously examine two lines, 11 ... ♗b7 and 11 ... ♘e5, which represent quite different plans. In the latter case Black intends repositioning his knight to d7, opening the diagonal for the b7 bishop. This line plans ... d5 at some stage. 11 ... ♗b7 is a more restrained line; Black concentrates on developing his pieces and waits to see what White intends. After 11 ... ♗b7 (or **11 ... ♗d7** 12 f3 ♕b8 13 ♕e1 ♖a7 14 ♕f2 ♖b7 15 ♖fd1 ♖d8 16 ♖ac1 ♗e8 17 ♔h1 ♘d7 18 ♕f1 ♗f6 19 ♘ab1 ♘c5 20 f4 ♗e7 21 b3 h6 22 ♖d2 ♖c8 23 ♖cd1 ♖d8, Matulovic–W. Schmidt, Vrnjacka Banja 1983, and now 24 ♖b2! is good for White, while **11 ... ♖e8** 12 ♖c1 ♘e5 13 f4 ♘ed7 14 ♗f3 will probably transpose to the main line of the game) 12 ♕b3 ♘d7 (12 ... ♘a5?! 13 ♕xb6 ♘xe4 14 ♘xe4 ♗xe4 15 ♕xd8 ♖xd8 16 ♖ad1 left Black under unpleasant pressure in Karpov–Kasparov, Moscow match 1984/5; nobody has cared to repeat this line) 13 ♖fd1 Black may play:

(1) **13 ... ♖c8** 14 ♖ac1 ♘a5 15 ♕a4 f5 16 exf5 ♖xf5 17 b4 ♗g5, Chandler–Kurajica, Sarajevo 1985, and now 18 ♗g4! ♗xe3 19 ♗xf5 ♗xc1 20 ♗xe6+ ♔h8 21 ♗xd7 is good for White according to Chandler, the point being that 21 ... ♕g5 22 ♘d5 ♖xc4 23 ♘xc4 ♘xc4 is met by 24 ♗h3!,

both defending g2 and threatening ♕e8 mate.

(2) **13 ... ♖e8** (a bit irrelevant) 14 ♖ac1 ♗f8 15 ♗f1 ♖c8 16 ♕c2 ♘ce5 17 h3 ♕c7 18 f3 with a typical slight plus for White, Karpov–Romanishin, USSR 1981.

(3) **13 ... ♖a7!?** 14 ♖d2 (14 ♘a4 ♘a5 doesn't achieve anything since 15 ♕c2 ♘c6 and 15 ♗xb6 ♘xb6 16 ♕xb6 ♕xb6 17 ♘xb6 ♗xe4 are not better for White) ♗a8 15 ♕d1 ♕b8 16 ♕f1 ♘f6, Nunn–Cebalo, Biel 1986, and now 17 f4 intending ♕f2 would have created awkward pressure against the b6 pawn.

(4) **13 ... ♕b8** 14 ♖ac1 ♗a8 15 ♖d2 ♖b7 16 ♕d1 ♕b8 17 ♕f1 ♘f6?! (Black's plan is similar to that in Nunn–Cebalo above, but this time White finds the right reply; 17 ... ♖c7 was more solid) 18 f4 ♖c7, A. Rodriguez–Kirov, Havana 1986, and now 19 ♕f2 ♖fc8 20 ♖cd1 followed by ♗f3 would, by defending b2 a second time, create a genuine threat to take on b6.

(5) **13 ... ♘c5** (the most important line) 14 ♕c2 *(109)* and now:

(5a) **14 ... ♗f6** 15 ♖ac1 and now:

(5a1) **15 ... ♘e5** 16 ♘ab1 ♕h4 17 g3 ♕f6 18 f4 ♗d4 19 ♕d2 e5 20 ♘d5 ♕d8 (20 ... ♕h6 21 ♘bc3 f5 22 exf5 ♖xf5 23 ♗g4 is good for White) 21 ♘bc3 ♗xe3+ (21 ... ♔h8 22 f5 ♘d7 23 ♗f3 ♗c5 24 ♔g2 f6 25 ♘e2 gave White the advantage in Karpov–

109
B

Olafsson, Amsterdam 1976) 22 ♕xe3 exf4 23 gxf4 ♖e8 24 b4 ♘d7 25 ♗f3 with a slight plus for White, Westerinen–Liberzon, Geneva 1977.

(5a2) **15 ...** ♗xc3 16 ♕xc3 ♘xe4 17 ♕d3 ♘e5 18 ♕d4 and White will regain the pawn while keeping the two bishops.

(5a3) **15 ...** ♘b4 16 ♕d2 (if White wants to avoid complications then 16 ♕b1 is a safe option) ♗xc3 17 bxc3 ♘xe4 18 ♕b2 ♘c6 19 f3 ♘f6 20 ♗xb6 ♕e7 21 ♘c2 ♖fc8 22 ♕a3 ♘d7 23 ♗f2 ♘c5 24 ♖d2 ♖d8 25 ♖cd1 f6 26 ♘d4 ♘e5 27 ♘b3 ♘xb3 28 axb3 with an edge for White, Mokry–Lobron, Reggio Emilia 1984/5.

(5b) **14 ...** ♕c7 and now there is plenty of flexibility about move order, for example:

(5b1) **15 f3** (the start of a slightly unusual plan based on preparing b4 by ♖ab1) ♖fe8 16 ♕d2 ♖ac8 17 ♖ab1 ♘d7 18 f4 ♘cb8 19 ♖bc1 (having persuaded the knights to retreat the rook may be repositioned) ♘f8 20 ♘c2 ♘bd7 21 ♘d4 ♕b8 22 b3 ♗d8 23 ♗f3 and Black's passive play gave

White the advantage in Yudas-hin–Dzhandzhava, Simferopol 1988.

(5b2) **15** ♖ac1 ♖ac8 (15 ... ♗f6 16 ♘ab1 ♖ac8 17 a3 ♕b8 18 b4 ♘d7 19 ♕d2 ♗e7 20 f4 ♖fd8 21 ♕e1 gave White his usual slight plus in Tseshkovsky–Hulak, Dubai Ol. 1986) 16 ♘ab1 (16 ♗f1 ♖fd8 17 ♕b1 ♘b4 18 ♘c2 ♘xc2 was roughly equal in Lobron–Liberzon, Ramat-Hash-aron 1982) ♘e5 17 ♘d2 ♘cd7 18 a3 ♖fe8 19 b4 ♘f6 20 h3 ♘g6 was played in Jadoul–Karpov, Brussels 1986. This position is slightly unusual in that Black's knight has moved away from the queenside to g6. The logical response would be for White to start action on the relatively bare left flank by 21 ♘b3 followed by a4–a5.

(5b3) **13** ♕d2 (this appears the most logical because it allows the a3 knight to return to the game via c2) ♘e5 (15 ... ♖ad8 16 ♘c2 ♘e5 17 f3 ♘cd7 18 ♖ac1 ♘f6 19 ♘d4 was slightly better for White in Karpov–Small, Lucerne Ol. 1982) 16 f3 with an edge for White in Akopian–Semkov, Erevan 1988. It is worth giving the rest of this game in full because it is an excellent example of how Black can be tortured in this variation. White goes round and round, an-noying Black with one little threat after another, always being care-ful not to allow Black to free himself. Finally White adopts the plan of a queenside breakthrough, which eventually proves decisive: 16 ... ♖ac8 17 ♖ac1 ♖fd8 18 ♕e1 ♘g6 19 ♕f2 ♗f6 20 b4 ♘d7 21 ♘a4 ♖b8 22 ♗f1 ♗a8 23 ♔h1 h6 24 ♕d2 ♗e7 25 ♘b1 ♕b7 26 a3 ♘ge5 27 ♕f2 ♖dc8 28 ♘d2 ♖c6 29 ♘b3 ♖bc8 30 ♘b2 ♖6c7 31 ♕d2 ♘f6 32 ♕d4 ♘ed7 33 ♖b1 ♕b8 34 ♗f2 ♘e8 35 ♕d2 ♗g5 36 ♗e3 ♗xe3 37 ♕xe3 ♘e5 38 ♖bc1 ♘d7 39 ♕d2 ♗b7 40 a4 ♖d8 41 a5 ♗a8 42 ♘a4 ♖dc8 43 axb6 ♘xb6 44 ♘xb6 ♕xb6 45 c5 dxc5 46 ♘xc5 ♗b7 47 ♖a1 ♖a8 48 ♘d7 ♕a7 49 b5 ♗c8 50 b6 ♖xd7 51 bxa7 ♖xd2 52 ♖xd2 ♔f8 53 ♖d8 ♔e7 54 ♖xc8 Resigns.

12 f4 ♘ed7

The knight transfer from c6 to d7 improves the position of Black's pieces, since he may exert pressure against e4 by ... ♗b7 and ... ♘c5, or he may play for ... d5. The defect is that it gives White extra time, and this allows him the chance to start a kingside attack.

13 ♗f3 ♗b7
14 ♕e2 ♖c8 *(110)*

Once again the move order is a matter of personal choice, but this move is bound to be played sooner or later, so Black may gain some flexibility by playing it first.

15 ♖ac1

It is unwise not to play this move, because a poorly defended knight on c3 is an invitation for Black to start a tactical storm by playing ... d5. This happened after 15 g4 h6 16 h4 d5! 17 exd5

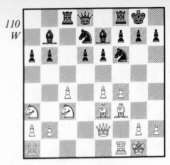

110
W

♗xa3 18 bxa3 ♘xd5 19 cxd5 ♖xc3 20 ♗d4 ♖xa3 21 g5 hxg5 22 fxg5 e5!, A. Rodriguez–Polugayevsky, Moscow 1985 and 15 ♖ad1 ♕c7 16 g4 d5! 17 cxd5 ♗xa3 18 bxa3 ♕xc3 19 g5 ♘xd5 20 exd5 ♗xd5 21 ♗xd5 exd5 22 ♗d4 ♕xa3, Hernandez–Renet, Thessaloniki Ol. 1988, with advantage to Black in both cases.

15 ... ♕c7
16 ♖fd1

It is an open question as to whether this further preparatory move is really necessary. The alternative is the immediate 16 g4 *(111)* and now:

111
B

(1) **16 ...** ♘c5 17 ♕g2 (after 17 ♗d2 h6 18 h4 ♘h7 19 b4 ♗xh4

20 ♔g2! ♘d7 21 ♖h1 ♗e7 22 g5 hxg5 23 ♖xh7! ♔xh7 24 ♖h1+ ♔g8 25 ♔g1 f5 the complications should have led to a draw in Gufeld–Georgadze, USSR 1985) d5 (Kasparov suggested 17 ... g5 18 fxg5 ♘fd7, but not surprisingly nobody has cared to try this) 18 exd5 (18 e5 ♘fe4 19 cxd5 exd5 20 b4 ♘xc3 21 ♖xc3 d4 was unclear in Tseshkovsky–Kasparov, USSR Ch. 1979) ♘d3 19 ♖cd1! ♘xf4 20 ♗xf4 ♗c5+ (20 ... ♕xf4 21 d6 wins a piece) 21 ♔h1 ♕xf4 22 g5 ♘e8 (22 ... ♘d7 23 dxe6 wins a piece) and now White has a pleasant choice: he can win a pawn for insufficient compensation by 23 dxe6, but 23 d6! appears even stronger to me.

(2) **16 ... ♕b8** (this appears too passive) 17 g5 ♘e8 18 ♗g2 g6 19 ♗h3 ♘g7 20 f5 exf5 21 exf5 gxf5 22 ♖xf5 ♘xf5 23 ♗xf5 ♘e5 24 ♕h5 ♘g6 25 ♗d4 ♖fe8 26 ♖f1 ♗f8 (26 ... ♖c5 27 ♘d5! is good for White after **27 ... ♗xd5** 28 ♗xg6 fxg6 29 ♕h6 or **27 ... ♖xd5** 28 cxd5 ♗f8 29 ♗e6! fxe6 30 ♖f7!) 27 ♗xc8 ♕xc8 28 ♖xf7 ♔xf7 (28 ... ♗h6! 29 ♖xh7! ♕f5 30 ♖h8+ ♘xh8 31 ♕xe8+ ♗f8 is the critical line, but it is doubtful if Black has enough compensation for the two pawns since White's king can flee to the queenside) 29 ♕xh7+ ♔e6 30 ♕xg6+ ♔d7 31 ♕f5+ ♔c7 32 ♕xc8+ ♔xc8, Chandler–Quinteros, Vienna Open 1986, and now simply 33 h4 would have been good for White.

(3) **16 ... h6!** 17 h4 ♘c5 18 ♕g2 d5 19 exd5 ♘d3 (19 ... exd5? 20 g5 hxg5 21 hxg5 ♘d3 22 gxf6 ♗xf6 23 ♗xd5 ♘xc1 24 ♘e4 wins for White, Geller–Franzoni, Berne 1987) with unclear complications. Note that the continuation of line 1 is ineffective here, since after 20 ♖cd1 (20 g5 ♗c5 is unclear) ♘xf4 21 ♗xf4 ♗c5+ 22 ♔h1 ♕xf4 the h4 pawn is attacked.

16	**...**	**♖fe8**
17	**g4**	**h6**

If Black plays 17 ... ♘c5, then 18 ♕g2 leaves him much worse off than in the last note. There are two reasons for this; firstly the rook on e8 takes away a flight square from the f6 knight, so that there is an immediate threat to win a piece by g5 and b4, and secondly there is no chance that ... d5 will work when the rook is on d1.

18	**h4**	**♘h7**

Black is trying to hold up g5 for as long as possible. Now 19 g5 hxg5 20 hxg5 e5 is fine for Black, so White must take time out to defend h4.

19	**♕h2** *(112)*	
19	**...**	**♕b8**

This passive move looks wrong, but Black has not had much luck with the alternatives:

(1) **19 ... ♘c5** 20 ♕h3 (defending the bishop on f3, for the immediate 20 g5 is met by 20 ... f5!) ♗f6 21 ♘ab1 (meeting the threat to the e4 pawn; White is finally ready for g5!) g6 22 ♖c2 ♗g7 23

112
B

🛇cd2 🛇f8 24 g5 h5 25 🛇f2 🛇c6 26 🛇a3 🛇d7? (26 ... ♛b7 was better, although the out-of-play knight at h7 gives White some advantage), Nunn–Cramling, Zurich 1984, and now 27 e5! is very good for White.

(2) **19 ...** ♛**d8** 20 🛇**f2 g5** (a drastic way to prevent g5 by White; although this gains Black the e5 square he still has problems along the h-file) 21 hxg5 hxg5 22 f5 🛇e5 23 ♚g2 🛇f6 24 🛇h1 🛇f8 25 🛇d4! 🛇a8 26 🛇cf1 ♛e7 27 🛇e2, Hellers–Wahls, World Junior Ch. 1986, and the threat of 🛇f3–h3 causes serious problems for Black.

20 g5
White decides to play g5 straight away, even though Black can reply with ... f5. The alternative was 20 ♛h3 as in line 1 of the last note.

20 ... f5
21 ♛g2
There is a choice of promising lines for White. Chandler decides to keep the h7 knight locked out, but the direct 21 gxh6 gxh6 22 exf5 🛇xf3 23 ♛g3+ ♚h8 24 ♛xf3 exf5 25 🛇d5 followed by 🛇d4 was also good.

21	...	hxg5
22	hxg5	fxe4
23	🛇xe4	d5
24	🛇f2	🛇c5!

Black defends well. By exchanging Black-squared bishops he exposes the weakness of f4.

25 🛇xc5 🛇xc5 (113)

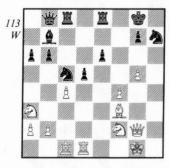

113
W

| 26 | 🛇d4 | 🛇f8? |

This move has disastrous consequences because it gives White the time he needs to revive his kingside attack. Black should have continued his policy of liquidation by 26 ... dxc4; after 27 🛇xc4 🛇xf3 28 ♛xf3 🛇cd8 White still has some advantage because of the h7 knight, but with each exchange White's attacking chances are reduced and he may soon have to look to the safety of his own king.

| 27 | g6 | 🛇f6 |
| 28 | ♛h3 | |

Black has no threat, and the free move enables White to create his own unpleasant threats of 29 b4 and 29 🛇g4.

28   ...   ♖fe8

Relatively best. **28 ... dxc4** 29 ♘g4 ♗xf3 (29 ... ♘cd7 30 ♖xd7) 30 ♘xf6+ ♖xf6 31 ♕h7+ ♔f8 32 ♕h8+ ♔e7 33 ♕xg7+ wins, as does **28 ... ♖ce8** 29 ♔g2 followed by ♖h1.

29   ♖e1

Stepping up the pressure on e6 renews the threat of b4. 29 ♘g4 ♘cd7 was less convincing.

29   ...   ♕d6
30   ♗g4

Black cannot bring any further support for e6 and he has no answer to the threat of b4 (30 ... a5 31 ♘b5).

30   ...   e5
31   fxe5   ♖xe5
32   ♖xe5   ♕xe5
33   ♗xc8   ♕xd4
34   ♗xb7   Resigns.

White has netted a clear piece since the recapture on b7 allows mate in 3.

9 Sicilian Four Knights

This rather antiquated system is not currently in favour, but fashions can change and it is advisable to be prepared even for less common variations. It experienced a brief surge of popularity when Chandler adopted it for a couple of years, but the generally passive nature of Black's position proved unattractive to other players and it has now virtually disappeared again. Black plays 1 e4 c5 2 ♘f3 e6 3 d4 cxd4 4 ♘xd4 ♘f6 5 ♘c3 ♘c6 (of course this can arise from other move orders, in particular via 2 ... ♘c6). In some ways this is akin to the Kan and Taimanov systems since Black leaves the f8–b4 diagonal open for his bishop, but instead of playing ... a6 he develops a piece. Naturally this is in Black's favour unless White has some direct method of exploiting the omission of ... a6, so 6 ♘db5 is the only move to cause Black problems. Black then very often continues 6 ... d6 and after 7 ♗f4 e5 8 ♗g5 we have transposed to the Pelikan, considered in Chapter 4. The point of this move order is that Black avoids the possibility that after 1 e4 c5 2 ♘f3 ♘c6 3 d4 cxd4 4 ♘xd4 ♘f6 5 ♘c3 e5 6 ♘db5 d6 White might play 7 ♘d5

or 7 a4. Since we are recommending the main line with 7 ♗g5 this transposition is not a worry and therefore 6 ... d6 just leads to the earlier chapter on the Pelikan. After 6 ♘db5, 6 ... d5 loses to 7 exd5 exd5 8 ♗f4 and 6 ... ♗c5 7 ♗f4 followed by ♗d6 is unpleasant for Black, so we need only consider 6 ... ♗b4 in this chapter. The tactical line recommended in the first edition has suffered a serious setback in recent years, so this time we only analyse the positional continuation 7 a3 ♗xc3+ 8 ♘xc3 d5 9 exd5, which either gives Black an isolated pawn after 9 ... exd5 or gives White a lead in development after 9 ... ♘xd5 10 ♗d2. This is a safe line for White in which he is likely to secure a small but permanent advantage. In practice it is easy for White to allow the position to slide towards a draw, and in some ways it is an annoying line to meet because instead of the sharp struggle typical of most Sicilian lines, White is trying to exploit a slight positional edge. Nevertheless it is even more unpleasant for Black, who can only win if White takes exceptional risks, and so this line is relatively unpopular.

Game 26
Mokry–B. Stein
Gausdal 1988

1	e4	c5
2	♘f3	e6
3	d4	cxd4
4	♘xd4	♘f6
5	♘c3	♘c6
6	♘db5	♗b4
7	a3	♗xc3+
8	♘xc3	d5
9	exd5	*(114)*

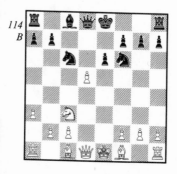

114
B

9 ... exd5
This has been almost the only move played during the past decade, but it is interesting to note that in a very recent game Ulf Andersson preferred the knight recapture. The analysis runs 9 ... ♘xd5 10 ♗d2 and now:

(1) **10 ... ♘xc3** 11 ♗xc3 ♕xd1+ 12 ♖xd1 f6 (12 ... e5 13 ♗d3 ♗e6 14 0-0 f6 15 f4 is similar, Ivkov–Gligoric, Amsterdam 1964) 13 f4 (for some reason Ehlvest preferred the passive 13 f3 and after 13 ... ♗d7 14 ♗d3 0-0-0 15 ♖d2 e5 16 ♗e4 ♗e6 17

♔e2 ♖xd2+ 18 ♔xd2 ♘e7 19 ♗b4 ♘d5 20 ♗xd5 ♗xd5 21 ♔e3 the players agreed to a draw in Ehlvest–Andersson, Skellteftea 1989) ♗d7 14 ♗c4 0-0-0 15 0-0 ♔c7 16 ♖de1 ♖he8 17 ♖f3 ♗c8 with a very unpleasant position for Black, Fischer–Addison, USA Ch. 1962–3.

(2) **10 ... ♕h4** 11 ♕f3 0-0 (**11 ... ♘e5** 12 ♕g3 and **11 ... ♘d4** 12 ♕d3 just make matters worse) 12 0-0-0 ♘xc3 13 ♗xc3 e5 14 ♗d3 ♗g4 (14 ... ♕g4 15 ♗e4 ♕xf3 16 ♗xf3 with the typical favourable ending for White, Minic–Gerusel, Halle 1967) 15 ♕e4 ♕h6+ 16 ♗d2 ♕g6 17 f3 ♗e6 18 ♕xg6 hxg6 19 ♗e3 and again White has a promising ending, Tal–Matulovic, Kislovodsk 1966.

(3) **10 ... ♕b6** 11 ♘b5 ♘d4 12 ♘xd4 ♕xd4 13 ♗b5+ ♗d7 14 ♗xd7+ ♔xd7 15 0-0 left Black's king badly placed in Kaplan–Siaperas, Siegen 1970.

(4) **10 ... ♕f6** 11 ♕h5 0-0 12 0-0-0 ♘xc3 (12 ... ♕xf2 13 ♘xd5 exd5 14 ♗d3 is no better) 13 ♗xc3 ♕f4+ 14 ♖d2 e5 15 ♗b5 with advantage, Matulovic–Kokkoris, Athens 1969.

(5) **10 ... 0-0** 11 ♕h5 ♘f6 12 ♕h4 ♕d4 13 ♗g5 ♖d8 14 ♕xd4 ♖xd4 15 ♗d3 b6 16 0-0-0 is the same story as in all the other lines, Gufeld–Hasin, USSR Ch. 1966.

10 ♗d3 0-0
Or 10 ... d4 (after 10 ... ♕e7+ 11 ♕e2 ♕xe2+ 12 ♘xe2 ♘e5 13 ♗b5+ ♗d7 14 ♗xd7+ ♔xd7,

Liberzon–Bronstein, USSR 1972, White could have played 15 ♗e3 ♖he8 16 ♗d4 with a slight advantage) and now:

(1) **11 ♕e2+** ♗e6 12 ♘e4 ♘xe4 13 ♕xe4 ♕d5 14 ♗f4 0-0-0 15 0-0 g5, Frolov–Maliutin, Jurmala 1989, and now 16 ♗d2 ♘e5 17 ♕xd5 ♗xd5 18 ♗f5+ is a little better for White according to Maliutin and Kimelfeld.

(2) **11 ♘e2** ♗f5 (11 ... 0-0 12 0-0 transposes into the main line) 12 0-0 ♗xd3 13 ♕xd3 0-0 14 ♗g5 h6 15 ♗h4 ♖e8 16 ♖ad1 ♖c8 17 c3! (more dynamic than 17 ♖fe1 ♖e6 18 ♔f1 ♕c7 19 ♗g3 ♕b6 20 b4 with just a microscopic advantage for White, Karpov–Kuzmin, Leningrad 1977) dxc3 18 ♕h3 ♕e7 19 ♘xc3 ♕e6 (19 ... ♕e5 20 f4 ♕e3+ 21 ♕xe3 ♖xe3 22 ♗xf6 gxf6 23 ♘d5 is very good for White) 20 ♕xe6 fxe6 (20 ... ♖xe6 21 ♗xf6 ♖xf6 22 ♖d7 b6 23 ♖e1 favours White) 21 ♗xf6 gxf6 22 ♘e4 with an endgame advantage for White, Estevez–Chaviano, Santa Clara 1983.

11 0-0 *(115)* **d4**

This is the most logical because it forces White to decide where his knight is going immediately. To avoid liquidation it seems that 11 ... d4 should be met by the relatively passive ♘e2; after other 11th moves White can usually arrange to meet ... d4 by the more active ♘e4, for example:

(1) **11 ... a6** 12 ♗f4 (12 ♗g5 is also promising) d4 13 ♘e4 ♘d5 (13 ... ♗f5 14 ♗c7! illustrates why Black should not have delayed) 14 ♗d6 ♖e8 15 ♗g3 f5? (suicide, but even 15 ... ♗f5 16 ♘d6 ♗xd3 17 ♕xd3 ♖e7 18 ♘f5 is very awkward) 16 ♘d6 ♖f8 17 ♗c4 ♗e6 18 ♖e1 ♕d7 19 ♘xb7 ♕xb7 20 ♖xe6 ♘a5 21 ♗a2 Resigns, Vukcevic–Ervin, USA 1976.

(2) **11 ... h6** 12 ♗f4 d4 13 ♘b5 (13 ♘e4 as in line 1 is also possible) ♘d5 14 ♕f3! ♗e6 15 ♖ad1 ♕d7 16 h3 ♖ad8 17 ♗h2 ♕e7 18 ♕g3 and White has a clear advantage, Ciric–Rossolimo, Vrsac 1969.

(3) **11 ... ♗g4** 12 f3 ♗e6 13 ♗g5 h6 (13 ... ♖e8 14 ♕d2 d4 15 ♘e2 a6 16 ♘g3, Planinc–Andersson, Sombor 1970 and 13 ... ♕b6+ 14 ♔h1 ♘d7 15 f4! f5 16 ♕f3, Matulovic–Benko, Vrnjacka Banja 1973 were also bad for Black) 14 ♗h4 g5 15 ♗f2 ♘h5 16 ♘b5 and according to Taimanov White has a clear plus.

12 ♘e2

The available evidence suggests that this offers the best chances for an advantage. After 12 ♘e4

♗f5 13 ♗g5 ♗xe4 14 ♗xe4 h6 15 ♗h4 (15 ♗xf6 ♕xf6 16 ♖e1 ♖ad8 17 ♕d3 ♘e5 18 ♕b3 b6 19 ♖e2 g6 20 ♖ae1 ♔g7 21 ♕b5 ♖fe8 22 ♗d3 ♘xd3 23 ♕xd3 ♖xe2 24 ♖xe2 ♖d5 was equal in Kudrin–Chandler, London 1987) g5 16 ♗xc6 bxc6 17 ♗g3 ♕d5 18 f4! ♘e4 (18 ... g4? 19 ♗h4 wins) 19 fxg5 hxg5 (19 ... ♘xg3?! 20 hxg3 hxg5 21 ♕d3 f5 22 ♖ae1 is dangerous) 20 ♕d3 f5 21 ♖ad1 ♖ad8 22 ♗f2 c5 23 c3 ♕b3! White's advantage was infinitesimal in Kir. Georgiev–Chandler, Leningrad 1987.

12   ...   ♗g4 *(116)*
Or 12 ... h6 (12 ... ♕d5 13 ♘g3 gives White an edge) 13 h3 (probably best, although 13 ♗f4 ♘d5 14 ♗g3 ♕f6 15 ♖e1 ♘de7 16 ♘f4 ♗f5 17 ♗c4 ♖ac8 18 ♕d2 ♖fd8 19 ♘d3 gave White an edge in Geller–Winants, Amsterdam II 1987; not, however, 13 ♗b5 ♗g4 14 f3 ♕b6!) a6 (because now ♗b5 is a real threat) and White may try:

(1) **14 ♗f4** ♖e8 (14 ... ♘d5 15 ♗h2 ♕f6 16 ♘g3 gives White an edge) 15 ♖e1 ♕d5 16 ♘g3 ♗d7 17 ♕d2 (threat ♗xh6) g5 18 ♗c7 b5? (Black should have started hacking rooks off) 19 f4 ♖ac8 20 fxg5 hxg5 21 ♘f5! ♖e3 22 ♘xe3 dxe3 23 ♕xe3 ♖xc7 (Black has material equality but too many loose pieces) 24 ♖ad1 ♔f8 25 ♖f1 ♔g7 26 ♗f5 and White wins, Carlier–Winants, Wijk aan Zee II 1987.

(2) **14 ♖e1** ♘d5 15 ♘f4 (15

♗e4 ♘de7 16 ♕d3 ♕b6 17 ♖d1 ♖d8 18 ♕g3 ♔h8 19 ♗f4 ♕b5 20 ♗d3 ♕d5 21 ♗c7 ♖e8 22 c3 dxc3 23 ♘xc3 was good for White in Ernst–Prasad, Subotica 1987) ♘xf4 16 ♗xf4 ♗e6 17 ♕h5 ♕d7 18 ♖e2 f5 19 ♖ae1 ♗f7 20 ♕f3 ♖ae8 21 ♖xe8 ♖xe8 22 ♖xe8+ ♗xe8 23 ♗g3 with a solid positional plus for White, Lobron–Gobet, Biel 1984.

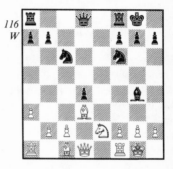

13   f3
This appears best, because the exchange on e2 often simplifies Black's defensive task. After the alternative 13 ♗g5 (13 ♗f4 ♖e8 14 ♖e1 ♕b6 15 b4 ♘e5 16 ♗xe5 ♖xe5 17 ♕d2 ♗xe2 18 ♖xe2 ♖xe2 19 ♗xe2 g6 20 ♖d1 ♖d8 21 ♗f3 gave White a small but lasting advantage in Lobron–Chandler, Biel 1987) ♕d6 14 ♖e1 (14 ♕d2 ♗xe2 15 ♕xe2 ♖fe8 16 ♕d1 ♘e5 offers White nothing, Short–Wiedenkeller, Esbjerg 1984) ♖e8 (after 14 ... a5 15 ♕d2 ♘d5 16 h3 ♗xe2 17 ♗xe2 h6 18 ♗h4 Black tried to imprison White's bishop by 18 ... f5 19 c4 ♘f4 20 ♗f3 ♘g6 21 ♗g3 f4 but

this rebounded after 22 ♗d5+ ♚h7 23 ♖e6 ♕d7 24 ♕d3 ♘ce7 25 ♗h2 ♘f5 26 ♖ae1 ♖ab8 27 ♕e4 b6 28 g3 ♕d8 29 h4 h5 30 ♕f3 ♗h6 31 ♕xf4+ ♚h7 32 ♕e4 ♖c8 33 ♕f3 ♚h6 34 ♖1e5 Resigns, R. Mainka–B. Stein, Dortmund II 1987) 15 ♕d2 (15 f3 ♗h5 16 ♘f4 h6 17 ♘xh5 hxg5 18 ♘xf6+ ♕xf6 19 ♕d2 ♘e5 20 ♖e4 Draw, Short–Chandler, Hastings 1987/8) ♗xe2 (better than 15 ... ♖ac8 16 ♘g3 with a clear edge for White) 16 ♖xe2 ♖xe2 17 ♕xe2 ♖e8 18 ♕f3 ♘e5 19 ♕f4 ♕b6 20 ♗xf6 ♘xd3 21 ♕g3 ♕xf6 22 ♕xd3 ♕b6 Black drew easily in Kudrin–Rogers, London 1988.

13   ...   ♗h5
14   ♗g5   ♕d6

The position is the same as in Short–Chandler above, except that the moves ♖e1 and ... ♖fe8 have been omitted. This difference favours White, as the main line of the game proves.

15   ♕e1

15 ♕d2 ♖ad8 16 ♖ad1 ♖fe8 17 ♗h4 ♗g6 18 ♗xg6 hxg6 19 ♗f2 ♘d5 was level in Zapata–Chandler, Amsterdam 1987. The move ♕e1 has the immediate threat of ♕h4, but White also intends to step up the pressure on d4 by ♕f2 and ♖ad1.

15   ...   ♗g6
16   ♖d1   ♖fe8

Black must not exchange on d3 as this gives White a free tempo to increase the pressure on d4 by ♕f2 and ♖fd1. However Black

might have tried to exploit the fact that White's queen is no longer defending the c2 pawn by putting a rook on c8.

17   ♕f2   ♖ad8
18   ♖d2   ♖d7

Black decides to meet White's plan passively, even though being forced on the defensive is usually a sign that an isolated pawn position has gone wrong. However Mokry's suggestion of 18 ... ♖e5 appears no better after 19 ♗h4 threatening ♗g3.

19   ♖fd1   ♖ed8

In the line 19 ... ♗xd3 20 ♖xd3 ♕e5 21 ♗xf6 ♕xe2 22 ♕xe2 ♖xe2 23 ♗xd4 ♖xc2 24 ♗c3 Black succeeds in exchanging his isolated pawn, but only at the cost of giving White a dominant bishop and good chances of penetrating to the seventh rank.

20   ♗b5!

Removing a vital defender increases the pressure on d4 intolerably. Black's reply leads to a fatal material loss, but even 20 ... ♕e5 21 ♗xc6 bxc6 22 ♗xf6 gxf6 23 f4 ♕b5 24 ♘g3, threatening f5, is very unpleasant.

20   ...   h6 *(117)*
21   ♘xd4!   hxg5

Black's moves are all forced, since 21 ... ♘xd4 loses to 22 ♗xd7.

22   ♘xc6   ♕xd2
23   ♖xd2   ♖xd2
24   ♘xd8   ♖xf2
25   ♚xf2   ♗xc2
26   ♘xb7

White is a pawn up and his

26	...	♗ b3
27	♘ a5	♗ d5
28	♘ c6	♗ xc6
29	♗ xc6	♔ f8
30	♔ e3	♔ e7
31	♔ d4	♔ d6
32	♗ b5	**Resigns**

Black did not wish to see the technical phase of the game.

active king makes the task of converting his material plus into a point relatively simple.

10 Lowenthal Variation

This line starts 1 e4 c5 2 ♘f3 ♘c6 3 d4 cxd4 4 ♘xd4 e5 and is slightly akin to the Pelikan in its use of an early ... e5. The 'old' Lowenthal runs 5 ♘b5 a6 6 ♘d6+ ♗xd6 7 ♕xd6 ♕f6 (7 ... ♕e7 8 ♕xe7+ is worse) and Black hopes that his lead in development will compensate for his black square weaknesses and lack of the two bishops. Current theory suggests that this is a vain hope and White should be able to maintain an advantage. Black has an interesting alternative which has been pioneered by Sveshnikov and other Soviet players. This runs 5 ♘b5 d6, and here White has the choice between 6 c4, aiming for a firm grip on d5, or 6 ♘1c3 as in the Pelikan. If White plays 6 ♘1c3 Black plans to reach a superior type of Pelikan variation in which ... ♘ge7 is played instead of ... ♘f6, thus avoiding the doubling of Black's f-pawns.

If, on the other hand, White plays 6 c4 Black will either aim for counterplay by ... f5 or try to exchange his bad bishop by ... ♗e7–g5. This line is still in a state of flux, so we give a more complete survey than usual, since at this stage it is impossible to judge which line is best for White.

Game 27
Liberzon–Franzoni
Biel (Open) 1980

1	e4	c5
2	♘f3	♘c6
3	d4	cxd4
4	♘xd4	e5
5	♘b5	a6

Or 5 ... d6 *(118)* (5 ... ♘f6 6 ♘1c3 transposes to the Pelikan, 5 ... ♗c5 6 ♘1c3 ♘f6 transposes to page 63 and 5 ... h6 6 ♘d6+ ♗xd6 7 ♕xd6 ♕e7 8 ♕d1 ♘f6 9 ♘c3 is good for White) and now there are two lines:

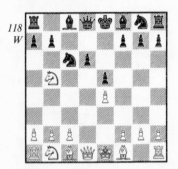

(1) **6 ♘1c3 a6** (6 ... ♘f6 is a Pelikan) 7 ♘a3 b5 8 ♘d5 ♘ge7 (after 8 ... ♘f6 White may transpose back to the Pelikan with 9 ♗g5, but unfortunately the resulting line is not part of our recommended repertoire; I therefore suggest 9 ♘xf6+ ♕xf6 10 c4

b4 11 ♘c2 ♗b7 12 ♗d3 ♕d8 13 0-0 ♗e7 14 a3 and White had an edge in Vitolinsh–Ambarcumian, USSR 1988; 8 ... ♗e7 9 c4 b4 10 ♘c2 a5 11 ♗e3 ♖b8 12 ♗e2 ♘f6 13 ♕d3 ♘d7 14 ♘xe7 ♔xe7 15 ♖d1 gave White an edge in Geo. Timoshchenko–Sveshnikov, Moscow GMA 1989) 9 c4 ♘d4 and now:

(1a) **10 cxb5** ♘xd5 11 exd5 ♗e7 12 ♗c4 axb5 13 ♘xb5 ♗a6 14 ♘a3 0-0 15 0-0 ♗f6 16 ♗e3 left Black struggling to find compensation for the pawn, Klovans–Kiselev, Frunze 1988.

(1b) **10 ♗e3** ♘xd5 11 cxd5 ♗e7 12 ♗d3 0-0 13 0-0 f5? (13 ... ♗f6 is only very slightly better for White) 14 ♗xd4 exd4 15 exf5 ♗xf5 16 ♘c2 and Black has no compensation for his weak pawns, A. Rodriguez-Estevez, Cuba Ch. 1988.

(2) **6 c4** ♗e7 (6 ... ♗e6 generally leads to a transposition) 7 ♘1c3 a6 8 ♘a3 and now:

(2a) **8 ... h6** 9 ♗e2 ♗e6 10 0-0 ♗g5 **11 ♘c2** transposes to line 2c below, but not **11 ♗g4** ♘f6 12 ♗xe6 fxe6 13 ♗xg5 hxg5 14 ♘c2 ♔f7! and Black is at least equal, Nikolenko–Sveshnikov, USSR 1987.

(2b) **8 ... ♘f6** (Black simply develops, abandoning the idea of ... h6 and ... ♗g5) 9 ♗e2 0-0 10 ♗e3 ♗e6 11 0-0 ♖c8 12 ♕d2 ♘a5 (12 ... h6 13 ♖ac1 was slightly better for White in Dolmatov–Guseinov, Klaipeda 1988) 13 ♘d5 ♗xd5 14 exd5 b6 15 ♖ac1 ♘b7 16 f4 ♘d7 17 ♘c2 a5 18 ♘a3 with advantage to White, Dolmatov–Minasian, USSR 1988.

(2c) **8 ... ♗e6** 9 ♘c2 h6 10 ♗e2 ♗g5 11 0-0 ♘f6 (11 ... ♘ge7 12 ♕d3! ♘g6 13 g3 ♗xc1 14 ♖axc1 ♕g5 15 ♘d5 ♗xd5 16 cxd5 with an edge for White, Geller–Lputyan, Moscow 1987) 12 ♕d3 ♗xc1 (12 ... ♕c7 13 ♖d1 ♖d8 14 ♗xg5 hxg5 15 ♖ac1 ♕b6 16 b3 is a little better for White, Geller–Lputyan, USSR 1987) 13 ♖axc1 0-0 14 ♖fd1 ♕b6! 15 ♕xd6!? (or 15 a3 ♘a5! 16 ♕xd6 ♘xc4 17 ♗xc4 ♕xd6 18 ♖xd6 ♘xc4 19 ♖b6 ♖ab8 20 ♘e3 ♗e6 21 ♖d1 ♖fe8 22 b3 ♔f8 with equality, Dvoiris–Tiviakov, USSR 1988) ♕xb2 16 ♕d3 ♕b6 17 ♖b1 ♕a7 18 ♘d5 ♘d7 19 ♘c7 ♘c5 20 ♕e3 ♖ab8 is unclear according to Tiviakov.

In practice 6 c4 has been the most popular response, but 6 ♘1c3 may be better, even though this allows Black the chance to transpose into the Pelikan.

    6   ♘d6+   ♗xd6
    7   ♕xd6   ♕f6 *(119)*
7 ... ♕e7 8 ♕d1 ♘f6 9 ♘c3 threatening ♗g5 is good for White.

    8   ♕d1
White has a wide variety of queen moves and most of them are good! There seems little doubt that **8 ♕c7**, which has always been highly regarded theoretically, gives White a good game but I have not recommended it

119
W

here because White must always be careful that his queen is not trapped, so the simpler ♕d1 seems preferable. One should note that 8 ♕xf6 is also quite good, e.g. **8 ♕xf6** ♘xf6 9 ♘c3 and now:

(1) **9 ... d5** 10 ♗g5 d4 (**10 ... ♘b4** 11 ♗xf6 gxf6 12 ♘xd5 ♘xc2+ 13 ♔d2 ♘xa1 14 ♘c7+ ♔e7 15 ♘xa8 ♗e6 16 ♘b6 ♗xa2 17 ♔c3 and **10 ... ♘xe4** 11 ♘xd5 0-0 12 ♗e3 are also good for White) 11 ♗xf6 dxc3 12 ♗xg7 ♖g8 13 ♗h6 ♘b4 14 0-0-0 ♘xa2+ 15 ♔b1 ♗e6 16 ♖d6 ♖g6 17 ♗e3 ♘b4 18 ♗c5 with advantage for White according to Gligoric.

(2) **9 ... ♘b4** and now:

(2a) **10 ♗d3** ♘xd3+ (**10 ... h6** 11 b3 d6 12 ♗a3 ♘xd3+ 13 cxd3 ♔e7 14 f4 ♔e6 15 f5+ ♔e7 16 ♖d1 ♖e8 17 d4 exd4 18 ♖xd4 ♔f8 19 ♗xd6+ ♔g8 20 0-0 b5 21 e5 Resigns was a drastic finish, Byrne–Evans, USA Ch. 1981) 11 cxd3 h6 12 b3 with an edge for White.

(2b) **10 ♔d2** d5 11 a3 d4 12 axb4 dxc3+ 13 ♔e3 ♘g4+ 14 ♔e2 f5 15 bxc3 ♘f6 16 ♖a5

♘xe4 17 f3! ♘d6 18 ♖xe5+ and Black has very little for the lost pawn, Velimirovic–Ristic, Yugoslavia 1979.

8 ... ♕g6
8 ... ♘ge7 9 ♘c3 0-0 (9 ... ♕g6 transposes to the next note) 10 ♗e3 b5 11 ♕d2 ♕g6 12 f3 d6 13 0-0-0 ♖d8 14 ♔b1 ♗b7 15 g f6 16 ♘d5 ♘xd5 17 ♕xd5+ is also good for White, Gligoric–Benko, Dublin 1957.

9 ♘c3 *(120)*

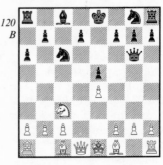

120
B

9 ... d5!?
For a time this move caused a revival of the Lowenthal, but now White has found a way to defuse the complications and liquidate to a favourable ending. The older line runs 9 ... ♘ge7 10 h4! h5 (**10 ... d5** 11 h5 ♕d6 12 h6! g6 13 exd5 and now **13 ... ♘d4** and **13 ... ♘b4** allow 14 ♘e4, while **10 ... h6** 11 h5 ♕f6 12 ♗e3 0-0 13 ♕d2 b5 14 0-0-0 b4 15 ♘a4 a5 16 ♘b6 ♖b8 17 ♕d6 gave White an excellent ending in Boleslavsky–Sakharov, USSR 1957) 11 ♗g5 d5 (the only move that makes sense, for example 11 ... b5 12

♕d3 ♗b7 13 0-0-0 ♖d8 14 ♕d6
15 ♖xd6 f6 16 ♗e3 ♘c8 17 ♖d2
♘6e7 18 ♗d3 d6 19 ♖hd1 was
very good for White in Hazai–
Csom, Warsaw 1987) 12 exd5 (the
tempting 12 ♗xe7 is met by 12 ...
d4!) ♘b4 (12 ... ♘d4 13 ♗d3
♗f5 14 ♗xf5 ♘exf5 15 ♕d3 f6 16
♗e3 is very good for White) 13
♗xe7 ♔xe7 14 ♗d3! (much
better than the often recommended 14 d6+ since White
reaches the same type of ending,
but with his d-pawn securely
defended) ♘xd3+ 15 ♕xd3
♕xd3 16 cxd3 and now:

(1) 16 ... b5 17 a3 and Black
cannot recover his pawn, for example 17 ... ♗f5 18 ♔d2! ♖h6
19 ♖he1 ♔d6 20 ♖ac1, Sveshnikov–Panchenko, USSR 1977 or
17 ... ♗b7 18 0-0-0 ♔d6 (suggested by Sveshnikov) 19 d4, or
finally 17 ... ♖b8 (suggested by
Baumbach) 18 0-0-0 b4 19 axb4
♖xb4 20 ♖he1 ♖xh4 (or else
♖e4) 21 d4!, and in all cases
White has a good ending.

(2) 16 ... ♖h6 17 0-0-0 ♖g6 18
♖he1! ♖xg2 (18 ... f6 19 d4 and
18 ... ♔d6 19 d4 are also good
for White) 19 ♖xe5+ (19 d4!? is
interesting) ♔d6 (19 ... ♔d8 20
♖de1 ♗d7 21 d6 threatens ♖xh5)
20 d4 followed by ♘e4+ and
again White has the advantage.

10   ♘xd5   ♕xe4+
11   ♗e3   ♘d4

This move, which is the only
reasonable reply to the threat of
♘c7+, is the idea behind 9 ...
d5!?

12   ♘c7+   ♔e7

12 ... ♔d8? allows White to
take the a8 rook, while after 12 ...
♔f8? White can either play 13
♖c1 or take the exchange by 13
♕d3 ♘xc2+ 14 ♔d2 ♕xd3+ 15
♗xd3 ♘xe3 16 ♘xa8 ♘d5 17
♖ac1 or take the rook—a
pleasant choice!

13   ♖c1!

Until this move was discovered
Black had been doing rather well
against 13 ♘xa8?! and 13 ♕d3.

13   ...   ♗g4

If Black moves the rook on a8
then 14 c3 is very strong.

14   ♕d3   ♕xd3
15   ♗xd3   ♖d8
16 h3 *(121)*

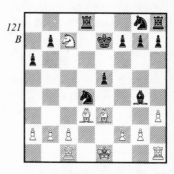

16   ...   ♗c8

The alternative is 16 ... ♗h5 17
f4 f6 18 ♔f2 ♔d6 19 c3 and now:
(1) 19 ... ♔xc7 is bad after 20
cxd4+ ♔b8 21 fxe5 fxe5 22 ♖c5.
(2) 19 ... ♘b3 20 axb3 ♔xc7 21
♗e4 ♘e7 22 ♖he1 ♘d5 23 fxe5
♘xe3 24 ♔xe3 fxe5 25 ♖f1 ♖de8
26 ♖f5 ♗g6 27 ♖g5 ♗xe4 28
♖xg7+ ♔c6 29 ♔xe4 with a
winning position for White, Mar-

janovic–Simic, Yugoslavia 1983.

(3) **19 ... ♞c6 20 ♗b6** exf4 **21 c4 ♞ge7 22 ♗e4 ♞c8 23 c5+ ♚d7 24 ♞d5 ♞xb6 25 cxb6 ♚d6 26 ♞xf4 ♗f7 27 ♖hd1+ ♚e5 28 ♚e3** with a clear plus for White, Winsnes–Hillarp, Rilton Cup 1988.

17	**f4**	**exf4**
18	**♗xf4**	**♞e6**

Otherwise White castles and Black is unable to develop his king's rook while e8 is covered.

19	**♞xe6**	**♗xe6**
20	**0-0**	

The outcome of the opening is very favourable for White. He has two active bishops supporting a queenside pawn majority and while so many pieces remain on the board Black's king is not well placed on e7.

20	**...**	**♞f6**
21	**a3**	**♞d5**
22	**♗d2**	**♖d7**
23	**♖ce1**	**♖c8**
24	**♖f3**	**b5**
25	**b3**	**h6**
26	**c4**	**bxc4**
27	**♗xc4?!**	

It was more important to drive away Black's centralized knight than to keep the queenside pawns intact. After 27 bc ♞f6 28 ♗b4+ White has a passed pawn and an attack against Black's king.

27... **♖a8?!** *(122)*

A passive and nervous move. 27 ... ♖c6 is better.

28	**a4**	

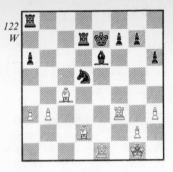

Preparing both ♗c1–a3+ and b4–b5.

28	**...**	**♚d6**

An attempt to bring the king over to help in the fight against White's queenside majority, but two rooks and two bishops are a formidable attacking force and the king soon runs into trouble.

29	**b4**	**♚c7**
30	**b5**	**axb5**
31	**♗xb5**	**♖d6**
32	**♖d1**	

With the sneaky threat 33 ♗f4 ♞xf4 34 ♖c3+ winning the exchange.

32	**...**	**♚b7**
33	**♗b4**	**♖dd8**
34	**♖fd3**	**♚c7**

Trying to unpin the knight.

35	**♖c1+**	**♚b6**

35 ... ♚b8 36 ♖c5 ♖a7 37 ♗c6 wins material.

36	**♗c5+**	**♚a5**
37	**♖cd1**	**♖ac8**
38	**♗e7**	**♖e8**
39	**♗xe8**	**♖xe8**
40	**♖xd5+**	**Resigns**

11 Pin Variation

There is no generally accepted name for this variation, which runs 1 e4 c5 2 ♘f3 e6 3 d4 cxd4 4 ♘xd4 ♘f6 5 ♘c3 ♗b4. There is certainly a pin involved, so 'Pin Variation' is a reasonable name. Until ten years ago this was thought to be a very poor line for Black, but round about 1979 it suddenly reappeared with Black's play being based on a new idea involving an exchange sacrifice. After a few years during which it was used in occasional Grandmaster games it entered a decline and is now very rarely seen. However it is worth studying because there are a lot of tricky tactics in the Pin Variation, and White players who do not know the correct antidote may well find themselves in trouble.

Game 28
Wagman–Barle
Biel (open) 1981

1	e4	c5
2	♘f3	e6
3	d4	cxd4
4	♘xd4	♘f6
5	♘c3	♗b4
6	e5	(123)

The only move to cause Black any difficulties.

| 6 | ... | ♘d5 |

123
B

Black's two alternatives are close to losing by force:

(1) 6 ... ♕a5 7 exf6 ♗xc3+ 8 bxc3 ♕xc3+ 9 ♕d2 ♕xa1 10 c3 (threat 11 ♘b3 ♕b1 12 ♗d3) ♕b1 11 ♗d3 ♕b6 12 fxg7 ♖g8 13 ♕h6 and wins.

(2) 6 ... ♘e4 7 ♕g4 ♕a5 (7 ... ♘xc3 8 ♕xg7 ♖f8 9 a3 and now the lines 9 ... ♗a5 10 ♗h6 ♕e7 11 ♘b3 and 9 ... ♕a5 10 ♘b3 ♕d5 11 ♗d3 are winning for White so Black must try 9 ... ♘b5+ 10 axb4 ♘xd4 11 ♗g5 ♕b6 12 ♗h6 ♕xb4+ 13 c3 ♘f5 14 cxb4 ♘xg7 15 ♗xg7 ♖g8 16 ♗f6 but White's black square pressure gives him a very favourable ending) 8 ♕xe4 ♗xc3+ 9 bxc3 ♕xc3+ 10 ♔d1 ♕xa1 11 ♘b5 d5 12 ♕b4 ♘a6 (12 ... ♕xe5 13 f4 ♘c6 14 fxe5 ♘xb4 15 ♘c7+ ♔d8 16 ♘xa8 b6 17 ♗a3

is winning for White) 13 ♘d6+ ♚d7 14 ♗xa6 bxa6 15 ♘xf7 ♖g8 16 ♚d2 d4 (or else ♗a3) 17 ♗b2 ♛xa2 18 ♖a1 ♛d5 19 ♖a5 and White has a decisive attack (analysis by Euwe).

7   ♗d2

Originally theory gave 7 ♛g4 as best, but after 7 . . . 0-0 (the new idea mentioned above) 8 ♗h6 g6 9 ♗xf8 ♛xf8 Black has reasonable compensation for the exchange with play against c3 and e5.

7   ...   ♘xc3

Or 7 . . . ♗xc3 8 bxc3 0-0 9 ♗d3 d6 10 ♛h5 (**10 exd6 ♛xd6 11 0-0** was at least slightly better for White, Geller–Tseitlin, Moscow 1982, while **10 f4** dxe5 11 fxe5 ♘d7 12 ♛h5 g6 13 ♛e2 ♛c7 14 c4 ♛b6 15 ♘f3 ♘e7 16 ♗c3 ♘c5 17 ♛d2 proved good for White in Epishin–Ulybin, Tbilisi 1989) g6 11 ♛e2 dxe5 12 ♛xe5 ♘d7 13 ♛d6 ♛f6 14 0-0 b6 15 ♘c6 ♘c5 16 c4 e5 17 ♛xe5 with a clear plus for White, Vogt–Ermenkov, Berlin 1982.

8   bxc3   ♗a5?!

A major decision point for Black. 8 . . . ♗a5 keeps the pressure against c3 but leaves the kingside dangerously bare. Black should adopt the alternative variation 8 . . . ♗e7 9 ♛g4 0-0 (**9 . . . g6** 10 h4 h5 11 ♛g3 ♘c6 12 ♘b5 was good for White in Rabar–Fuster, Munich 1942, while the remarkable **9 . . . g5** 10 h4 h5 11 hxg5!? hxg4 12 ♖xh8+ ♗f8 was played in Grosar–De Waal, Sas

van Gent 1986, and now 13 g6 fxg6 14 ♗h6 ♛f7 15 ♖xf8+ ♛xf8 16 ♗xf8 ♚xf8 17 ♗e2 is good for White) 10 ♗h6 g6, but the main line still favours White after 11 h4! *(124)* and now:

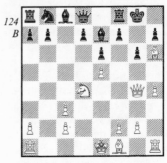

124
B

(1) **11 . . . d6** 12 h5 ♛a5 (12 . . . dxe5 13 ♗d3! exd4 14 hxg6 fxg6 15 ♗xg6 wins) 13 0-0-0!? dxe5 (**13 . . . ♛xc3** 14 ♖h3 ♛a1+ 15 ♚d2 ♛xa2 16 ♗d3 ♛a5+ 17 c3 ♛xe5 18 hxg6 fxg6 19 ♗xg6 ♖xf2+ 20 ♚c1 and **13 . . . ♛xe5** 14 hxg6 fxg6 15 ♗d3 ♖f6 16 ♖de1 ♛d5 17 ♗g5 ♖f7 18 ♗xe7 ♖xe7 19 ♗xg6 are winning for White) 14 ♘b5 a6 15 hxg6 fxg6 16 ♗xf8 ♗xf8 17 ♖xh7! ♚xh7 18 ♗d3 wins for White.

(2) **11 . . . ♛a5** 12 ♛g3 ♖d8 (after 12 . . . d6 13 exd6 Black may play **13 . . . ♗xd6** 14 ♛xd6 ♖d8 15 ♛b4 ♛xb4 16 cxb4 ♖xd4 17 c3 with the better ending for White or **13 . . . ♗f6** 14 0-0-0 ♛xa2 15 h5 ♘c6 16 ♘xc6 ♛a3+ 17 ♚d2 bxc6 18 ♗xf8 ♚xf8 19 hxg6 hxg6 20 ♗c4 and White has the advantage) 13 h5 d6 14 hxg6 fxg6 15 ♗f4 dxe5 16 ♗xe5 ♖d5

17 f4 ♘d7 18 ♗c4 ♘xe5 (after 18
... ♖xe5+ 19 fxe5 ♕xe5+ 20
♕xe5 ♘xe5 21 ♗b3 the e6 pawn
is too weak) 19 ♗xd5 ♕xd5 20
fxe5 ♕e4+ 21 ♔d2 ♗d7 22
♖ae1 d5, Wedberg–Pokojowc-
zyk, Copenhagen Open 1984, and
now 23 ♖xh7! ♔xh7 24 ♖h1+
♔g7 25 ♕h2 ♔f7 26 ♕h7+ ♔e8
27 ♕xg6+ ♔d8 28 ♖h8+
should win for White.

9 ♕g4

White can also use the move
order 9 ♗d3 d6 10 ♕g4 after
which Black has nothing better
than 10 ... 0-0 transposing into
the game.

9 ... 0-0
10 ♗d3 d6
11 ♘f3

Byrne and Mednis suggest 11
♗g5 with the lines **11 ... ♗xc3+**
12 ♔f1 f5 13 exf6 ♖xf6 14 ♖d1
and **11 ... ♕c7** 12 ♗f6 ♕xc3+
13 ♔e2 ♕d2+ 14 ♔f1 g6 15
♖d1. This has never been tried in
practice but looks good to me.

11 ... g6

Or else ♗xh7+ is crushing, for
example 11 ... dxe5 12 ♗xh7+
♔xh7 13 ♕h5+ ♔g8 14 ♘g5
♖e8 15 ♕xf7+ ♔h8 16 ♕h5+
followed by ♕h7+, ♕h8+,
♕xg7+ and ♘f7+ picking up
the queen.

12 h4!

The latest twist—White just
plays for mate. 12 ♘g5?! h5! (not
12 ... dxe5? 13 ♘xh7! ♔xh7 14
♗g5 ♗xc3+ 15 ♔e2 ♕d4 16
♕h3+ ♔g8 17 ♗f6) 13 ♕g3
dxe5 14 ♘e4 ♘d7 15 0-0 ♔g7

enabled Black to defend in
Peters–Arnason, New York 1980,
while 12 0-0 dxe5 (Sigurjonsson
gives the attractive line 12 ... ♘c6
13 ♗g5 ♕c7 14 ♗f6 ♗xc3 15
♕h4 ♘xe5 16 ♘g5 h5 17 ♕xh5)
13 ♘xe5 followed by f4 only gave
White an edge in Sigurjonsson–
Arnason, Iceland 1980.

12 ... dxe5

12 ... h5 is met by 13 ♕g3 or 13
♕f4.

13 h5 f5 *(125)*

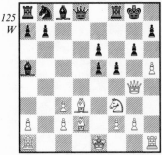

14 ♗xf5! exf5

14 ... ♖xf5 15 hxg6 h5 16
♖xh5 ♕f6 (16 ... ♖xh5 17 ♕xh5
♕c7 18 0-0-0 wins, while otherwise Black can hardly meet the
threat of ♖h8+) 17 0-0-0 followed by ♖dh1 with a decisive
attack.

15 ♕c4+ ♖f7

15 ... ♔g7 16 hxg6 ♔xg6 17
♘xe5+ wins.

16 hxg6 hxg6
17 ♘g5 ♕c7

If the queen defends the rook
from any other square White wins
by 18 ♘xf7 ♕xf7 19 ♖h8+.

18 ♕h4 ♔f8
19 ♘xf7?

Having conducted the attack so well up to here it is surprising that White should miss 19 ♕h8+ ♚e7 20 ♘xf7 when he is material up with a mating attack. Fortunately White is still winning even after 19 ♘xf7?

| | 19 | ... | ♚xf7 |

19 ... ♕xf7 20 ♕h8+ ♚g8 21 ♕f6+ wins the queen.

| | 20 | ♕h7+ | ♚e6 |

20 ... ♚f6 21 ♗g5+ ♚e6 22 ♕xg6+ ♚d5 23 0-0-0+ ♚c5 24 ♗e3+ ♚b5 25 ♖d5+ is even worse.

	21	♕xg6+	♚d5
	22	♖h6	♘c6
	23	♕g8+	♚c5
	24	♖b1!	

White correctly adheres to the rule applying to king-hunts that it is more important to cut off the king's escape route than to give check.

	24	...	b5
	25	♗e3+	♘d4
	26	♗xd4+	exd4
	27	♕f8+	

White misses it the first time round ...

	27	...	♚c4
	28	♕g8+	♚c5
	29	♖xb5+!	

... but spots it the second!

	29	...	♚xb5
	30	♕d5+	♚c5
	31	a4+	Resigns

It is mate next move.

12 2 ... ♞f6

Although this move surfaces from time to time, its appearances at the Grandmaster level are very rare. White has a range of possible lines against 2 ... ♞f6, which have all achieved good practical results. The variation 3 ♞c3, which was analysed in the first edition of this book, has performed well in the intervening years, while the more recent idea 3 e5 ♞d5 4 ♞c3 e6 5 ♞e4 has also acquired a good reputation. However, in this second edition, we will return to the 3 e5 ♞d5 4 ♞c3 e6 5 ♞xd5 exd5 6 d4 variation which was recommended in the first edition. Concentrating on this one line I will give a more detailed coverage and show that White can be sure of at least a slight advantage against 2 ... ♞f6.

Game 29
Rhine–Sprenkle
USA 1981

1	e4	c5
2	♞f3	♞f6
3	e5	♞d5

3 ... ♞g4 4 h3 ♞h6 may be met by 5 d4 or 5 c3, with advantage to White.

| 4 | ♞c3 | e6 |

Or 4 ... ♞xc3 (**4 ... ♞b4** 5 ♗c4 and **4 ... ♞c7** 5 d4 cxd4 6 ♛xd4 ♞c6 7 ♛e4 g6 8 ♗c4 ♗g7 9 0-0 0-0 10 ♖e1, Kindermann–Ostl, Bundesliga 1987, are good for White) 5 dxc3 *(126)* and now:

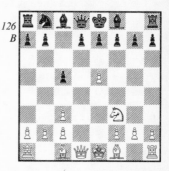

126
B

(1) **5 ... d5** 6 exd6 ♛xd6 (6 ... exd6 7 ♗c4 ♗e7 8 ♗f4 0-0 9 ♛d2 followed by 0-0-0 puts severe pressure on the backward pawn) 7 ♛xd6 exd6 8 ♗f4 ♗g4 (8 ... d5 9 0-0-0 ♗e6 10 ♞g5 followed by g3 and either ♗g2 or ♞xe6 and ♗h3, when Black's central pawns will be fortunate to survive) 9 0-0-0 ♞d7 10 ♗c4 (even better than ♗xd6, since ... 0-0-0 is prevented) followed by ♗xd6 winning a pawn.

(2) **5 ... ♞c6** 6 ♗f4 h6 (6 ... e6 7 ♛e2 ♛a5?! 8 ♞d2! ♛c7 9 ♞c4 f6 10 ♞d6+ ♗xd6 11 exd6 ♛a5 12 h4 was good for White in van der Wiel–Bjelajac, Novi Sad 1982)

7 ♕e2 ♕c7 8 0-0-0 b6 9 ♕e3 e6 10 ♘d2 ♘e7 11 ♘c4 ♘f5 (11 ... ♘d5? 12 ♖xd5 exd5 13 ♘d6+ ♔d8 14 e6 wins) 12 ♕h3 ♗b7 13 ♖g1 intending g4 and White has some advantage, van der Wiel–Murei, Moscow 1982.

(3) **5 ... g6** 6 ♗c4 ♗g7 7 ♗f4 0-0 8 ♕d2 followed by 0-0-0 and h4 gives White a strong attack.

(4) **5 ... b6?** 6 e6! dxe6 (6 ... fxe6 and 6 ... f6 are both met by 7 ♘e5!) 7 ♕xd8+ ♔xd8 ♘e5 ♔e8 9 ♗b5+ ♗d7 10 ♘xd7 ♘xd7 11 ♗f4 and White is close to winning already.

5	**♘xd5**	**exd5**
6	**d4**	**♘c6**

If Black doesn't like to sacrifice a pawn he can try 6 ... d6, but after 7 ♗b5+ *(127)* Black cannot equalize, as the following analysis shows:

127 B

(1) **7 ...** ♗d7 8 ♗xd7+ ♕xd7 (not 8 ... ♘xd7 9 dxc5) 9 0-0 ♘c6 10 exd6 ♗xd6 (10 ... ♕xd6 11 dxc5 ♕xc5 12 ♗e3 is also good for White) 11 ♖e1+ ♘e7 12 dxc5 ♗xc5 13 ♗g5 0-0 14 ♕d3 f6 (14 ... h6 15 ♗xe7 ♗xe7 16 ♖ad1

♖ad8 17 c4 ♗f6 18 cxd5 ♗xb2 19 d6 and White's passed pawn is very dangerous) 15 ♗e3 and Black has a poor isolated pawn position in which he has no active pieces to compensate for the static weakness.

(2) **7 ...** ♘c6 8 0-0 ♗e7 (8 ... ♗e6 is also met by 9 c4 when Black has nothing better than to transpose by 9 ... ♗e7) 9 c4 ♗e6 (**9 ... dxc4** 10 exd6 ♕xd6 11 d5 a6 12 ♗xc4 and **9 ... a6** 10 ♗xc6+ bxc6 11 cxd5 cxd5 12 exd6 ♕xd6 13 dxc5 ♕xc5 14 ♗e3 are very good for White) 10 ♗e3 ♕b6 (White threatened exd6) 11 a4 a6 12 a5 ♕c7 13 exd6 ♕xd6 14 dxc5 ♕d8 15 ♗xc6+ bxc6 16 ♘e5 ♕c7 17 ♕a4 with a horrid position for Black, Unzicker–Pomar, Bad Aibling 1968.

7	**dxc5**	**♗xc5**
8	**♕xd5**	**♕b6**

Here there is an important alternative: 8 ... d6 9 exd6 ♕b6 *(128)* (giving up another pawn to allow Black's pieces to come into play more rapidly) and now:

(1) **10** ♗e3!? (for brave players

128 W

only) ♛xb2 (10 ... ♗xe3 11 fxe3
♛xe3+ 12 ♗e2 ♗e6 13 ♛g5 is
good for White) 11 ♗b5!? and
now **11 ... ♛xa1+** 12 ♔e2 ♛c3
13 ♗xc6+ bxc6 (not **13 ... ♔f8?**
14 ♛xc5 nor **13 ... ♔d8?** 14
♛xf7) 14 ♛xc6+ ♔f8 15 ♛xa8
♛xc2+ 16 ♘d2 ♗xd6 17 ♖b1
leads to an advantage for White.
11 ... ♛xb5 12 ♛xc5 is depressing for Black, while **11 ... 0-0** 12
0-0 ♗xe3 13 fxe3 ♗e6 14 ♛c5
was good for White in Boll–Lanz,
corr. 1982, so the best line is **11 ...
♗b4+** 12 ♔e2 ♛xc2+ 13 ♘d2
♗e6 with a total mess.

(2) **10 ♛e4+** ♗e6 (10 ... ♔d8
11 ♗g5+ f6 12 0-0-0! ♖e8 13
♛h4 is good for White) 11 ♛h4!
(11 ♗c4!? is an interesting recent
idea, when van der Wiel–Short,
Wijk aan Zee 1990 continued 11
... ♛b4+ 12 ♘d2 0-0 13 0-0
♖ae8 14 c3 ♛b6 15 ♘f3 h6 16 b4
♗xd6 17 ♗e3 ♛c7 18 ♗xe6
♖xe6 19 ♛c4 and Black has insufficient compensation for the
pawn) with the variations:

(2a) **11 ... f6** 12 ♗d3 0-0-0 (12
... ♘b4 13 d7+! ♗xd7 14
♛h5+ followed by 0-0 is good
for White) 13 0-0 and there is a
further branch:

(2a1) **13 ... ♗xd6** 14 ♗e3
♛xb2 15 ♖ab1 ♛a3 16 ♗c4 gives
White good attacking chances for
no sacrifice.

(2a2) **13 ... ♖xd6** 14 ♗e3 (I am
not sure that it was necessary to
return the pawn since Black has
no immediate threats; 14 a3
intending b4 appears promising)

♗xe3 15 fxe3 ♛xe3+ 16 ♔h1
♛c5? (16 ... ♛b6 is just slightly
better for White) 17 ♖ae1 ♗d7
18 ♛g3 g6 19 ♘d2! f5 20 ♘b3
♛b4 21 a3 winning material,
Chandler–Arnold, Bundesliga
1987.

(2a3) **13 ... h5** 14 ♗e3 ♗xe3 15
fxe3 ♛xe3+ 16 ♔h1 ♗g4 (16 ...
♖xd6 17 ♖ae1 ♛b6 18 ♖xe6
♖xe6 19 ♗f5) 17 ♛g3 (17 ♖ae1
♛c5 18 ♗e4 is good for White
according to Gutman) ♛c5 18
♖ad1 ♔b8 19 ♗e4 ♘e5 20 ♘xe5
♖xd1, Hansson–Fernandes, London 1984, and although this game
has appeared a number of times in
print, nobody seems to have
noticed that after 21 ♛xg7 Black
can quite reasonably resign.

(2b) **11 ... ♖xd6** 12 ♗e2 (even
12 ♗d3 ♘b4 13 0-0 ♘xd3 14
cxd3 0-0 15 ♛e4 h6 16 ♗e3 ♛xb2
17 ♖fb1 was slightly better for
White in Hellers–Ivarsson, Sweden 1985) ♗e7 (12 ... ♘b4 13 0-0
is good for White after **13 ... 0-0**
14 c3 or **13 ... ♗e7** 14 ♛e4 f5 15
♛e5 ♘xc2 16 ♗g5) 13 ♛e4 0-0-0
14 0-0 ♗d5 (after 14 ... ♘d4 15
♘xd4 ♖xd4 16 ♛e3 ♗c5 17 ♛c3
White stands very well) 15 ♛g4+
♔b8 (15 ... ♗e6 16 ♛a4),
Chandler–Bartsch, Bundesliga
1985, and now 16 c4! is good for
White.

9	♗c4	♗xf2+
10	♔e2	0-0
11	♖f1	♗c5

Black has regained the sacrificed pawn, but now f7 is exposed
to attack.

129
B

12 ♘g5 *(129)* **♘d4+**

Transferring the knight to e6 in order to shield f7. 12 ... ♘xe5? (12 ... d6? 13 ♖xf7! ♘d4+ 14 ♔d1 ♗g4+ 15 ♖f3+ ♔h8 16 ♕g8+ and mate) 13 ♕xe5 d5 14 ♕xd5 ♖e8+ (14 ... ♗g4+ 15 ♖f3 ♗g1 16 ♔f1! ♖ad8 17 ♕e4 ♖d1+ 18 ♔e2 ♗xf3+ 19 gxf3 ♖fd8 20 ♗xf7+ ♔f8 21 ♘xh7+ ♔xf7 22 ♘g5+ ♔f8 23 ♕f5+ ♔e7 24 ♕f7+ ♔d6 25 ♗f4+ ♔c6 26 ♕c4+ ♔c5 27 ♕xc5+ ♗xc5 28 ♖xd1 ♖e8+ 29 ♘e4 Resigns was Prokopchuk–Kuznetsov, USSR 1972) 15 ♔f3 ♕f6+ 16 ♔g3 ♗d6+ 17 ♖f4! ♗e6 18 ♘xe6 ♖xe6 19 ♕xd6 ♕g6+ 20 ♖g4 ♖e3+ 21 ♗xe3 ♕xd6+ 22 ♔f2 ♖e8 23 ♖f4 ♖e7 24 ♗b3 ♕e5 25 ♖e1 g5 26 ♖f3 ♔g7 27 ♖d1 f6 28 ♔g1 g4 29 ♗d4 Resigns, Spassky–Ciric, Marianske Lazne 1962.

13 ♔d1 ♘e6
14 ♘e4

Here White has various possibilities, but this move attacking c5 and restraining ... d6 looks best.

14 ... d6

14 ... ♗e7 is too passive and in Savkin–Tseitlin, corr. 1972 White obtained a strong attack after 15 c3 (15 ♘d6 is also good) d6 16 exd6 ♖d8 17 ♕c2 ♗xd6 18 ♖xf7! ♔xf7 19 ♘g5+ ♔e8 (19 ... ♔g8 20 ♕e4 h6 21 ♗e3 ♕a5 22 ♗xe6+ ♗xe6 23 ♕h7+ and ♖f1+ wins) 20 ♘xe6 ♕f2+ 21 ♔b3 ♕b6+ 22 ♗b5+ ♗d7 23 ♘c7+! and Black resigned without waiting to see one of the lines **23 ... ♕xc7** 24 ♕g8+ ♗f8 25 ♗f4! or **23 ... ♗xc7** 24 ♕g8+ ♔e7 25 ♗g5+ ♔d6 26 ♖d1+.

15 exd6 ♖d8

15 ... ♗xd6? is a miscombination which rebounds after 16 ♘xd6 ♖d8 17 ♗f4 ♘xf4 (Black saw the danger in Zaretdinov–Pugachevsky, USSR 1977 but still lost after 17 ... h6 18 ♗e5 ♘g5 19 ♖xf7 etc) 18 ♕xf7+ ♔h8 ♕g8+ Resigns, Unzicker–Sarapu, Siegen 1970.

16 ♗d3 ♗xd6
17 ♕h5 f5
18 ♘xd6 ♕xd6

After 18 ... ♖xd6 19 ♕xf5 the threats to f7 and h7 force 19 ... ♖xd3+, but Black does not have enough compensation.

19 ♕xf5 *(130)*
19 ... ♕xh2

Or 19 ... ♘f8 (19 ... g6 20 ♕f7+ ♔h8 21 ♕f6+ ♔g8 22 ♗f4 liquidates to an ending in which White has a clear extra pawn) 20 ♕f7+ ♔h8 21 ♕f4 and now:

(1) **21 ... ♕c5** 22 ♗e3 ♕h5+ (22 ... ♗g4+ 23 ♔d2 ♕a5+ 24

After this move White can gain a clear endgame advantage with no risk. The critical move is 22 . . . ♕xg2! 23 ♕h5! *(131)* (I gave 23 ♖f2 in the first edition, but 23 . . . ♕g4+ 24 ♔d2 ♕b4+ 25 ♔d1 ♘g5! is good for Black) and now:

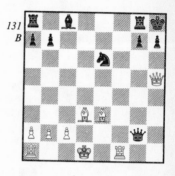

b4 ♕h5 25 ♕g5 exchanges queens) 23 ♔d2 ♗e6 24 ♕g5 (24 ♗d4! looks very good to me since **24 . . . ♘g6** allows 25 ♗xg7+ ♔xg7 26 ♕f6+ and **24 . . . ♕d5** 25 ♕e5! ♕xg2+ 26 ♖f2 ♕g4 27 h3! is a disaster) ♕e8, A. Rodriguez–Diaz, Cuba Ch. 1983, and now 25 ♖f4 intending ♗d4 gives White a clear advantage.

(2) **21 . . . ♕e7** 22 ♕g5 ♕e8, Short–Minic, Banja Luka 1985, and now Minic gives the line 23 ♗d2 ♗e6 (23 . . . ♕a4 24 ♗c3! ♖xd3+ 25 ♔c1 ♘g6 26 ♖f8+ mates) 24 ♗c3 ♘g6 25 ♔d2 ♖d5 26 ♕g3 ♕d7 27 ♖ae1, assessing the final position as slightly better for White. I suspect that White's advantage is considerably greater than this; he is a pawn up with the two bishops, and if he consolidates with ♔c1 he must be winning. Therefore Black should play 27 . . . ♗f5, but after 28 ♖e3 followed by ♔c1 White is a pawn up for nothing.

20	♕f7+	♔h8
21	♗g5	♖g8
22	♗e3!	♘d8

(1) **23 . . . ♘f8?!** 24 ♖f4! (intending ♖h4 and mate on h7) ♕h3 (seemingly forced) 25 ♕xh3 ♗xh3, Odeev–Varlamov, corr. 1987, and now 26 ♔d2 ♗g2 (26 . . . ♖d8 27 ♖h1 ♗g2 28 ♖h2 ♗c6 29 ♖fh4 h6 30 ♗d4 wins the exchange) 27 ♖g1 ♗c6 28 ♖h4 (intending ♖g3–h3) ♖d8 29 ♖g3 ♗d7 30 ♗d4 and White has a large advantage.

(2) **23 . . . g6** 24 ♕h4! (24 ♗d4+ ♘g7 25 ♗xg7+ ♔xg7 26 ♕e5+ ♔h6 is a draw) ♘g7 (**24 . . . ♖d8** 25 ♕f6+ ♔g8 26 ♕f7+ ♔h8 27 ♗d2! and **24 . . . ♗d7** 25 ♖f7 ♖g7 26 ♗e4! are very good for White) 25 ♖g1 ♕f3+ (25 . . . ♕d5 26 ♖xg6 threatening 27 ♕xh7+ ♕xh7 28 ♖h6 mate is crushing) 26 ♔d2 ♗f5 reaching a position in which White has a

very strong attack for the pawn. I have not been able to find a forced win for White, but Black has a difficult defence in prospect, e.g. 27 ♖g3 ♛d5 28 ♖h1 h5 29 ♗d4 (29 ♛g5? ♖gd8!) ♗xd3 (the threat was 30 ♛xh5+) 30 cxd3 ♔h7 (to defend against both ♖xg6 and ♖g5 followed by ♖xh5+) 31 ♖g5 ♛e6 (31 ... ♛f7? 32 ♛e4 ♘f5 33 ♖hxh5+ gxh5 34 ♖xf5 wins) 32 ♖e5 ♛c6 33 ♖c1 ♛g2+ 34 ♖e2 ♛d5 (34 ... ♛g4 35 ♛xg4 hxg4 36 ♖e7 wins) 35 ♖c5 ♛d6 36 ♖e7 ♖ad8 37 ♔c3 and Black is in big trouble since 38 ♖cc7 is threatened and 37 ... ♖c8 fails to 38 ♖xg7+ while 37 ... ♖d7 loses after 38 ♖xh5+.

23   ♛f2?!

As Rhine correctly points out, 23 ♛f4! ♛xf4 (23 ... ♛xg2 24 ♖g1 ♛d5 25 ♔d2 and ♖h1) 24 ♖xf4 would have given White a very favourable ending at no risk.

23   ...   ♘c6
24   ♔d2   ♛d6?

The bishop on d3 is the main enemy and Black should have tried to eliminate it by 24 ... ♘e5, when 25 ♗xh7 (25 ♖h1 ♘xd3) ♖d8+! (25 ... ♘c4+ 26 ♔c3 ♛e5+ 27 ♗d4 ♛a5+ 28 ♔xc4 ♗e6+ 29 ♔d3 and White evades the checks) 26 ♗d3 ♘xd3 27 cxd3 ♛d6 28 ♛h4+ ♔g8 29 ♛e4 leaves White with some advantage, but in view of the opposite coloured bishops it isn't clear how many winning chances he has.

25   ♖h1   h6
26   ♗c5!   (132)

White's ambition is to gain f4 for his queen, when a sacrifice on h6 will be inevitable.

26   ...   ♛d5

26 ... ♛c7 is spectacularly refuted by 27 ♛f6! 26 ... ♛e5 27 ♖ae1 ♛g5+ 28 ♗e3 followed by ♗xh6 also loses quickly.

27   ♛f4   ♖d8

27 ... ♛xg2+ 28 ♔c3 doesn't help Black in his efforts to combat ♖xh6+.

28   ♖xh6+   ♔g8
29   ♖h8+!   ♔xh8
30   ♛h4+   ♔g8
31   ♛h7+   ♔f7
32   ♛g6+   ♔g8
33   ♛h7+   ♔f7
34   ♖f1+   ♗f5

34 ... ♔e6/e8 35 ♛g6+ ♔d7 36 ♖f7+ mates.

35   ♖xf5+   ♛xf5
36   ♛xf5+   ♔g8
37   ♔c1   Resigns

Quite apart from his material disadvantage there is no defence to the threat of ♗c4+.

13   2 ... a6

This is often called the O'Kelly Variation after the late Belgian Grandmaster who played it with some regularity. Since ... a6 is almost universal in the Sicilian, Black gets it over with as soon as possible, reserving his options as to which Sicilian system to adopt. White should not play 3 d4? cxd4 4 ♘xd4 ♘f6 5 ♘c3 e5 when Black has a favourable version of the Najdorf in which his king's bishop can emerge actively at c5 or b4. 3 c3 is a sensible reply, which tends to lead to 2 c3 Sicilian positions in which Black has played the unusual move ... a6, which is perhaps not the best way to spend a tempo. However the strongest reply of all is 3 c4, which either leads to Maroczy Bind positions or to a sort of hedgehog.

In view of the rare occurrence of 2 ... a6 in practice, it perhaps does not rate a chapter of its own, but this did give me the excuse to include another of my own games in the book!

Game 30
Nunn–Surtees
Basingstoke Open 1977

1	e4	c5
2	♘f3	a6
3	c4 *(133)*	

133
B

3		♘c6

Or:

(1) **3 ... d6** (this may lead to a type of hedgehog) 4 d4 cxd4 (4 ... ♗g4 is an interesting move, since **5 dxc5** ♗xf3 **6 ♕xf3** dxc5 leaves Black with a grip on d4 to compensate for the two bishops; 6 gxf3! dxc5 7 ♕xd8+ ♔xd8 8 ♘c3 is possible, but the simplest line is **5 d5** with a positional edge for White) 5 ♘xd4 ♘f6 6 ♘c3 b6 (6 ... e6 7 ♗d3 leads to positions from Chapter 6, so we concentrate here on Black's attempt to develop early pressure against e4, which is unique to 2 ... a6) 7 ♗d3 ♗b7 8 0-0 (it is more accurate to play 8 ♕e2 ♘bd7 9 b3—see next note) ♘bd7 9 ♕e2 e6 (9 ... ♘e5 is interesting since 10 ♗c2 ♖c8 11 ♗a4+ ♘fd7 is unclear, so White would have to allow Black to take on d3) 10 b3 (10 f4 ♕c7 11 ♔h1

♗e7 12 ♗d2 is also good, when Nunn–Franklin, London 1985, continued 12 ... h5 13 ♖ae1 h4 14 f5 ♘f8 15 fxe6 fxe6 16 ♘d5! ♛d8 17 e5 dxe5 18 ♛xe5 ♘xd5 19 ♘xe6 ♛d6 20 ♛xd6 ♗xd6 21 cxd5 Resigns) ♛c7 11 ♗b2 ♛c5?! (Black plays too ambitiously with his king stuck in the centre—11 ... ♗e7 followed by ... 0-0 is better) 12 ♖ae1! (exploiting the tactical point 12 ... ♛xd4 13 ♘a4 White prepares a breakthrough by ♘d5) b5 (12 ... ♛h5 13 ♛d2 g6 14 f4 ♗h6 15 ♛f2 g5 16 ♗e2 g4 17 ♛g3 ♖g8 18 ♗d1! was also good for White in Nunn–Franklin, London 1977, since e5 is imminent, while Franklin's later suggestion of 13 ... g5 allows 14 ♘d5! with added effect as the f5 square is now available) 13 cxb5! ♛xd4 14 bxa6 ♗c6 15 ♘b5 ♛b6 16 ♗d4 ♛b8 17 ♖c1 ♘c5 18 a4! (this nullifies the threat of ... ♘xd3 and prepares to break open the c-file by b4) e5 19 ♗e3 ♗e7 20 b4 ♘xd3 21 ♖xc6 ♘xb4 22 a7 ♛b7 23 ♖b6 (heading for b8) ♛xe4 24 ♘c7+ ♔d7 25 ♛b5+ ♔xc7 26 ♖c1+ ♘c2 27 ♖xc2+ Resigns, Nunn–Franklin, Nottingham 1979, as 27 ... ♛xc2 28 ♖b7+ ♔d8 29 ♖b8+ ♔c7 30 ♗b6 is mate.

(2) **3 ... e6** 4 ♘c3 ♘c6 5 d4 cxd4 6 ♘xd4 ♗b9 (6 ... ♘f6 7 ♘c2! is good for White) reaching an unusual position which does not seem to be considered by theory. **7 ♘c2** ♗xc3+ 8 bxc3 is one possibility, but I like **7♘xc6.**

Then **7 ... bxc6** 8 ♛d4 looks very awkward since 8 ... ♘f6 and 8 ... ♛f6 are both met by e5, so **7 ... dxc6** 8 ♛xd8+ ♔xd8 is best. Then White plays 9 ♗f4, intending 0-0-0+ and ♘a4 with good play against the weak black squares at c5 and b6. If Black exchanges at c3 White had the dream square d6 for his bishop.

4	**d4**	**cxd4**
5	**♘xd4**	**♘f6**

Or 5 ... e5 (**5 ... e6** 6 ♘c2 is still good for White, and **5 ... g6** allows 6 ♘xc6 and 7 ♛d4) 6 ♘f5 d5 (6 ... ♘f6 7 ♘c3 transposes to Nunn–Surtees) 7 cxd5 ♗xf5 8 exf5 ♘d4 9 ♘c3 ♘e7 (again 9 ... ♘f6 transposes) 10 ♗d3 (10 f6 is also promising) ♘exf5 11 0-0 ♗d6 12 f4 with a dangerous initiative for White.

6	**♘c3**	**e5**
7	**♘f5**	**d5**

After 7 ... d6 8 ♗g5 (8 ♘e3 controlling d5 is also good) ♗xf5 9 exf5 ♘d4 10 ♗d3 White's control of e4 and d5 gives him an excellent position.

8	**cxd5**	**♗xf5**
9	**exf5**	**♘d4**
10	**♗d3**	**♘xd5**
11	**0-0** *(134)*	**♗b4**

Black has tried a variety of moves in this position, but without coming close to equality, for example **11 ... ♘xc3** 12 bxc3 ♘c6 (once the knight has to move from d4 the only asset of Black's position vanishes) 13 ♖b1 ♖b8 14 ♛f3 ♛c7 15 ♗e4, Ravinsky–Kliascicki, USSR 1966, **11 ...**

♘f6 12 ♖e1 ♘c6 13 ♕b3 ♗b4 14 ♖d1 ♕e7 15 ♗g5, Rogacovski–Konovalov, corr. 1972 or **11 ... ♗e7** 12 ♗e4 ♘xc3 13 bxc3 ♘c6 14 ♖b1 ♕c8 15 ♕g4, Matanovic–Perez, Belgrade 1961 with a clear plus for White in every case.

12	♗e4!	♘xc3
13	bxc3	♗xc3
14	♖b1	0-0

In Altshuler–Fink, corr. 1960 Black tried to hold on to the pawn but after 14 ... ♖b8 15 ♕g4 g6 16 ♗g5 gxf5 17 ♗xf5 f6 18 ♕h5+ White had a winning position.

15 ♖xb7

This simple move was suggested by Gligoric and Sokolov as an improvement over the unclear continuation 15 ♕g4 ♕d6 16 ♖d1 ♖ac8 (but not 16 ... ♖ad8? 17 ♖d3 ♗b4 18 f6!) 17 ♖d3 ♖c4 in which White lacks a knock-out blow.

15 ... ♕d6 *(135)*

White's main threat was 16 ♗a3, driving the rook away from the defence of f7, followed by ♕h5 and if Black manages to defend f7 White still has the crushing blow f6 in reserve.

Black's ... ♕d6 is of course designed to prevent ♗a3, but unfortunately the move loses by force. He had to try 15 ... ♖b8 although 16 ♖xb8 ♕xb8 17 f6 gives White a strong attack with no material investment.

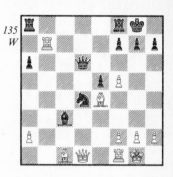

16 ♖b3!

White utilizes the undefended queen to threaten ♗xa8, ♖xc3 and ♗a3. Black's reply is forced.

16	...	♖ac8
17	♗a3	♕d8

If the queen moves anywhere else 18 ♗xf8 ♘xb3 19 ♗xg7 wins a pawn and demolishes Black's kingside.

| 18 | ♖b7 | ♖e8 *(136)* |

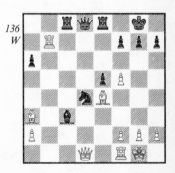

19   ♖xf7

A piece of rather unnecessary flashiness since 19 ♕h5 ♕f6 (or 19 ... ♖c7 20 f6) 20 ♗d5 wins quite easily.

19   ...   ♕g5

19 ... ♔xf7 20 ♕h5+ ♔g8 (20 ... ♔f6 21 ♕xh7 ♔f7 22 ♕h5+ forces the king to g8 in any case) 21 f6 g6 22 ♗xg6 ♕d7 23 f7+ wins, but Black can hardly hope to survive long after losing the vital f7 pawn.

20   ♗d5   ♔h8

21   f6   g6

21 ... gxf6 22 ♗e7 costs material.

22   ♕a4   e4

Losing at once, but Black's king would have succumbed soon in any case.

23   ♖xh7+   Resigns

After 23 ... ♔xh7 24 ♕d7+ ♔h6 25 ♕g7+ ♔h5 26 ♕h7+ ♔g4 (26 ... ♔h6 27 g4+ ♔g5 28 f4+ exf3 29 ♗c1+) 27 ♕h3+ ♔f4 28 ♗d6+ ♖e5 29 ♕xc8 the position speaks for itself.

14   Unusual Lines

The material in the first 13 chapters will be sufficient to prepare the reader for the vast majority of the games he will have as White against the Sicilian, but there remain a substantial number of unusual variations which Black players might adopt. Only a few have any pretentions to respectability and we concentrate on these few in this chapter. Wilder eccentricities are usually best dealt with by an application of common sense and straightforward development. The following breakdown of lines considered in this chapter will aid the reader in locating the variation he is looking for.

A   The pseudo-Dragon 1 e4 c5 2 ♘f3 ♘c6 3 d4 cxd4 4 ♘xd4 ♘f6 5 ♘c3 g6.
B   Unusual lines involving 2 ... ♘c6 apart from the pseudo-Dragon: 1 e4 c5 2 ♘f3 ♘c6 3 d4 cxd4 (3 ... d5) 4 ♘xd4 ♘f6 (4 ... a6, 4 ... d5, 4 ... ♕c7, 4 ... ♕b6) 5 ♘c3 ♕b6.
C   Unusual lines involving 2 ... d6: 1 e4 c5 2 ♘f3 d6 3 d4 cxd4 3 ... ♘f6) 4 ♘xd4 ♘f6 5 ♘c3 e5 (5 ... ♘bd7) 6 ♗b5 + .
D   Unusual lines involving 2 ... e6: 1 e4 c5 2 ♘f3 e6 3 d4 cxd4

(3 ... d5) 4 ♘xd4 ♗c5 or 4 ... ♗b4 + .
E   Unusual Black second moves: 1 e4 c5 2 ♘f3 g6 (2 ... ♕c7, 2 ... b6).

A

1	e4	c5
2	♘f3	♘c6
3	d4	cxd4
4	♘xd4	♘f6
5	♘c3	g6 (137)

137
W

This is an attempt by Black to reach accelerated Dragon positions without allow White the option of playing the Maroczy bind. It has been played a few times in Grandmaster chess, but White can obtain a clear advantage with accurate play.

	6 ♘xc6	bxc6

Or 6 ... dxc6 7 ♕xd8 + ♔xd8 8 ♗c4 ♔e8 (not 8 ... b5? 9 ♗xf7 e6 10 ♗g5 ♗e7 11 0-0-0 + winning, while **8 ... ♗g7** 9 ♗f4 ♔e8 10 0-0-0 ♘d7 11 ♗c7! is good for White since Black is not allowed to castle) 9 e5 ♘g4 10 f4 h5 (after 10 ... ♗f5 11 h3 ♘h6 12 g4 Black has to go back since 12 ... ♗xc2 13 ♖h2 ♗a4 14 ♘xa4 b5 15 ♗b3 bxa4 16 ♗xa4 ♖c8 17 ♖c2 ♔d7 18 ♗e3 is winning for White) 11 ♗d2 h4 (or 11 ... ♗f5 12 h3 ♘h6 13 0-0-0 ♗g7 14 ♖he1 with advantage to White) 12 ♘e4 ♘h6 13 ♗c3 h3 14 e6 ♖g8 15 exf7+ ♘xf7 16 0-0-0! with a clear plus for White, Maus–Schlick, Bundesliga 1987.

7 e5 ♘g8

After 7 ... ♘d5 8 ♘xd5 cxd5 9 ♕xd5 ♖b8 10 e6! (with ♕e5 if the pawn is taken) f6 11 ♗f4 ♖b4 12 ♗d2 ♖b6 13 ♗b5 ♖d6 14 ♕c4 White has a winning position.

8 ♗c4 *(138)*

8 ... ♗g7

Other moves are no better:

(1) **8 ... d5** 9 exd6 ♕xd6 (9 ... exd6 10 ♕f3 d5 11 ♘xd5 cxd5 12 ♗xd5 ♕e7+ 13 ♗e3 ♖b8 14 0-0 ♗g7 15 ♗f4 with a decisive at-

tack) 10 0-0 ♕xd1 11 ♖xd1 ♗h6 12 ♗xh6 ♘xh6 13 ♖d2 ♘f5 14 ♘e4 is very pleasant for White, Geller–Stein, USSR Ch. 1966–7.

(2) **8 ... ♕a5** 9 0-0 and now:

(2a) **9 ... ♕xe5** 10 ♖e1 ♕a5 (or 10 ... ♕b8 11 ♕d4 f6 12 ♘e4 ♗g7 13 ♗f4 ♕b6 14 ♘d6+ ♔f8 15 ♕d3 ♗b7 16 ♗xg8 ♖xg8 17 ♕c4 Resigns, Tiviakov–Mugerman, Pinsk 1989) 11 b4 ♕d8 leaves Black in a dreadful mess. In Karaklajic–Ivanovic, Yugoslavia 1974, White won Black's queen by 12 ♘e4 e6 13 ♗b2 f6 14 ♗xe6 dxe6 15 ♘xf6+ ♔xf6 16 ♗xf6 ♘xf6, which proved sufficient in the end, but I would not be surprised if White had an even stronger continuation.

(2b) **9 ... ♗g7** 10 ♕f3 f5 (**10 ... e6** 11 ♗f4 and **10 ... f6** 11 ♖e1 are also good for White) 11 ♗f4 leads to the note to Black's 10th move below.

9 ♕f3 f5

Relatively best, for example 9 ... e6 10 ♗f4 ♕a5 11 0-0! ♕xe5 12 b4 ♕c7 13 ♘b5 ♕b8 14 ♗xe5 ♕xe5 15 ♖ad1 d5 16 ♖fe1 ♕b8 17 ♗xd5 cxd5 18 ♕xd5 ♔f8 19 ♕d8+ ♔g7 20 ♘c7 ♘f6 21 ♕e7 and White wins.

10 ♗f4 e6

Or 10 ... ♖b8 (10 ... ♕a5 11 0-0 ♗xe5 12 b4 ♕c7 13 ♘b5 ♕b8 14 ♗xe5 ♕xe5 15 ♖fe1 ♕b8 16 ♕c3 is now instantly decisive) 11 0-0 e6 12 ♖ad1 followed by ♖fe1 and just as in the main line White has an unpleasant bind, Andersson–Bilek, Teeside 1972. Black has no way to solve the problem of his backward d-pawn and the g7 bishop is inactive. White players must be on the lookout for the exchange sacrifice ... ♖b4xf4, which can be good for Black if he can get the e5 pawn, but provided White keeps his bind on Black's position he can be optimistic about the future.

11 0-0

The correct choice; in other games White played 0-0-0, but this gives Black counterplay down the b-file.

11 ... ♘h6

We give the rest of the game Short–Sosonko, Wijk aan Zee 1986, which is a model example of how to play such positions. Black is never allowed to free himself and is finally overcome by the problems resulting from the backward d-pawn: 12 ♖ad1 ♕c7 13 ♖fe1 ♘f7 14 ♕g3 0-0 15 h4 ♔h8 16 ♘a4 a5 17 b3 ♖e8 18 ♕e3 h6 19 g4! ♖g8 20 ♗g3 ♗f8 21 ♕b6 ♖a7 22 f3 ♕xb6+ 23 ♘xb6 ♗c5+ 24 ♗f2 ♗xf2+ 25 ♔xf2 fxg4 26 fxg4 ♔g7 27 ♘a4 g5 28 h5 ♖f8 29 ♔g3 ♘d8 30 ♘c5 ♖f4 31 a4 ♔f8 32 ♗d3 ♔e7 33 ♗g6 ♖a8 34 ♖e3 ♖b8 35 ♖ed3 ♖bb4 36 ♖xd7+ ♗xd7 37 ♖xd7+ Resigns.

B 1 e4 c5
2 ♘f3 ♘c6
3 d4 cxd4

3 ... d5 4 exd5 ♕xd5 5 ♘c3 ♕e6+ (or 5 ... ♕h5 6 d5) 6 ♗e3 cxd4 7 ♘xd4 ♕d7 8 ♘db5 ♖b8 9 ♕e2 and White is probably winning already, Boleslavsky–Gurgenidze, USSR 1960.

4 ♘xd4 ♕b6

4 ... a6 c4 transposes to Chapter 13, 4 ... d5 5 ♘c3 dxe4 6 ♘xc6 ♕xd1+ 7 ♔xd1 bxc6 8 ♘xe4 ♗f5 9 ♗d3 0-0-0 10 ♔e2 e6 11 ♗f4 ♔b7 12 ♖ad1 is just good for White and 4 ... ♘f6 5 ♘c3 ♕b6 transposes to the main line. That leaves 4 ... ♕c7, which can be met by 5 ♘b5 ♕b8 6 c4 ♘f6 7 ♘5c3 e6 8 f4 (8 ♗e3 allows either **8 ... ♗d6!?** or **8 ... b6** followed by ... ♗c5) d6 (8 ... ♗c5 9 e5 ♘g8 10 ♘e4) 9 ♗e2 ♗e7 10 ♗e3 0-0 11 0-0 b6 (White has a favourable version of Chapter 8 in which Black has lost time with his queen) 12 ♘d2 ♗b7 13 ♗f3 ♖d8 14 a3 (better than 14 ♖c1 ♗f8 15 ♕e2 d5!? with unclear play, Chandler–Barlov, Haninge 1988) ♗f8 15 ♗f2 ♘d7 16 b4 with advantage to White, Karpov–Kurajica, Hastings 1971/2.

5 ♘b3 ♘f6
6 ♘c3 e6
7 ♗e3 ♕c7
8 ♗d3 *(139)*

139
B

8 ...   ♗e7

Or 8 ... a6 (8 ... ♗b4 9 0-0 0-0 10 ♘b5 ♛b8 11 f4 was good for White in Gheorghiu–Forintos, Monte Carlo 1968) 9 f4 d6 10 ♛f3 (**10 ♛e2** is also possible, as in some examples below, while White may start his kingside pawn advance immediately, e.g. **10 g4** b5 11 g5 ♘d7 12 ♛d2 ♗b7 13 0-0-0 ♘c5 14 ♛f2! with some advantage to White, Belyavsky–Gufeld, Suhumi 1972) b5 (if Black plays ... ♗e7 we transpose to the main line below) 11 0-0-0 ♗b7 12 ♚b1 ♘a5 13 ♘xa5 ♛xa5 14 g4 0-0-0 15 g5 ♘d7 16 a3 ♚b8 17 ♛f2 ♗e7 18 ♗d4 e5 19 fxe5 dxe5 20 ♗a7+ ♚a8 21 ♘d5 with a clear plus for White, King–Wirthensohn, Berne 1988.

9 f4   **d6**
10 ♛f3

It is useful for White to delay committing his king, since he can reasonably castle on either side. However, there is an argument for developing the queen to e2, for example 10 ♛e2 a6 and now **11 0-0-0** 0-0 12 g4 ♖e8 13 g5 ♘d7 14 ♖f3 g6 15 ♖af1 b5 16 ♖h3 b4 17 ♘d1, A. Rodriguez–Carlier, Amsterdam 1987 or **11 0-0-0** b5 12 ♚b1 ♘b4 13 g4 ♘d7 14 g5 ♗b7 15 a3 ♘xd3 16 cxd3 g6 17 ♖c1 ♘c5 18 ♘d4 ♛d8 19 h4, Todorovic–Bosic, Novi Sad Open 1988, with good attacking chances for White in both cases. In Wedberg–Benko, New York Open 1989, the continuation 10 0-0 0-0?! (castling into the storm is wrong; 10 ... a6 was better) 11 g4 (White is even better off than in the main line, as his queen may go directly to h5) ♘d7 12 g5 ♖e8 13 ♖f3 a6 14 ♖h3 gave White a massive attack; the finish was 14 ... ♘f8 15 ♛h5 ♘b4 16 ♖f1 ♗d8 17 a3 ♘xd3 18 cxd3 b5 19 f5 exf5 20 ♘d5 ♛d7 21 ♗d4 fxe4 22 ♖h4 e3 23 ♘xe3 ♖e6 24 ♖hf4 ♖g6 25 ♖xf7 ♛xf7 26 ♖xf7 ♖xg5+ 27 ♛xg5 ♗xg5 28 ♖xg7+ Resigns.

10 ...   **a6** *(140)*

Black also delays castling since 10 ... 0-0 11 g4 ♖e8 12 g5 ♘d7 13 h4 ♘b4 14 h5 ♗f8 15 0-0-0 a6 16 g6 gave White an immense attack in Jansa–Martinovic, Vrnjacka Banja 1982.

140 W

11 g4

White has a choice of good lines. After 11 0-0 0-0 (not **11 ... b5** 12 e5, but castling invites the kingside pawn storm, so **11 ... ♗d7** may be best) 12 g4 (in some games White played ♖ae1, but this preparation is not necessary) Black has fared very badly in practice, for example **12 ... ♖e8**

13 g5 ♘d7 14 ♕h5 ♘f8 15 f5 ♘e5
16 f6 ♗d8 17 ♘d4 b5 18 ♖f2
♗b7 19 ♖af1 b4 20 ♘ce2 ♘fg6
21 ♘g3, Hawelko–Sznapik,
Slupsk 1988 or **12 ... ♘b4** 13 g5
♘d7 14 ♕h5 g6 15 ♕h6 ♖e8 16
♖ad1 b5 17 a3 ♘xd3 18 ♖xd3
♗f8 19 ♕h4 ♗b7 20 ♗d4, G.
Mainka–Martinovic, Dortmund
II 1988, and White's attack is
overwhelming in both cases.

11 ... b6

This rather odd move is
designed to support c5 in anti-
cipation of the manoeuvre ...
♘d7–c5. **11 ... h6** 12 0-0-0 b5 13
♖hg1 ♘d7 14 ♕f2! (this possibility explains Black's preference
for ... b6 in the main line, since
once he has played ... b5 the
knight on d7 is hard to redeploy)
♗b7 15 ♔b1 ♗f6? (Black's ... 6
renders the kingside too dangerous for ... 0-0—he should have
played 15 ... ♘b4) 16 e5! dxe5 17
♗xb5 0-0 18 g5 hxg5 19 fxg5
♗e7, Estrin–Kopylov, USSR
1973, and now 20 ♕h4! axb5 21
♖g3 would have given White a
decisive attack according to
Estrin. Perhaps Black should try
11 ... b5 but White still has the
advantage.

12 g5 ♘d7

13 0-0-0 ♘c5 14 ♔b1 (to
answer ... ♘xd3 by cxd3) ♗d7
15 h4 ♕b7 16 ♗e2! (now the c5
knight isn't doing much) ♘a7 17
f5 ♘b5 18 ♗d4 ♗c6 19 fxe6
♘xc3+ 20 ♗xc3 ♘xe6 21 ♖hf1
0-0 22 ♗d3 b5 23 a3 ♘c5 24
♘xc5! dxc5 25 ♕f5 ♖ae8 (or 25

... c4 26 ♕e5 f6 27 gxf6 ♗xf6 28
♕e6+ ♖f7 29 ♖xf6!) 26 ♗xg7!
♗d7 (26 ... ♔xg7 27 e5) 27 ♕e5
♗d8 28 ♕d6 ♔xg7 29 ♕h6+
♔h8 30 e5 f5 31 exf6 ♗e6 32
♖de1 c4 33 ♗g6 ♖f7 34 ♗xf7
♕xf7 35 g6 ♕xg6 37 f7 Resigns,
Kavalek–Hübner, Buenos Aires
1978.

C 1 e4 c5
2 ♘f3 d6
3 d4 cxd4

Black quite often plays 3 ...
♘f6 in order to avoid the line 3
... cxd4 4 ♕xd4. White should
reply 4 ♘c3 when Black is obliged
to play 4 ... cxd4 5 ♘xd4 transposing to normal lines.

4 ♘xd4 ♘f6
5 ♘c3 e5 *(141)*

Or 5 ... ♘bd7 6 ♗c4 ♘b6
(Black's development is not easy
because ... e6 and ... ♗e7 will
allow a ♗xe6 sacrifice, while 6 ...
g7 7 f3 ♗g7 8 ♗e3 0-0 9 ♕d2 is a
Dragon in which Black has developed his knight to the inferior
square d7) 7 ♗b3 e5 8 ♘de2 ♗e6
9 ♗g5 ♗e7 10 ♗xf6 ♗xf6 11
♘d5 ♘xd5 12 ♗xd5 ♕b6 13

141
W

♗b3 0-0 14 ♘c3 and White's control of d5 gives him a clear advantage, R. Byrne–Cuellar, Siegen 1970.

6   ♗b5+

One of the points of 5 ... a6 is to prepare ... e5 by preventing this move, so it is the only logical reply to 5 ... e5.

6   ...   ♘bd7

After 6 ... ♗d7 7 ♗xd7+ ♕xd7 8 ♘f3 (8 ♘f5 allows Black to complicate the issue by 8 ... ♘xe4) the exchange of white-squared bishops enhances the weakness of d5.

7   ♘f5   a6

8   ♗xd7+   ♕xd7 *(142)*

142
W

The critical moment. White has a number of possible plans, but it is not clear which is the best:

(1) **9 ♗g5** ♘xe4 10 ♘xg7+ ♗xg7 11 ♘xe4 and now:

(1a) **11 ... d5?!** 12 ♘f6+ ♗xf6 13 ♗xf6 0-0 (13 ... ♖g8 14 0-0 is also very bad) 14 ♕d3 e4 15 ♕d4 ♖e8 16 g4! ♕d6 17 0-0-0 ♕f4+ 18 ♔b1 ♖e6 19 g5 ♖e8 20 ♗h8 f6 21 gxf6 ♕f5 22 ♖hg1+ ♔f7 23 ♖g7+ ♔e6 24 ♕b6+ Resigns, Camacho–Cruz Lima, Cuba 1986.

(1b) **11 ... 0-0** (this pawn sacrifice is the point of the variation, but it may not be correct) 12 ♕xd6 f6 (12 ... ♕f5 13 ♘f6+ ♗xf6 14 ♕xf6 ♕e4+ 15 ♔f1 ♗h3 16 f3 ♕c4+ 17 ♔e1 ♕b4+ 18 ♗d2 is good for White) and I doubt if Black has enough for the pawn. After 13 ♗e3 ♕g4 14 ♘c3! ♗f5 15 ♕d5+ ♗f7 16 h3 ♕g6 17 0-0-0! ♖c8 (17 ... ♗xc2 18 ♖d2 ♗f5 19 g4 is good for White) 18 ♖d2, Klovan–Mocalov, USSR 1981 or **13 ♕xd7** ♗xd7 14 ♗d2 ♗f5 15 f3 ♗g6 16 0-0-0 ♖ac8 17 ♗c3 b5 18 a3 ♖c6 19 ♖d7 ♗f5 20 ♖a7 ♗h6+ 21 ♗d2 ♗xd2+ 22 ♔xd2, Perenyi–Bielczyk, Berlin Open 1988, White had the advantage and although Black managed to draw the first of these games the ending cannot be pleasant for him.

(2) **9 ♘e3** ♕c6 and now:

(2a) **10 ♕d3** (this gives White a small but safe advantage) ♗e6 11 0-0 ♖c8 12 ♗d2 (12 a4 ♗e7 13 ♘cd5 ♗xd5 14 exd5 ♕c7 15 a5 g6 16 b3 0-0 17 ♘c4 ♖fe8 18 ♗e3 ♗f8 was equal in Popovic–Rajkovic, Vrsac 1987) ♗e7 (12 ... g6 is possible, but White is still slightly better) 13 ♘cd5 ♗d8 (now 13 ... ♗xd5 14 exd5 ♕c7 15 ♘f5 is good for White; ♗d2 is much more useful than a4) 14 c4 0-0 15 ♖ac1 ♖e8 16 b3 ♘d7 17 ♘b4 with some advantage for White, Ehlvest–Kupreichik, Moscow TV 1987.

(2b) **10 ⊘ed5** ⊘xd5 11 ⊘xd5
♗e6 0-0 ♖c8 13 c4!? ♕xc4 14
⊘b6 ♕xe4 15 ⊘xc8 ♗xc8 16
♖e1 ♕g4 17 f3 with a small plus
for White, Krnic–Jovanovic,
Yugoslavia 1982.

(2c) **10 0-0** ⊘xe4 (10 ... ♗e6 is
probably better, when White may
have nothing better than 11 ♕d3
transposing to line 2a) 11 ⊘xe4
♕xe4 12 ⊘d5 ♖b8 13 b3 ♗f5 14
c4 f6 15 ♗a3 ♚f7 16 ♕d2 ♖d8 17
♖fe1 ♕g4 18 ⊘e3 ♕g5 19
♕d5+ with advantage to White,
L. Schneider–Bator, Sweden Ch.
1986.

(2d) **10 ♕f3!?** b5 11 0-0 ♗b7 12
⊘cd5 ⊘xd5 13 ⊘xd5 ♕xc2 14
♗g5 ♗xd5 15 exd5 f6 16 ♖ac1
♕g6 17 ♗d2 ♗e7 18 ♖c7 with
good compensation for the pawn,
Kudrin–Conquest, London 1986.

D **1 e4   c5**
    2 ⊘f3   e6
    3 d4   cxd4

3 ... d5 4 exd5 exd5 5 ♗b5+
⊘c6 gives Black an uncomfortable isolated pawn position after
6 ⊘c3 or 6 0-0.

    4 ⊘xd4   ♗c5

Or 4 ... ♗b4+, when White
can transpose to chapter 11 by 5
⊘c3 ⊘f6, but it is also possible to
play 5 c3 ♗e7 6 c4, with a Maroczy bind position.

The idea of 4 ... ♗c5 is to
reach a position similar to that
after 1 e4 c5 2 ⊘f3 e6 3 d4 cxd4 4
⊘xd4 a6 5 ♗d3 ♗c5 (see game
21), but without wasting a tempo
on ... a6. Naturally this exposes
Black to the possibility of ⊘b5 at

some point, but attempts to
exploit this directly don't work.
White has to be a bit more careful
to gain the advantage against 4
... ♗c5.

    5 ⊘b3   ♗b6 *(143)*

143
W

    6 ⊘c3

Simple development guarantees
at least a slight advantage. The
ambitious 6 c4 is also promising,
for example 6 c4 ⊘e7 7 ⊘c3
(White must prevent ... d5) 0-0
(or 7 ... ⊘bc6 8 ♗f4 e5 9 ♗g5 f6
10 ♗d2 d6 11 ♕h5+ ♚f8 12
♗d3 ♗e6 13 0-0 and White is
better, Howell–S. Arkell, London
1986) 8 ♗f4 (it is essential to
reach d6 with the bishop before
Black prevents it with ... f5, e.g. 8
♗e2?! f5 and ♗f4 is impossible)
f5 9 ♗d6 ⊘bc6 10 ♗e2 and now
if Black plays **10 ... fxe4** 11 c5
♗c7 12 ⊘xe4 White's hold on d6
cannot be broken, while after **10
... f4** aiming to play ... ⊘g6–e5
(after a rook move, of course)
White might even consider 11
♗h5!?

    6 ...   ⊘e7
    7 ♗d3

Or 7 ♗g5!? f6 8 ♗h4 0-0 9 ♕h5 ♘bc6 10 0-0-0 ♘e5 11 ♗g3 ♘7g6 12 ♔b1 f5 13 f4 ♘c6 14 ♗c4 ♕f6 15 e5 ♕e7 16 ♘b5 a6 17 ♘d6 ♔h8 18 h4 ♘a5 19 ♘xa5 Resigns, Sibarevic–G. Welling, Lugano Open 1989. Weak play by Black, but this direct plan could be dangerous.

7 ... 0-0

8 0-0 ♘bc6 9 ♗f4 f5 (9 ... d5 10 exd5 ♘xd5 11 ♘xd5 ♕xd5 12 c4 ♕d8 13 ♗d6!) 10 ♗d6 f4 11 ♕h5 f3 12 g3 ♗c7 13 e5 g6 14 ♕g5 ♗xd6 15 exd6 ♘f5 16 ♕xd8 ♘xd8, Wedberg–Nunn, Helsinki 1983, and now 17 ♗xf5 ♖xf5 18 ♘d4 ♖f8 19 a4! a5 20 ♖a3 would have been good for White.

E 1 e4 c5
2 ♘f3 g6

One of the most important lines in this chapter, since it has occurred many times in Grandmaster chess and White can probably only secure an edge against it. Other second moves are very unusual and can be met by normal development, e.g. **2 ... b6** 3 d4 cxd4 4 ♘xd4 ♗b7 5 ♘c3 ♘c6 (or 5 ... a6 6 ♗d3 g6 7 f4 ♗g7 8 ♘f3 d6 9 0-0 followed by ♕e1–h4 with attacking chances) 6 ♗f4 ♖c8 7 ♘xc6 dxc6 8 ♕f3 ♕d4 9 ♖d1 ♕c5 10 e5 ♖d8 11 ♖xd8+ ♔xd8 12 ♗e2 ♔e8 13 0-0 f5 14 e6 ♘f6 15 ♖d1 ♘d5 16 ♗e5 Resigns, Belyavsky–Quinteros, Vienna Open 1986, or **2 ... ♕c7** 3 c3 (it is probably not a good idea to play 3 d4 since 3 ... cxd4 4 ♘xd4 ♘f6 5 ♘c3 a6 followed by

... e5 gives Black a type of Najdorf position in which his king's bishop can still be developed actively at c5 or b4) ♘f6 4 e5 ♘d5 5 d4 cxd4 6 cxd4 d6 7 ♘a3 a6 8 ♗d3 e6 9 ♘c4 dxe5 10 dxe5 b5 11 ♘e3 ♗b7 12 0-0 followed by a4 when Black's queenside pawn structure will be weakened.

3 d4

The attempt to reach a Maroczy bind position by 3 c4 ♗g7 4 d4 can be met by 4 ... ♕a5+, when it is not at all easy for White to maintain any advantage.

3 ... ♗g7

3 ... cxd4 4 ♘xd4 transposes to lines examined earlier, for example 4 ... ♘c6 5 c4 and 4 ... ♗g7 5 c4 end up in Chapter 7, 4 ... ♘f6 5 ♘c3 d6 is chapter 5, and 4 ... ♘f6 5 ♘c3 ♘c6 leads to line A in this chapter.

4 dxc5 ♕a5+ (144)

4 ... ♘a6 5 ♗xa6 ♕a5+ 6 c3 ♕xa6 7 ♕e2 ♕c6 8 ♗e3 ♕xe4 9 ♘bd2 ♕c6 10 0-0 ♘f6 11 ♘d4 ♕c7 12 ♘b5 ♕d8 13 ♗f4 was good for White in Rajna-Nagy, Hungary 1960.

144 W

5 ♘c3

Natural, but 5 c3 may be stronger, for example 5 ... ♕xc5 6 ♗e3 ♕c7 7 ♗d4 e5? (7 ... ♘f6 8 e5 ♘g4 9 ♘a3! is better, but White can still claim a modest advantage) 8 ♗e3 ♘f6 9 ♘a3! 0-0 10 ♘b5 ♕c6 11 ♘xe5 ♕xe4 12 ♘xf7! with a large plus for White, Maric–Tringov, Bar 1977.

5 ... ♘f6

Or 5 ... ♗xc3+ (5 ... ♕xc5 6 ♘d5 e6 7 b4 ♕f8 8 ♘c7+ ♔d8 9 ♘xa8 ♗xa1 10 ♗g5+ ♗f6 11 ♗xf6+ ♘xf6 12 ♕d4 ♕e7?! 13 ♗b5 b6 14 ♘xb6! axb6 15 ♕xb6+ ♔e8 16 0-0 was very good for White in Mohrlok–Breazu, corr. 1987) 6 bxc3 ♕xc3+ 7 ♗d2 ♕xc5 8 ♗d3 (8 ♗e2 ♘f6 9 e5 ♘g4 10 0-0 ♘xe5 11 ♗e3 ♘xf3+ 12 ♗xf3 ♕c7 13 ♕d4 was also promising in Petrov–Limonikov, corr. 1974) ♘f6 (8 ... d6 9 0-0 ♗g4 10 ♖b1 ♕c7 11 ♖b3 ♘d7 12 ♖c3 ♘c5 13 h3, Ambrosz-Petran, Czechoslo-

vakia 1979 gave White more than enough for the pawn) 9 0-0 0-0 10 e5 ♘g4 11 ♖b1 ♘xe5 12 ♖b5 ♘xf3+ 13 ♕xf3 ♕c7 14 ♗h6 ♖e8 15 ♖f5 ♖f8 (*New in Chess* gave ... f6 as unclear, but 16 ♖e1! appears crushing after 16 ... ♕c3 17 ♗c4+! ♕xc4 18 ♖xf6) 16 ♗xf8 gxf5 17 ♗xe7 d5 18 ♖e1 ♗e6 19 ♗f6 ♘d7 20 ♗d4 ♕d6 21 ♗xf5 ♗xf5 22 ♕xf5 ♘f8 23 ♕g5+ ♘g6 24 h4 ♖f8 25 h5 Resigns, Frivaldszky–Monostori, corr. 1986.

6 ♗d3 ♕xc5
7 ♗e3 ♕a5

7 ... ♕h5 is possible, but I cannot find any practical examples of it.

8 ♕d2 ♘c6

9 0-0 0-0 10 h3 d6 11 a3 ♗e6 12 ♘g5 d5 (12 ... ♗d7 13 f4) 13 exd5 ♗xd5 14 b4 ♕d8 15 ♖ad1 and White has a slight advantage, Sveshnikov–Romanishin, USSR ch. 1977.

Index of Variations

Now:
B1 5 ... e6
B2 5 ... g6
B3 5 ... a6
For 5 ... ♘c6 *see* A and for 5 ... e5 and 5 ... ♘bd7 *see* p. 163.

B1

5	...	e6
6	g4	h6

6 ... e5 *32*
6 ... ♘c6 7 g5 ♘d7 8 h4 *33*
6 ... a6 7 g5 ♘fd7 8 h4 *36*
6 ... ♗e7 7 g5 ♘fd7 8 h4 *37*

7	h4	♘c6

7 ... ♗e7 *20*
7 ... a6 8 ♗g2 *21*

8	♖g1	h5

8 ... ♗d7 *26*
8 ... d5 *26*

9	gxh5	♖xh5 *28*

B2

5	...	g6
6	♗e3	♗g7

6 ... a6 *78*

7	f3	0-0

7 ... a6 *78*
7 ... ♘c6 *78*

8	♕d2	♘c6

8 ... d5 *79*

9	♗c4	♗d7

9 ... a6 *80*
9 ... a5 *80*
9 ... ♘xd4 *80*
9 ... ♕a5 *80*
9 ... ♘d7 *80–1*

10	0-0-0	♖c8

10 ... ♕c7 *82*
10 ... ♕b8 *82*
10 ... ♕a5 11 ♗b3 *83*

11	♗b3	♘e5

12	h4	h5

12 ... ♕a5 *85*
12 ... a5 *85*
12 ... ♘c4 *86*

13	♗g5	♖c5

13 ... a6 *87*
13 ... ♘h7 *87*
13 ... ♘c4 *87*

14	♔b1 *90*	

B3

5	...	a6
6	f4	e5

6 ... ♘c6 *2*
6 ... g6 *2*
6 ... e6 7 ♕f3 *2*
6 ... ♘bd7 7 ♗e2 *3*
6 ... ♕c7 7 ♘f3 ♘bd7 (7 ... e6 8 ♗d3 *6*) 8 ♗d3 *7*

7	♘f3	♘bd7

7 ... ♕c7 8 a4 *9*

8	a4	♗e7

8 ... ♕c7 *9*
8 ... d5 *12*

9	♗d3	0-0
10	0-0 *12*	

C

2	...	e6
3	d4	cxd4

3 ... d5 *165*

4	♘xd4	a6

4 ... ♗c5 *165*
4 ... ♗b4+ *165*
4 ... ♘c6—*see* A
4 ... ♘f6 5 ♘c3 ♗b4 (5 ... d6—*see* B1; 5 ... ♘c6 *134*) 6 e5 *145*

5	♗d3	♘f6

5 ... ♘c6 *94*
5 ... g6 *95*
5 ... ♘e7 *96*